Haponski, William C.
New horizons.

NEW HORIZONS

NEW HORIZONS

THE EDUCATION AND CAREER PLANNING GUIDE FOR ADULTS

William C. Haponski, Ph.D.,
and Charles E. McCabe, M.B.A.

Peterson's Guides
Princeton, New Jersey

To Nettie Marie Jones

In this second edition we again
dedicate our efforts to you
for your lifetime support of lifelong learning.

Contents

PART I
DECIDING AND PREPARING

PART II
SUCCEEDING

Contents

x

Preface and Acknowledgments

As a college professor, William Haponski tried to guide adult students to written material that would be helpful to them in making decisions on college and careers. In his office, in his classes, and at coffee breaks he listened to their aspirations for success, coupled sometimes with their problems of coping. When, after a determined search, he found no single, comprehensive source of information that would assist these people, the idea for this book was born.

About that time, sitting in one of Professor Haponski's classes at Adelphi University was Charles McCabe. Having himself experienced frustration at finding little information, Chuck was excited by the thought of collaboration. The two prospective authors sketched an outline and soon knew they were committed to the book.

Later, Bill went on to become a college vice president and dean, and then developed his own business in education, training, and career services and products. Chuck, while enrolled in a doctoral program, is also managing a large commercial enterprise. Their experiences since meeting in that classroom have led them always in search of new horizons, just like the people for whom this book is written.

The predecessor to this book, *Back to School: The College Guide for Adults,* seems to have achieved our ends. According to many reviewers, it was the concise, indispensable guide that we hoped it would be. Yet we felt some things were lacking in the book. For one thing, in its concentration on colleges and universities and degrees, it did not cover the full spectrum of adult educational opportunities. And, although it contained sections on career matters, it did not integrate career and educational concerns as closely as they are integrated in the lives of most adults who seek more satisfaction in their personal and professional lives. Consequently, in our new book we have broadened our treatment to include guidance for those millions of you who will

xii   benefit from higher education programs that don't necessarily award a college degree. In addition, new developments in nontraditional education, computers, and some other areas call for new or expanded treatment, which we have provided.

This book is thus a concise, integrated career and education guide for that once-neglected species, the adult, a person who needs this type of guidance probably even more than the young person on whom all the guidance was once lavished. Although the book is intended as a manual, we hope that it is also highly readable, even humorous and irreverent on occasion. The approach is sequential, taking you from those early nagging doubts about your future through the various steps and experiences that will lead you on your way to new horizons. Part I is for you while you are in the process of preparing for major changes in your career and personal life, and are deciding on the steps to bring them about. Part II is for you while you are enrolled in courses of study and training that will help you to meet your career and personal goals. Throughout this book you will find profiles of adults who, for career and personal reasons, have gone on to some form of higher education. Within this gallery of successful adults you will recognize elements of yourself, your trials and aspirations.

From the beginning, when we wrote the predecessor to this book, we wanted it to reflect not only our own thoughts, experiences, and research but the broadest possible range of all adult experiences that are concerned with careers, personal relationships, and higher education. Consequently, we invited career counselors, instructors and administrators in higher education settings, and adult students from all over the United States and Canada to contribute. The response was overwhelming. Over 40 people contributed to the earlier book. Many more have joined their ranks in contributing to this one. Unfortunately, we cannot acknowledge all of these people here. But we can extend our thanks especially to the individuals and organizations mentioned in the text, and to Philip M. Backlund, Carol Mackintosh, and Nancy Hawks for their major contributions, to Janet Wagner for her bibliographical work, and to Tony Farma for his unflagging support of our efforts.

We also are indebted to the staff of Peterson's Guides for their professional handling of this book.

All of us who have contributed to the book believe it will be a major aid for adults for many years to come, being revised as conditions change. But in order for us to serve adults well in future editions, we need your help. We want your comments on the strengths and weaknesses of this book, and your suggestions for inclusion or elimination of material in future editions. Most of all, whether you are an adult with career concerns, or an adult student, career counselor, academic counselor, teacher, or administrator in a higher education institution, we would like to have your descriptions of the problems you have had and the solutions you have found in reaching new horizons. Please send your comments on this book and material for consideration for the next edition to William C. Haponski, Ph.D., ETC Associates, 507 Rider Road, Clayville, NY 13322. By doing so, you will serve adults in the future better, quite certainly, than you have been served in the past. And that's a significant contribution.

William C. Haponski
Charles E. McCabe

Introduction

NEW HORIZONS FOR ADULTS

More opportunities exist today than ever before for adults who seek to enhance their careers or gain personal satisfaction by continuing their education beyond high school. Turn on your television set, and along with the soap and beer commercials you are quite likely to see advertisements by local colleges or trade schools that are seeking enrollments of adults. Open your mail and you may find a brochure from a distant correspondence school that hopes to interest you in starting your own tax preparation business or becoming an electronics technician. Wherever you turn you will find educational opportunity beckoning.

Are adults responding to such calls from the many institutions and agencies that seem to offer them a path to a brighter future? And how! Prompted by a perceived need to prepare themselves for greater opportunities and more satisfaction, adults are enrolling in a bewildering variety of higher education programs at a record pace. They are taking classes during the day, in the evening, on the weekend, in the summer. They are pursuing programs of study on college campuses, in their homes, at their places of work. In fact, if you are considering higher education or are already enrolled, you are an important part of the educational phenomenon of our times—the growing tide of adult students.

The National Center for Education Statistics reports that by 1992, students 25 years and older are expected to account for 49% of the 11.8 million students enrolled, compared with 39% in 1982 and 31% in 1972. Whereas the enrollment of students under 25 years of age is expected to drop 20% from school year 1982–1983 to 1992–1993, the enrollment of those over 25 years of age is expected to increase by about the same amount. The College Board predicts that by the end of this century, there will be more students over 25 years of age on college campuses than under 25 years of age. Part-time enrollment of adults is expected to continue to outnumber full-time enrollment, and enrollment of adult women—now over one-half of the total adult enrollment—is expected to increase faster than that of adult men. So you can see that statistics confirm how important you, the adult, are in the higher education scene. Great change has been occurring in the educational marketplace, and you, the adult consumer, are the cause of much of this flux. Adults have awakened to higher education, and it is unlikely that they will ever again consider it the privileged territory of the young.

How did the adult student achieve such preeminence? Before World War II, higher education generally was viewed as a four-year period between the end of high school and the beginning of a profession. Most students studied the liberal arts. Then, for a while after the war, veterans taking advantage of the GI bill made the enrollment of adult men and some women quite common. They signed up for technical as well as liberal arts fields, and often for programs lasting only a few months instead of four years.

The veterans graduated and the higher education scene began to resume its "normal" character, but the stage had been set and after a few years adults again began to enroll in growing numbers and in a variety of programs—from skills-oriented, relatively short programs such as welding and hair styling to professional programs such as medicine that required years of advanced study.

Looking back from our viewpoint in the mid to late 1980s, we see the 1960s, '70s, and early '80s as a dynamic era. The complexity of going about modern business and living brought large numbers of adults back into education. They wanted to upgrade their skills and equip themselves for an even more complex future. At the same time, new opportunities for education were opened to the previously disadvantaged, and each year these people were attracted to higher education programs by the hundreds of thousands. Community colleges bloomed. In the early '60s, about 300 of these public two-year institutions existed. By the late '70s the number had tripled. A major reason for this amazing growth was the adult learner, restricted in mobility to the community by job and family considerations, without much money to spare, but with legislators and community college administrators and faculty sympathetic to this person's needs and dependent upon him or her for enrollments. Programs for delivery of higher education by nontraditional means blossomed, and people who could not afford the time or cost of enrollment in classes were able to fulfill their educational needs while maintaining their regular employment. Learning centers came into being, and, with improved and more accessible counseling, the increasing flow of information on higher education opportunities brought adults into both traditional and nontraditional programs. In 1976, Congress passed the Lifelong Learning Act, stating, "American society should have as a goal the availability of appropriate opportunities for lifelong learning for all its citizens." During the 1970s and early 1980s, state legislatures supported many adult education programs, and corporations, labor unions, and foundations provided grants that immensely benefited the adult learner. Whereas in earlier years only a few colleges and universities had faculty that specialized in teaching adults, and there was little training for this specialty, universities began graduating men and women with doctorates in adult education. Today, adult students are widely recognized as higher education's "new learners," a distinction they will soon lose as enrollments increase and adults come to outnumber younger students.

One might think that with so much attention now being given to adult learning, adults would feel perfectly comfortable in their role as students. As we prepared this second edition we thought we might be able to deemphasize our treatment of the greatest problem that had faced earlier students, that of the anxiety most adults experience both while contemplating enrollment and during the early stage of resumed studies. After all, with so many stories in newspapers and on radio and TV about the successes of adults as learners, one might assume that the anxiety problem would disappear. Unfortunately, this is not the case. And, because of the many pressures adults will continue to face even as they become the majority in higher education, anxiety may always rank as the most serious obstacle to overcome.

One of the greatest fears, which has moderated somewhat since the first edition of this book, is that they cannot compete with younger students. Adults have begun to discover that this concern is not borne out by the facts, yet it remains a pervasive and destructive myth. We hope that by the time we prepare the next edition that myth will have been permanently dispelled, and we won't even have to mention it. But for now, for those of you who still need reassurance, let's deal with it and also begin to allay some of the other concerns that contribute to anxiety.

YOU CAN SUCCEED!

As you read this book, many reasons why you can succeed academically will be highlighted, but for now, let's take just four. In the first place, you may not be competing with younger students, which most adults seem to fear. Many institutions have established divisions or schools of continuing education, and their primary if not sole clientele are adult students. The people sitting next to you might not be teenage students, but, like you, working or retired adults.

Second, even if you should find yourself in classes with younger students, the situation is so normal on campuses by now that you may be the only one who thinks anything about it. And old dogs *can* learn new tricks. Not even advanced age can be taken any longer as an excuse for not continuing to learn. In a pamphlet called "Is My Mind Slipping?" by the Andrus Gerontology Center of the University of Southern California, the first sentence reads: "Let's get the facts straight right now: barring an illness, you can expect your mind to stay strong and healthy well past the age of 80. You'll be able to learn, to think, to remember, to enjoy."

Third, institutions have made special efforts to adjust to the needs of adult students, so your task may not be as difficult as it might have been a few years ago. For instance, a recent publication of the Board of Regents of the University of the State of New York states that "Many higher educational institutions are making adjustments in their programs, schedules, and even locations to serve the special needs of an adult, non-resident, generally part-time student body."

Finally, many instructors are aware of your concerns and will do all they can to get you over the hurdle of initial anxiety. As contact with adult learners has increased in these past several years, more and more instructors have discovered that they even prefer teaching adults.

Our contacts with adult students around the United States and in Canada reveal that almost all of them show amazement at first when they learn they can compete. Linda Mitchell of Brescia College in Ohio describes her anxiety in encountering her first class: "I glanced around the room and was dismayed to find that I was the only 'older' student there. Turning back slowly toward my new biology professor, I really panicked when I realized that even *he* was younger than I." Yet Linda succeeded in that first class and the ones after that. In fact, her success inspired her husband later to enroll in the same college.

But if you have never taken a course in a higher education setting, your anxiety is quite natural. The grandiose image projected by some schools can be intimidating. Here is what author Charles McCabe feels about his experience:

As an adult entering college for the first time, I remember the feeling quite vividly. I hadn't before seriously considered attending, and I'd never asked anyone what college was like. The few people I knew who had gone to college did not discuss their college experiences with me. Perhaps they sensed my embarrassment about my lack of formal education (I was a high school dropout), and they avoided the subject. College seemed completely out of reach for me, so I chose to disregard it.

My eventual enrollment in college was caused by an abrupt break in my professional career as a manager, an event that initiated a major self-reevaluation. I decided that my lack of academic credentials was a serious shortcoming I would have to correct in order to achieve career advancement and mobility. Fortunately, I learned of a special college degree program for adults. I applied and was accepted as a nonmatriculated student pending my qualifying for the New York State High School Equivalency Diploma by successfully completing 24 college credits.

Here I was, a high school dropout, beginning my first college course, Interpersonal Behavior and Group Dynamics. Most, if not all, of my eighteen classmates had previously attended college or had been in the program for some time. I was concerned about my ability to keep up with the class. Classroom participation was thoroughly enjoyable, but I found the readings extremely difficult; my vocabulary was limited, my reading comprehension was poor, and the psychology texts (there were *three* of them) contained much unfamiliar jargon. By attending all of the free college writing and study skills workshops, I was able to do well on the examinations and assignments. I worked very hard, but my efforts paid off—I earned an A in my first college course. Two years later I graduated summa cum laude with a bachelor of science degree. I ranked number one in my class of 141 evening and adult students. Since then I have gone on to complete my M.B.A. and am now working for a doctorate, all part-time since I have a family and a management position in business.

You can be assured that my success as an adult student had little to do with my level of intelligence; I am not exceptionally smart. However, success in studies, as in life, is not entirely dependent upon an individual's so-called I.Q. More important are certain intangible qualities such as motivation, organizational ability, discipline, and perseverance. The world is full of highly intelligent failures. The most successful people are often those who put everything they have into something they really want to achieve. If you are an adult entering higher education for the first time, your potential for success is just as good as anyone else's.

So much for the idea that you may not be able to compete with younger students if you find them in your program. In this book you will find numerous examples of how adults have met this challenge. Now what about the many other concerns you may face? These might include trying to determine what your career goals really are and what higher education you need to achieve them; sorting out all the possible approaches so you end up with the right program; getting accepted into the program of your choice; financing your education; balancing all those demands placed on you by your current employment, your family and friends, and your studies when you are enrolled; and getting the most you can possibly get out of your chosen program. Well, that's what the rest of this book is all about. Read on!

Part I:

DECIDING
AND
PREPARING

1.
Assessing Yourself and Your Career Goals and Options

What can I do with the rest of my life, and how can I reduce the risks in making crucial decisions?

THE MOST IMPORTANT CONSIDERATION–YOURSELF

We all know that mature, intelligent people often make bad decisions. Most of us, no doubt, have made more poor choices in important matters than we care to remember. We have bought the wrong automobile, perhaps the wrong house, or even married the wrong person, and our life has been changed at least for a while for the worse.

Now you are considering another important, probably crucial, matter—how to make the most out of your life, and how higher education may be a key element in your decision. If you make the right choices, you could gain long-term, profound satisfaction.

You stand alone in making your choices, for ultimately, of course, no one but you can decide. There is no reason, though, for you to go without help in arriving at your decisions, as so many people do.

The Greek philosophers believed that true insight begins with self-knowledge: "Know yourself." And we believe that you are most likely to achieve satisfaction in making decisions on higher education if you first start with yourself. Who are *you*, what are *your* goals, how are *you* going to set about achieving them?

We have found in our examination of adult student motivations that there are two primary concerns most often expressed when adults consider going on for further education: The personal satisfaction they will achieve and the effect it may have on their career. Let's look at each in turn.

3

4   PERSONAL SATISFACTION

A strong motivation for adults' seeking further education has been the personal satisfaction it brings. This motivation often is not related to career concerns, and sometimes is not easily explained by those who have it. Many times a crisis or specific set of painful circumstances causes an adult to start investigating his or her options. Just as often, though, the impetus can be simply a long-standing dissatisfaction with the way things have been going, or with the way a person thinks of himself or herself. Helen H. Probst, formerly administrative assistant to the president at Adelphi University, and a recent graduate of the university, reports:

> I graduated from high school 14 months after the 1929 crash, and the depression was very real. It was a question of whether I would be permitted to enter Cornell, where I had been accepted, or would have to settle for a year's secretarial school and then go out into the working world to help put my brother, who was a year behind me, through college. This is what happened, and believe me I was very disappointed and secretly resentful that I had to follow this course and attend New York University downtown in the evening. Why couldn't my brother have followed the same course? He attended Fordham University each day. I didn't think that at all fair. After my first semester at NYU I was forced to drop out due to the overtime requirements of my position at a law firm. Part of my earnings, however, continued to be used to help pay my brother's tuition. Then I married and helped my husband through law school. He passed on right after my daughter started college and my son was still in high school. After I got my children through, I suddenly realized I had been on Adelphi's campus for 22 years and had never sat in one of its classrooms.

We have heard from many adults, especially older ones who are retired, who share Mrs. Probst's motivation. They have no plans for using higher education for career reasons. Rather, they are fulfilling a dream, picking up where they left off many years ago, or they simply want to set new challenges for themselves and gain the satisfaction of meeting them.

Many adults also enjoy the social and cultural opportunities provided through continuing their education. Attaining and enjoying higher social status and prestige among friends, relatives, and associates is often important to adult students, as are the exciting and new experiences they gain while pursuing their programs. Dale E. Reich, director of information services at the University of Wisconsin–Whitewater, tells of Zelda Stanke, born in 1905 on a farm near Belleville, Wisconsin. Zelda audited 32 courses during four years at Whitewater. She became so excited about college life that she brought along her 92-year-old mother! Mrs. Stanke said: "I like the fellowship of the students. You don't feel lonely. There's always someone to talk to, to exchange ideas with."

Personal satisfaction, then, is one of the best reasons for furthering   5
one's education. Maura B. Gregory knows what this means to her.
Maura, a postal employee, was 53 when she got her bachelor's degree
in independent studies (B.I.S.) from George Mason University in Fairfax, VA. She sums up her feelings about going to college this way:
"Chances are I will chug along in my present job until I retire. But later,
when I'm sitting and rocking, too feeble to do anything else, I hope
there'll be something in my brain besides recipes and musty nostalgia."

CAREER GROWTH

In a course called Writing and Social Issues, at Adelphi University,
the authors (one the professor, the other the student) surveyed their
class by questionnaire and asked the members to rate the importance
they placed on various possible reasons for the surge of adults into
higher education. Career-related reasons proved strongest, with the
following three reasons clearly rated as most important:

1. to qualify for a more challenging position in the same field of
   work, with either a present employer or a new employer
2. to qualify for a new or different occupation, including entering
   or reentering the job market and changing careers.
3. to increase earnings potential because of either financial need or
   a desire for a higher standard of living, or both.

Since taking that limited survey, the authors have discovered through
research that the career concerns and beliefs of that class are quite
typical of those in the adult student population as a whole. For example, Helen E. Marshall, who completed her studies at Essex County
College in Newark, New Jersey, and transferred to a four-year college
for work toward the baccalaureate, reports:

> It was mandated by the board of nursing in my state that to continue prac-
> ticing as a licensed practical nurse, all of us would have to return to school.
> Not being old enough to retire, I had no alternative. So, caught in the middle,
> 58 years young with this mandate hanging over me, I proceeded posthaste to
> an institution of higher learning and was accepted at Essex County College.

Does higher education pay? If a person is considering getting more
of it because of career concerns, then it seems reasonable enough to
expect a return on the investment of time and money.

Recent studies by government and other agencies confirm that
higher education translates into higher earnings and improved career
standing for the average individual. According to U.S. Department of
Labor statistics, about 40% of the labor force aged 25 to 64 have
completed a year or more of college, and almost 25% have completed
four years. According to a department economist, "Education levels
are rising for virtually every occupation. Your chances of being un-

6   employed are greater if you don't have the necessary education." The National Center for Education Statistics reports that 60% of the courses taken by the more than 20 million adult men and women participating in adult education activities were taken to advance in a job or to get a job. Several years ago, in his book, *Investment in Learning,* Dr. Howard R. Bowen concluded that the economic returns to an individual more than offset the costs of higher education. We have seen no studies since then that would dispute that finding. Even successful business people have felt the lack of higher education. Some years ago the president of one of the largest stock brokerage firms in the United States took his life. According to newspaper accounts, in an interview the day before the incident he had seemed depressed, complaining that his lack of a college education was keeping him from being as competitive as he wanted to be in his business. Although this is an extreme case, there is no doubt that higher education is very important to adults across the country and from all walks of life for career reasons. Statistics substantiate their beliefs that advancement within a present career, successful career change, improved earnings, and the ability to succeed are enhanced by appropriate higher education credentials.

The less tangible values of higher education to a career should also be considered. For many people, success at their studies provides confidence in addition to useful information and skills. Even if the credential you receive is not directly related to your career goals, the way you feel about it and yourself may help you succeed in your career.

ANALYZING YOUR CAREER ASPIRATIONS AND YOURSELF

What have I done in my career? Where am I right now? Where am I going? What should I be doing now to get there? All concerned adults at one time or another have pondered such questions.

Unfortunately, too many adults allow these questions to nag at them and cause unease, without purposefully assessing their situation. They become confused and discouraged, and they fail to realize their full potential. Then later in life, when it is too late, they wonder what went wrong.

To achieve maximum success and satisfaction you should basically enjoy your work. Sure, there will be "those days" in any occupation, but if you hate going to work every day probably you are not making full use of your capabilities at work, or you are in the wrong field, or you are working for the wrong employer. Perhaps you should ask whether self-employment, or maybe a career change, is right for you.

Especially if you are not currently employed or are considering a career change, and you are weighing higher education as a means to qualify for a new trade or profession, it should be relatively easy for you to be objective when considering career alternatives. Whether you are employed or not, you may come up with several occupations in your career assessment that you think you would enjoy and be good at. But how can you be sure if you've never tried them? Of course you can't be sure that any job would be right for you, but you can vastly increase the probability of being right by being as objectively introspective as possible. You should try to think in a completely unbiased and unemotional way. Your feelings cannot be ignored; indeed, you must clarify and define your feelings and opinions about many things. But in doing so, you must take stock of your assets and liabilities as objectively as possible in terms of your interests, reasoning skills, and technical abilities, and try to evaluate your potential realistically.

"What a task!" you say. That's true, but think of the alternative—stabbing into the dark and hoping you come up with the right choices. Very few adults realize that there is a vast array of devices and services available to help them. Your problem will not be to find them, since we are going to help you, but to choose the ones that can be most useful to you.

CAREER PLANNING AND PLACEMENT SERVICES

Whatever means you ultimately employ in your career planning, you should realize that although assessment instruments and references can be extremely helpful, they are most effective if administered in a comprehensive career-planning program by a trained career counseling staff. Several types of career advisory services for the adult are generally available: nonprofit public or private agencies of various types, commercial agencies, offices for career planning and placement in higher education institutions, and human resource offices of large companies.

Career counseling services often are made available by school districts, libraries, local governments, local offices of your state or federal government, and independent community organizations. You may find programs in your area by consulting your local library, city hall, institutions of higher education, local offices of elected state and federal representatives, state departments of education and labor, or the yellow pages of your telephone directory under "vocational guidance" or a similar heading. Although it may take some detective work to locate all of the potential agencies that might help you, your time will be well spent. Counseling services by nonprofit agencies often are effective, and free or low cost.

Commercial career counselors can be found in most major metropolitan areas. Such organizations usually cater primarily to experienced executives and professionals who are either unemployed or

8   wish to change their present jobs or careers, although sometimes they serve a more general clientele. Fees may range from several hundred dollars for appraisal of qualifications and capabilities to several thousand dollars (usually about one month's salary) for handling a complete executive-level, job-finding campaign, from definition of career objectives through acceptance of a position and planning for future career growth. Bernard Haldane Associates (at 598 Madison Avenue, New York, NY 10022, and in other major U.S. cities), like many agencies, offers a choice of a complete package or something less, such as a selection from Haldane's "Checklist of Services," which follows:

- Analysis of career potential
- Determination of long-range career direction
- Planning immediate objective
- Résumé preparation
- Letter-writing
- Portfolio development
- In-company advancement program
- How to make contacts and get interviews
- Interview strategy
- Salary negotiation
- Negotiation of title, benefits, etc.
- Evaluation of offers and job acceptance
- Plan for the future
- Special problems

If you are interested in hiring a commercial career consultant, you would be wise to shop around to compare prices and services. Also, you should ask for references to make sure the firm is reputable. You will find agencies advertising their services in *The New York Times, The Wall Street Journal,* and many other large-city newspapers.

Another option is for you to visit the office for career planning and placement at a local institution of higher education. Although their services are normally provided only to current students or graduates, you may be able to get some guidance, particularly if you are considering enrolling there. If they cannot provide services for you, they might be willing to refer you to an appropriate counseling service. (More on career services provided by institutions of higher education will be found in the last chapter.)

If your employer is a large corporation, you may find career counseling available. More and more companies are beginning to offer career services. They feel that they will have more satisfied employees and greater productivity even if they should lose some employees as a result of their counseling. So if you are employed by a company with a human resources office, you may wish to visit it for help.

COMPUTER-ASSISTED INFORMATION AND GUIDANCE SYSTEMS   9

If you either cannot find an appropriate counseling service in your area or choose not to use it, you have an alternative in computer information and guidance systems. They may be most helpful when used in conjunction with a trained counselor, but even when used alone they have proved of great value to many people. They vary from those that primarily give information to those that primarily give guidance. You do not need computer skills to use such a system. If you can hunt and peck your way around a typewriter keyboard and follow the easy directions that come up on a screen, you can use any of these systems.

Many career and educational guidance systems are on the market. Several have been used for years and have been considerably improved since they first appeared. Most of them were developed for the 17- or 18-year-old graduating high school student, but several have proved useful for adults as well. Some of the suppliers of these services recently have recognized the need for programs specifically to meet the needs of adults, and they have developed, or are now developing, versions for adult use. To find which systems are in your area and whether they are applicable for adults, call the career guidance offices of your local school district, local colleges, and your library. Also try the nearest office of your state department of labor. Maybe you will find that more than one system is accessible, and that you will be able to use them free of charge or for a small fee. Field studies of National Career Information System have shown that most schools are happy to help adults, especially parents and unemployed community members, on an individual basis as time permits. They do not often publicize this fact, however, since to serve the community on a regular basis they would need additional staff, equipment, and training.

Sometimes, administrators feel they should not make their system available to adults in the community. If this is the case in your area, you might want to remind those in charge that as a taxpayer you should be able to use such facilities. If that doesn't work, go higher up, and if that fails, try to get a community action group to work on the problem. By helping to make these useful systems known and available to adults generally, you will be doing a real community service.

As we indicated, some of the systems provide career or educational information only, rather than guidance. These systems are certainly useful, and we'll discuss them in chapters 2 and 14. (If you need to choose a program or school or get a job right now, skip ahead to those sections.) However, if you are trying to sort out long-term career and educational options, the systems that will be most useful to you at this stage are those that give career guidance. To use them, you sit down at a computer terminal, and, following simple instructions, type responses to computer prompts that appear on the screen. Normally

10 you will be guided in relating your interests and values to possible occupations or schools that might meet your goals. You will make choices between types of things you like to do and don't like to do. Some of the questions that will appear on the screen may seem only indirectly related to occupational concerns. Your responses, though, will build up a pattern that will be used later to lead you to career possibilities. With a sufficient amount of interaction at the keyboard, you will be able to see more clearly how your interests and personality traits relate to occupations, and you will be led to explore occupations, some of which, no doubt, you had not previously considered. At some point you will be given information on the type of skills and education you will need in order to pursue certain occupations, and you will be able to identify potential sources of that training and education, including the names and addresses of institutions offering programs that might fit your needs. Usually you will spend at least one-half hour using the system, and no doubt you will want to spend more, probably in more than one session. A printer is usually linked to the computer so that you will have a hard copy of your questions, the responses, and other information to study at your leisure. If you feel you have not properly defined certain personal traits or wish to repeat any section, you will probably be able to do this. You might even want to come back another time and do the whole thing again just to be sure.

Since systems vary in their approaches and emphases, if you can use two or more systems this will be to your advantage. Even if any or all of the systems available in your area were intended for younger people and have not been updated for adults, they will probably give you some useful guidance.

We cannot cover all of the systems in detail. If you want full information, contact ACSCI Clearinghouse, University of Oregon, 1787 Agate Street, Eugene, OR 97403. We will, however, outline two that should have adult versions in operation by the time you read this book. If you cannot find one of these or a comparable version locally, you can contact the program director at the address given for each, and this person will supply the location of the office nearest you that has the system.

DISCOVER for Adult Learners, created by the American College Testing Program in Iowa, consists of six modules. In Module 1—Weathering Change, the user is helped to describe his or her current situation, outline a desirable future, and define the steps needed to effect desired changes. Module 2—Assessing Self offers four assessment tools: an interest inventory, a self-rating of skills, an assessment of experiences, and an inventory of work-related values. The user receives a list of job families and specific occupations and programs of study. A summary function pulls together the occupations and shows

overlaps. Module 3—Gathering Occupational Information allows the
user to read about various occupations and get detailed descriptions
of those identified in Module 2 as potentially appropriate. Module 4—
Making Decisions gathers information from the first three modules
and integrates it into a useful decision-making model. This module
helps the user develop decision-making skills. In Module 5—Drafting
Educational Plans, the user gathers information about traditional and
nontraditional alternatives for obtaining higher education and is helped
to develop an action plan for reaching the educational goal. Module
6—Getting a Job provides general information about job seeking and
detailed coverage of résumé writing and job interviewing. In the résumé
section, the computer is used as a word processor to facilitate the
user's development of a personal résumé. For additional information,
contact the Director, DISCOVER Services, Educational Services Division, ACT, 2201 North Dodge Street, P.O. Box 168, Iowa City, IA
52243.

SIGI PLUS is also a very useful system for adult users. With it you
will be guided in assessing your values, interests, and skills. The Values
section is your first step, and it may turn out to be a real eye-opener.
You are asked to assign weights to each of these values: High Income,
Prestige, Independence, Helping Others, Security, Variety, Leadership,
Interest Field, Leisure, and Early Entry. The total number of points
cannot exceed a certain maximum, so you may have to go back
through your choices, adjusting weights until you get that maximum.
For example, although you would like to assign a high weight to
Helping Others, you find there is no room if you also want high
weights assigned to High Income and Prestige. Your forced choices
may be painful, but they are also the basis for much greater insight
into your true values and thus helpful in choosing a satisfying career
path. At any point in the program, if you feel you have not assigned
the proper weights to the values, you may go back and reassign weights
and rework the exercises. SIGI PLUS also has a skills analysis that will
allow you to assess your level of competence in certain areas and find
out what occupations utilize similar skills. After comprehensive self-
exploration, SIGI PLUS generates individualized lists of occupations
for you to explore and allows you to compare occupations. You can
ask specific questions about selected occupations and get answers
from an up-to-date, thoroughly researched data bank. SIGI PLUS describes educational programs of study in detail; it allows you to see
the kinds of courses that are typically required in any given major
and to receive course descriptions. It also lists the kinds of skills to
be mastered in each course. SIGI PLUS will help you to develop a
strategy for achieving your goals. Blair Ruller, a student at the Culinary
Institute of America in Hyde Park, New York, benefited considerably from using SIGI, the earlier version of SIGI PLUS. Adrift in un-

12 certainty, he was able to define a career direction and the type of schooling he needed. Blair got an associate degree in the food service field, decided *en route* that he wanted to be a chef, went on to the Institute, and is well satisfied with his career choice. Adults attending back-to-school seminars conducted by the authors also have been greatly enthusiastic about SIGI. We anticipate that the newer SIGI PLUS will prove to be an even more valuable guidance system. For additional information, contact the SIGI Office, Educational Testing Service, Rosedale Road, Princeton, NJ 08541.

DIAGNOSTIC INSTRUMENTS FOR ASSESSING YOUR INTERESTS, VALUES, ACHIEVEMENTS, APTITUDES, AND PERSONALITY

If you do not have access to computer-assisted resources for career exploration, or if you wish to supplement those resources with written survey instruments, you may be interested in the wide array of diagnostic tests that are available. Each test has its own particular strengths and weaknesses so far as applicability to your unique situation is concerned. We cannot possibly cover the spectrum of such tests, but we will try to guide you to certain of them that we feel are particularly useful in many situations. Remember, though, that you will do well to contact counseling offices to get more detailed guidance and determine what tests might be available to you locally. (Should you have to order the tests, the first three that are listed currently cost under $10.00. You will get the exact cost of a test by contacting the company that administers it.) You may also wish to request a catalog from the company since some of their other assessment instruments might be helpful to you.

The Self-directed Search

This survey is self-administered and self-scored. It consists of an Assessment Booklet that leads you in an evaluation of your abilities and interests, and an Occupations Finder that guides you in exploring possibilities in the world of work. It should take you only about an hour to complete and a few additional hours to follow up on occupational exploration from sources recommended in the booklet. This widely used survey should be available free or at low cost from counseling offices. If you cannot locate a source, contact Consulting Psychologists Press, Inc., 577 College Avenue, Palo Alto, CA 94306.

Career Assessment Inventory

This is an interest inventory for individuals who wish immediate career entry or want to enter occupations requiring some higher education, such as that provided by a technical or trade school, business school, or community college. It is self-administered but computer-scored. You will get a detailed printout of data and narrative to help you gain insight into yourself and occupations that could be of interest to you. Contact National Computer Systems, Box 1416, Minneapolis, MN 55440.

Strong-Campbell Interest Inventory

This diagnostic test is a classic, having been developed over 50 years ago, used by millions, and updated to reflect new occupational areas. It, too, is self-administered and computer-scored, with a detailed printout being returned to the user. It is recommended for those people interested in careers that will require advanced technical or college study. If it is not available at a local counseling office, contact Consulting Psychologists Press or National Computer Systems at the above addresses. Note that although the preceding two tests are computer-scored, they are not computer-assisted guidance systems such as SIGI PLUS or DISCOVER for Adult Learners.

Personal Skills Map

This assessment instrument is different from the ones above in that it does not point the user toward any particular occupation to explore nor does it assess interests. Rather, it helps you assess your personal and life skills, and is based on the belief that the skills are directly related to personal and career success. The purpose is to provide you with a "map" for personal and professional growth and change. The self-administered and self-scored instrument takes about one hour to complete plus an hour or so for assessing results. The results are depicted on a "Personal Skills Map" and measure the user's perception of his or her self-esteem, assertiveness, interpersonal comfort, empathy, drive strength, decision-making skills, time management, sales orientation, commitment ethic, stress management, and physical wellness. In addition, the results depict perceived effectiveness in personal communication style and astuteness in recognizing how much need there may be for personal change. Thus the Personal Skills Map may be helpful at an early stage when you are considering further development in a chosen career, or career change, and can assist you as you explore potential occupations and educational approaches. You will need the Personal Skills Map (Self-Scorable version), the Interpretive

14   Guide/Planning Workbook, and Creative Living Skills monograph.
(The cost of the material, including shipping and handling, is currently
$17.50.) Order from the Institute for the Development of Human
Resources, Inc., 1201 Second Street, Corpus Christi, TX 78404.

REFERENCES TO HELP YOU IN CAREER PLANNING

If you want to witness an exercise in utter frustration, go to a large
library, find the career section, and watch an adult plunge in with no
guidance. The mass of publications on career matters is overwhelming.
Our purpose in this section is to outline a few of the most useful references to get you started, and guide you to other references from
which you will be most likely to get the specific guidance and information you need for fulfilling your unique needs.

We think that a good place to start is with an overview, and the
best resource is appropriately entitled *Where to Start: An Annotated
Career-planning Bibliography,* by Madeline T. Rockcastle, Coordinator
of Career Center Library Resources at Cornell University. This book,
which is periodically updated, describes the publications used by
Cornell University's Career Center, one of the best in the country.
Particularly useful is the section entitled "Career Planning." It lists
many resources, including books that will help you systematically to
go about assessing your career potential and the direction to take. (If
the book is not available in your library, it may be ordered from
Peterson's Guides, Dept. 4102, P.O. Box 2123, Princeton, NJ 08540,
$11.95 plus $2.00 shipping and handling.)

If you already have an idea of the type of career you believe you
want, a basic resource is *Occupational Outlook Handbook,* published
annually by the U.S. Government Printing Office (be sure to ask for
the most current edition). For each of the many occupations included
in the book, you will find information on the nature of the work,
working conditions, employment (numbers, types, locations), training, other qualifications, advancement, job outlook, earnings, related
occupations, and sources of additional information. Supplementing
the *Handbook* is *Occupational Outlook Quarterly.* Published four
times a year, it provides articles on new occupations, training opportunities, salary trends, career counseling programs, and results of new
studies from the Bureau of Labor Statistics. You may also want to refer
to a recent copy of *Occupational Outlook for College Graduates.* Even
if you have not yet gotten the higher education you might need, this
publication may be able to guide you in the direction appropriate to
your long-term goals. If you cannot find copies in your library (shame
on them!), write to Superintendent of Documents, Department 33,

U.S. Government Printing Office, Washington, DC 20402, and request   **15**
their catalog. In it you will also find other publications that might be
useful.

Finding an appropriate career will be a great step for you, but what
about actually getting a job in that career field? If you need a job or
want to change jobs while you are preparing yourself for a career,
you may want to skip ahead to the last chapter, where we treat job
hunting and references. Also, if you are waiting to see a copy of
Where to Start, you may want to scan Appendix A of this book,
"Career References." It lists resources that might be helpful regardless of where you are in your career-planning process.

In this chapter we have tried to get you thinking about important
long-range considerations as you ponder how higher education might
help you achieve a more satisfying life. And we have provided information on resources that might assist you. If you go through a deliberate career analysis and discover the direction you want to take,
and it involves higher education, your next task will be to determine
the type of program that is most appropriate for you. That's the subject of the next chapter.

2.

Assessing Your Educational Goals and Options

What course of action would be right for me? Where do I get information about programs?

WHICH PROGRAM?

Choosing the program that is right for you will be crucial to your success. Many adults, like younger people, drop out of educational programs. Although statistics on reasons for dropping out are inconclusive, we believe that many adults do not finish because they did not assess their educational goals and options and thus did not well understand why they embarked upon a particular program in the first place. Obviously, once you commit yourself to a program you don't want to be one of the dropouts. Therefore you will want to assess your interests in regard to available programs as carefully as possible, preferably before you begin, but certainly before you have committed yourself so far that modifying your approach would be extremely difficult and costly.

At the end of this chapter and in the next two chapters we will explore specifics in both traditional and nontraditional approaches to higher education, which are the two basic avenues to useful credentials and experience. But for now, let's look at general considerations which apply to either approach.

DETERMINING THE NECESSARY EDUCATIONAL CREDENTIALS TO MEET YOUR GOALS

If you have made a deliberate career assessment along the lines we suggested in the preceding chapter, your educational goals probably

16

have become much clearer to you. If not, as a minimum you should **17** surely ask youself, "What are the goals I hope to reach, and what type of higher education will I require to achieve them?" Let's assume, for example, that you do not have a college degree but your goal is to earn a responsible position in the management of a corporation. You have found that having a Master of Business Administration degree (M.B.A.) will be an asset, so you assume that gaining an undergraduate degree in a business field would be the first logical step. Before choosing your undergraduate curriculum, though, you would be wise to explore some M.B.A. programs and find out what preparation would be best for you. You might be surprised to learn that an undergraduate course of study in business is not the only, and not necessarily the best, preparation for an M.B.A. program. Many leading graduate schools of business seek applicants with a broad liberal arts education, including undergraduate course work in such subjects as English, history, and mathematics.

Similar considerations apply to other career fields. In the nursing profession, for example, a registered nurse with a diploma from a nursing school may be faced with stiff competition for higher-level nursing positions and little opportunity for advancement because many hospitals now require their nurses to have a Bachelor of Science in Nursing degree (B.S.N.) in order to be considered for their top positions. Therefore, a person preparing for a career in nursing would do well to try to establish as early as possible the level of position that would provide satisfaction. Obtaining a higher-level position will probably require a different educational approach than obtaining a position at a lower level.

Imagine your frustration if, after struggling to get higher education credentials, you find you are no better off than before because your goals were not well understood or you did not choose the type of educational program that would enable you to achieve them. Establishing your ultimate objective and investigating ways of getting there will help you to define short-term goals, choose a logical curriculum, and improve your chances of avoiding costly mistakes.

HOW MUCH EDUCATION IS ENOUGH?

You have heard that you can never have too much education. If "learning" is the translation for "education" in that saying, no doubt that is true. Or if you seek more education for other than career reasons, it may be true. But if formal education, measured by courses, certificates, and degrees, is the intended meaning, and you are trying to improve your career potential, then we believe that is false. Higher education is costly in time, sometimes in lost job promotions while the person is getting it, and often in dollars. We believe that it makes good sense for persons interested in their careers to take higher edu-

18   cation one step at a time. If a single course will get you the job or
promotion you want, to us it seems to make sense that you should
take only that course now instead of enrolling in a full program. Or if
an associate degree will do, why get a bachelor's? This may sound
heretical, coming from authors of such a book as this, and it may even
sound contradictory to what we stated in paragraphs above. But we
have found that the one-step-at-a-time approach is practical *provided
that whatever you do now will allow you to take the next step at an
appropriate time or to take a side step and a new direction if your
interests change or something happens en route to cause you to take
another approach out of necessity.* The key is to keep as many options
open as you can at each step along your educational path. But if you
are sure of your goals, and taking only one step will waste your time
and resources and not lead smoothly to the second step, that is another
matter. So, in essence we feel that you should get what you need,
but only what you need; keep your options open; and reassess your
goals and progress frequently. Realize that you will be a somewhat
different person at the end of the program from what you were in
the beginning, and you will still be able to go on to higher educational
levels if your goals remain unchanged.

CREDIT OR NONCREDIT PROGRAM

Should you choose a credit-bearing program, or will a noncredit
program better meet your needs?

When we speak of "credit" courses, we are referring to those courses
that are normally accepted as part of a degree program. Most courses
at accredited junior or community colleges, four-year colleges, and
universities are in this category, although these same institutions certainly offer numerous noncredit courses as well. Read the catalogs
carefully. Courses at accredited trade and technical schools, business
institutes, and other occupational schools, even when part of an associate degree program, may or may not be accepted for transfer at accredited colleges and universities. If you think you might want courses
you take to be accepted for a degree program or to allow you to enter
a higher level of study at some point in the future, check into the matter before you enroll. Ask an officer at the institution you are considering enrolling in to help you plan properly.

Credit may mean everything to you, or it may mean nothing. Zelda
Stanke found her noncredit courses at the University of Wisconsin–
Whitewater the key to "joy, excitement, and self-esteem." Older adults
such as Zelda tend to rate credit lower than the learning experience
itself. And, for younger, career-minded adults, some of the best career-
enhancing programs are noncredit, and they look great on a résumé.
The American Management Association (AMA), for example, offers

several noncredit programs leading to a certificate. The certificate is **19** awarded jointly by the AMA and the local college or university with which the AMA is associated. Or you can take their courses by independent study through their Extension Institute. Contact the American Management Association, 135 West 50 Street, New York, NY 10020, for their extension catalog or information on the institution of higher education nearest you that offers their program. For information on types of noncredit programs offered by associations that serve various career areas, consult the *Encyclopedia of Associations* at your library. Find the category of your interest, read the descriptions of the associations in that category, and write to the association that seems closest to your area of interest.

There is another source for excellent noncredit experiences. Most colleges and universities with continuing education divisions, and some other higher education institutions, offer courses on a continuing education unit (CEU) basis. A CEU is awarded for each 10 hours of instruction in these courses or programs, and the student receives a CEU certificate for the total number of units earned. Although CEUs are not normally accepted later for credit, in some instances they are, depending on the nature of the instruction.

DEGREE OR NONDEGREE PROGRAM

Lynn Gallagher describes the problem she faced before enrolling in Baldwin-Wallace College in Berea, Ohio:

> A secretary for three years, I was in a rut. I felt like a mechanical part of the office—you could feed work in one side and, in time, pick up the finished product from the other. It was time to do something for me! My supervisor and I discussed my career and future assignments. I had the ambition, and intelligence, and the attitude necessary. But I didn't have "that little piece of paper"—a college degree. I hadn't realized how important it was. "That little piece of paper" is the key that can open many doors of opportunity.

Lynn knew what her goals were, and only a degree would satisfy her. But how can you decide whether you need a degree? After all, there are many fine programs that lead to a certificate or a diploma instead of a degree, and there are excellent single courses which might suffice to overcome what you perceive to be a deficiency in your education.

Certificate or diploma programs in the United States generally are of two types. One type is for people who already have a degree, usually a bachelor's degree, and provides specialized training at an advanced level. The medical education field, for example, offers many certificate programs for health care specialists. We will come back to these certificates in the last chapter. The other type usually

20   provides enough background for people without sufficiently developed skills in an intended career area to qualify them for entry into a trade or technical or business field of work at a low to middle level. You can find certificate or diploma programs that require relatively few hours of study and practice, and you can find extensive programs requiring weeks, months, and even a year or more. Let's take the case of a woman who decided she wanted to change careers and find work in the automotive trade. She could enroll in a noncredit certificate program taught, for instance, two nights a week for ten weeks in the adult education program of the local public school. Or she might decide to make a greater commitment and seek an associate degree in automotive mechanics at a local trade institute or community college. Or she might even decide to go for a four-or five-year bachelor's degree program in an engineering field related to the automotive trade. If her goal is to work on repairing automobiles, the certificate program probably would meet her needs. If she wanted to get involved in design or management in the automotive field, she would probably do well to take the associate program. And if she wanted to reach for high-level opportunities in management or design she would need the bachelor's degree and even perhaps an advanced degree. She might earn about the same initially, regardless of which course of action she took, but quite certainly in the long run she would earn more and have more responsibility and opportunity for creative work if she chose to get the more advanced degrees.

So, in summary, how can you decide between credit and noncredit, degree and nondegree? To answer this you have to review your goals. At what level of responsibility would you be comfortable? How much would you have to earn to be satisfied? What working conditions would meet your expectations? Can you stand the stress that often accompanies higher-level responsibilities? If career concerns are causing you to consider getting more education, you want to advance to middle or high levels in a career, and you do not yet have a degree, we believe you would do well to seek one rather than pursue noncredit certificates and CEUs. The time and cost might not be much more, and the potential for long-term gains would be greater. But if none of those conditions apply, then the noncredit or nondegree approach might be just right for you.

FULL-TIME OR PART-TIME STUDY

Should you enroll full-time or part-time? Full-time study usually implies a minimum of 12 credit hours per semester or quarter, with the normal load being 15–17 credit hours, depending upon the program. You may believe that you cannot study full-time and maintain

your job and family responsibilities. And you may be right. Some **21**
schools, though, offer full-time study programs that are compatible
with the lifestyles of adult students, and it is possible that you would
finish your program as quickly as if you quit your job and went to
school during the day. You must expect, however, to be an extraordi-
narily busy person.

A problem with adult offerings, generally, is that the range of degree
options often is restricted. A college or school might have a variety
of programs in its day division for full-time students, but in the evening and on weekends it simply might not have the teaching resources
to accommodate as many programs. The more a program is tailored
specifically to meet adult needs, the more general the degree it is likely
to offer compared to programs in the day division. For example, in
the day division you might be able to get bachelor's degrees in biology,
chemistry, physics, and mathematics, but in the evening division you
might find none of these degree offerings and have to settle for a program in general science. (Additional curriculum concerns regarding
full-time versus part-time enrollment are addressed in chapter 9.)

Another factor you should weigh is the relative cost of part-time
versus full-time enrollment. Tuition rate structures often vary between
full- and part-time study in the same institution. Whereas part-time
enrollment may be more expensive than full-time at some institutions,
at others it is just the opposite. Some private colleges and universities,
especially, have lowered part-time evening and weekend rates in
recent years in order to compete with the rate structure of nearby
public institutions.

Another aspect to check out is the financial aid available to you.
Although legislators have begun to address the problem, you may
find that you are eligible for far less financial aid if you choose part-
time attendance. Conceivably your total education costs could be less
if you go full-time because of a better financial aid package available
to you. Commuting and baby-sitting costs also could be less if you
take more courses in fewer trips to campus.

Most adults are part-time students. Possibilities for part-time study
can be investigated in *Who Offers Part-Time Degree Programs?* (Peterson's Guides, Inc., P.O. Box 2123, Princeton, NJ 08540, paperback,
$7.95 plus $1.25 for postage). This publication offers a complete
overview of the part-time degree opportunities—daytime, evening,
weekend, summer, and external degree programs—available from accredited colleges and universities in the United States.

KEEPING YOUR JOB OR GIVING IT UP

If you are considering nontraditional programs, this is a situation
you will probably not face. These programs, in fact, may give you

22 credit for your current as well as past work experience, depending on the nature of the program and the work you do. (See Chapter 4.)

If you are considering a traditional approach and full-time attendance, then you will have to evaluate your situation more carefully. If you need the money in order to pay for higher education, then you may have to keep your current job. Before you decide this is the case, though, go over your circumstances with a financial aid officer at a local institution. You may be surprised to find that it could be to your advantage in terms of the financial aid you would receive to quit your job and spend full time in study (see Chapter 7 for additional guidance on financial aid). If you are changing your career field, and continuing work in your present job will not give you additional career credentials, then you might be wise to quit and get the academic credentials you want as soon as possible. If, however, you are planning to remain in the same line of work, either with your current employer or another employer, then you have to consider whether you would be gaining or losing promotion potential if you were to quit and go to school full-time.

ACCREDITATION

What is accreditation? "Accreditation is a system for recognizing educational institutions and professional programs affiliated with those institutions for a level of performance, integrity, and quality which entitles them to the confidence of the educational community and the public they serve" (Council on Postsecondary Accreditation). You may be considering programs in an academic area in which accreditation is given. What are the sources of legitimate accreditation, and how important is it that your institution or program be accredited?

We believe that most educators depend on one or both of two ultimate sources of approval or accreditation: the U.S. Department of Education and the Council on Postsecondary Accreditation. These two sources do not directly accredit institutions; rather, agencies recognized by them are held responsible for evaluating various accrediting authorities. Those authorities in turn accredit individual institutions, elements of institutions, and individual programs. The list of accrediting authorities can be found in two annual directories: *Nationally Recognized Accrediting Agencies and Associations,* put out by the U.S. Department of Education, and *Accredited Institutions of Postsecondary Education,* published by the American Council on Education for the Council on Postsecondary Accreditation (COPA). (The latter may be more useful since it lists accredited institutions and programs. Both directories should be available in your local college library or registrar's office, or in major public libraries.

There are two types of accreditation: institutional and specialized.   **23**
The government's directory states: "Institutional accreditation normally applies to an entire institution, indicating that each of its parts
is contributing to the achievement of an institution's objectives, although not necessarily all on the same level of quality. . . . Specialized
accreditation normally applies to evaluation of programs, departments
or schools which usually are parts of a total collegiate or other postsecondary institution. The unit accredited may be as large as a college
or school within a university or as small as a curriculum within a
discipline." Of all the programs offered by accredited institutions,
only a small percentage usually will be subject to specialized accreditation. The directory published by the American Council on Education states: "The listings do not indicate all curricula offered by an
institution. For example, curricula in anthropology, English, physics,
and many other disciplines are not listed because no recognized specialized accreditation exists in those fields." In most cases, the U.S.
Department of Education and the Council on Postsecondary Accreditation are in agreement about which accrediting authorities they will
recognize. In a few cases, only one of them will list a particular accrediting authority.

The concept of accreditation, if not necessarily accreditation itself,
should be of concern to you. As you will see, depending on your goals
it could be crucial that your program or institution be accredited, or
it might be of no importance.

First, let's consider institutional accreditation. If you are seeking
a credential which you later wish to apply to a higher-level credential
in a certificate, diploma, or degree program, we believe that it could
be risky for you to enroll in a program from a nonaccredited institution. Normally, accredited institutions will accept credit for transfer
only from other accredited institutions. (In fact, since acceptance of
credit is entirely an institutional prerogative, sometimes an accredited
institution will not even accept the credit of another accredited institution.) If you find the institution listed in the COPA directory, it is
likely that your credit will be good when you seek to transfer it.

Now what about your program within the institution? First, you
have the problem of determining whether or not your intended field
is in a category that could receive accreditation. Unfortunately, this
can be a time-consuming process, but its importance is so great that
it will be worth your time. If you have already settled on an institution that is accredited, and you have confidence in what they tell
you, you can save time just by asking the director of the program. If
you are still searching for an institution, though, you will have to
start with COPA's directory. In an appendix it lists categories and accrediting agencies which involve specialized accreditation (in the section beginning with "Allied Health" and ending with "Veterinary
Medicine"). If you find your intended field listed, then write to the

24   accrediting authority to get the addresses of accredited programs. If you do not find your intended field listed, either it is not in a category to which accreditation applies or, instead of being covered by a specialized accrediting authority, it falls under the purview of one of the national authorities that accredit institutions. How can you tell which is the case? If you are considering a program from an accredited four-year college or university, you probably need go no further if you do not find the category listed. It is quite likely that no specialized accreditation applies to your category of program. If, however, you are considering a program from a bible college, trade or technical institute, business institute, or proprietary two-year college, or an occupational or home study program, you will want to investigate further. In our next two chapters, when accreditation might be of concern, we come back to the question as applicable to certain types of institutions, and we provide the address of the national accrediting authority when appropriate. This should help you to identify the authority for your intended field and determine whether or not accreditation is an issue that should have serious impact on your decision.

What if you are considering a program within an accredited institution, and, although specialized accreditation could apply to the program of that institution, the program is not accredited. Does this mean you should avoid the program? Not necessarily. Write to the accrediting agency. And then put their reply in perspective. They will probably be inclined to tell you that you should enroll in an accredited program, but what you may have to do is to get more points of view. Ask a variety of people in the profession. You will find from them that in certain fields accreditation status has critical ramifications. In other fields you will get mixed reactions: "Who cares?" said one general business employer. "I just want people who can perform." Some very fine programs are not accredited, often because the directors of these programs do not desire program accreditation or because the college or university itself is prestigious. The graduates of these programs often get good jobs and are readily accepted by graduate schools.

If your intended field is one of those represented by an accrediting body, carefully investigate the importance of accreditation as it may apply to the programs in the particular institutions you are considering. Ask the directors of those programs for their opinions. Once you assess those opinions and have this kind of background information, you may elect an accredited program for specific career reasons, or you may choose a nonaccredited program with full confidence that your certificate, diploma, or degree will be well accepted professionally.

GETTING INFORMATION ABOUT PROGRAMS

Too many adults never pursue their higher education interests because they do not know how to go about getting information. Since

they may never develop their potential, this certainly is unfortunate **25**
for all of us, but it is worse for them. And it is ironic that this should
be the case, for the information they need exists all around them.

Where can you begin your search?

In the preceding chapter we discussed computer information and
guidance systems primarily in relation to career guidance and indicated
that there are other systems that primarily give information. Some,
like CIS (Career Information System) and GIS (Guidance Information
System), combine academic and career information. Others, like
Peterson's College Selection Service, provide a directed college choice
program. To locate these systems, check in your area with the types
of counselors we recommended earlier. If you have difficulty finding
a service, you might write to one or more of the following:

CIS (Career Information System)
1787 Agate Street
Eugene, OR 97403

C-LECT (Computer Linked Exploration of Careers and Training)
Chronicle Guidance Publications
Moravia, NY 13118

GIS (Guidance Information System)
Time Share Corporation
630 Oakwood Avenue
West Hartford, CT 06110

Peterson's College Selection Service
Peterson's Guides
P.O. Box 2123
Princeton, NJ 08540

The place to look for printed references, of course, is your public
library or the library of the largest institution of higher education that
is close to you. Do you believe you have to be a registered student in
order to use a library on campus? This is probably not the case. Many
schools permit people who are not their students to use at least the
reference section of the library, and some will even allow local residents to check out books.

The sources of program information you may find most helpful
will probably be in the reference section, and the reference librarian
will get you started. Right now we want to emphasize that *your most
important resource in a library is the librarian.* Too many adults fumble
around, trying to do things they are not equipped to do. In chapter
10 we will come back to this important point in more detail. *Ask
your librarian to assist you!*

You may want to look in one or more of the helpful guides that the
librarian will point out. There are several standard reference books

26   about colleges and their programs, giving important information on majors, costs, student services, and other matters. You can ask for Peterson's *Guide to Four-Year Colleges* or *Guide to Two-Year Colleges* in your library (see the section preceding the back cover of this book for a listing of titles).

Once you have identified the schools that carry your program, you can ask for their catalogs or bulletins to learn more about their programs. Libraries ordinarily will have some current catalogs and bulletins on the shelves, and probably hundreds of others on microfiche (transparent sheets on which material is printed in miniature). In a few minutes of practice with the microfiche machine, you will be reading about programs almost anywhere in the United States or Canada, or indeed the world.

Another place to look is in the reference book section of your local bookstore, especially if it is a store owned by one of the large chains such as B. Dalton, or Waldenbooks. College guides are often grouped in a "Study Aids" section.

What are your other local sources of information? The training or personnel office of a large business or of a labor union will probably help you as a public service. Military bases have education offices filled with good career and education information. Most bases have easy access for civilians, and you will probably find the people in the education office quite helpful even though you are not in the military. Veterans Administration offices also may be willing to help the non-veteran. They do a large business in education information. Women's centers are especially good about supplying up-to-date education information and advice. (To men too! Ask and find out.) Newspapers you can buy locally may have an education section. Periodically, some large newspapers also run education supplements. And go to your local public school—the guidance office might help.

You can also receive help locally from your state university system and the education departments of your state and federal governments. Some states have a statewide system of education information centers operated by either the state university or the state government. Many states have free telephone networks to satisfy your needs for education information. The United States government has established Educational Opportunity Centers in several large cities.

How can you find out about such places? Look in your telephone directory under federal, state, or territorial government headings. Make some calls, and don't take "I don't know" or "I'm sorry we can't help you" for an answer. With perseverance you will locate the right agency and get the right answers.

And don't forget your elected representatives. If for some reason you are not getting the information and help you need elsewhere, they

have enormous resources and are usually readily responsive to your **27**
needs.

One of the best ways of getting detailed information, though, is to locate a seminar held specifically for this purpose at a school or college near you. These seminars usually range from a few hours to several weeks in length and are either free or low in cost. They present facts on adult higher education, build confidence that you, the adult, can compete, discuss sources of information on schools and programs, and explore costs, financial aid, admission, and other considerations. Individual counseling sessions often are included, as well as courses in basic academic skills and English as a second language for students who need them. (See chapter 10 for further discussion of basic skills.)

You should call or write nearby colleges and universities to determine what is offered that is similar to these seminars. Later in this chapter we will discuss what you can do if the program you want is not available locally, or if you have no school within commuting distance.

Information on higher education is all around you. Reach out for it.

SPECIAL CAREER AND EDUCATIONAL OPPORTUNITIES FOR MEMBERS OF THE ARMED FORCES, THEIR DEPENDENTS, AND DEFENSE DEPARTMENT EMPLOYEES

The United States defense establishment, taken in its totality, is the largest educational institution in the world. Its many career and educational programs often are the envy of the civilian educational community. Such programs as the Servicemembers Opportunity Colleges (SOC) Program make it possible for service members to get a higher education while moving from station to station. This program is a network of over 400 colleges and universities that have adopted policies and programs especially designed to assist people in the service. Some programs also serve dependents of service members and employees of the Department of Defense. We cannot go into detail on all of these programs. Virtually every section of this book applies to service members, their families, and defense employees. We especially direct your attention to chapter 4, Considering Nontraditional Higher Education, and chapter 5, Getting Credit for What You Already Know. External degrees and correspondence courses (chapter 4) are particularly suited to people who move around a lot, and many people in our defense establishment have gotten their higher education in this way. Also, the excellent training you get in service-related activities can be worth a lot of credit toward your higher education credentials (chapter 5), and there is a formal documentation procedure which has been established just for you.

28   The sources of financial aid outlined in chapter 7 apply to you, and in many cases you will be able to get special assistance. Rather than try to document all of the sources of career and educational assistance (would it even be possible?), we urge you to visit the education office at your station. Even if you are in such a remote area that you have no local office, you can be sure that an office somewhere serves you. Ask for it, and you will find it.

The authors are especially enthusiastic about encouraging service members to take the utmost advantage of their opportunities. William Haponski is a graduate of West Point and several service schools. He got his doctorate from Cornell University under the auspices of the Army's educational program, served twice on the faculty at West Point, and headed ROTC units at two universities. Since retirement he has guided many service members in pursuit of higher education. He can testify from personal experience that to take advantage of the opportunities available to you can indeed lead you to new horizons.

POTENTIAL DISADVANTAGES OF HIGHER EDUCATION

Up to this point we have been dealing with the advantages of higher education. It increases earning potential, brings you into contact with people at higher levels of responsibility, and can be an important ingredient in personal growth. But, conceivably, higher education might bring an individual no advantages and, indeed, in some instances might result in harm.

Broken marriages have resulted when one partner sacrifices some elements of a personal relationship in order to have time for higher education. In some instances, the partner who has gained the credentials has later decided that they were not worth the loss of a spouse. Some people, too, have found that higher education has not been the magic ticket to greater career opportunities for them, and they have come to resent the time and money they spent. Other people with credentials in hand may change careers or get promoted, then discover they were happier before.

Higher education, then, is not a panacea; for most people, it is a door-opener to new options. But perhaps the pursuit of something besides educational credentials will provide the options you seek, and might be better suited to your needs. Since seeking higher education, and particularly a degree program, almost certainly will cause some low moments for you at some point in your journey, you will want to make certain you have explored all the alternatives and be convinced you are doing the right thing.

THE TWO BASIC ROUTES TO HIGHER EDUCATION: 29
TRADITIONAL AND NONTRADITIONAL

At the beginning of this chapter we said that you have two main paths to your educational goals: traditional and nontraditional higher education programs. Let's pause a moment to consider what we mean by these terms.

You will find various, and often conflicting, definitions of "tradiional" higher education. The term once referred to the type of education that was offered primarily, almost exclusively, to recent high school graduates. Although some educators might disagree with us, we feel reasonably safe in saying that traditional higher education today implies on-campus education, characterized by guided study in a classroom environment. Students are of all ages, and they go to school both full-time and part-time.

The term "nontraditional" was used in the early 1970s to refer to programs offered specifically to meet the needs of adults. Often these programs granted credit for work and other experiences and were conducted at hours that met working adults' needs, in the evenings and on weekends. Sometimes special services accompanied the programs, such as child care and extended library hours. These programs became so popular and so many schools offer them that we, the authors, and many other educators no longer think of them as nontraditional.

Another route to higher education credentials that also developed in the 1970s from earlier beginnings was the off-campus program based primarily on independent study. The home or workplace became the "classroom," and instead of having a readily available instructor, the student received guidance by telephone, letter, or cassette tape. These programs are relatively inexpensive for the student, and they are convenient. (However, if the student lacks the self-discipline for independent study, they are also difficult or impossible to complete.) When we use the term "nontraditional," we are referring to such programs, ones that require no, or minimal, classroom participation, and rely largely on independent study and/or testing for completion. If they lead to a certificate or degree, they usually allow significant credit for noncollegiate experiences.

Which would be best for you, a traditional or nontraditional approach? The next two chapters should help you decide.

3.

Considering Traditional Higher Education

*Which traditional program or course of
action would best fit my needs?*

THE DIFFERENCES AMONG INSTITUTIONS
OF HIGHER EDUCATION

Let's assume you have some choice in the matter of selecting a school, and that you are not restricted by circumstances to the one closest to home. How will you choose?

You are making a big decision. The results of that choice will be with you in a significant way for the rest of your life.

For example, there are over 3,000 licensed or accredited colleges and universities in the United States and Canada that have at least a two-year curriculum. In addition, there are many other postsecondary institutions that do not award degrees but offer programs leading to certificates and diplomas. Like a person, each institution is unique. Each has an ambiance, a reputation. Each takes on some of the character of its surroundings as well as the character of the people who come there to administer, teach, and learn. In a curious way, schools change as the years change, yet they seem to remain constant.

If you are considering the type of curriculum offered at trade and technical schools, business or specialized schools, or other occupational schools, your options are almost limitless. Programs run the gamut from hairstyling to medical assistance and are offered all across the country by schools and institutes of every size and reputation. Or, if you are considering a two- or four-year degree program or graduate school, what would you be—a mining engineer, a meteorologist, a museum curator? Depending on your program, you might have

a choice between a college or university in Washington, D.C. (American   **31**
University) or one in the state of Washington (Whitworth College);
between one in Texas (University of Texas) or one in Missouri (North-
east Missouri State). You might apply to a university of world renown,
such as Yale, or to a college that is not so famous, such as Defiance
College in Ohio. You can find a college offering a two-year degree, a
four-year degree, or a graduate degree. You can mingle with 40,000
students or with fewer than a thousand. Your college might be public
or private, located in the country or in the city; it might offer a large
amount of financial aid or very little and have small classes or large,
ramps for wheelchairs or none, a party atmosphere or a serious study
environment. What is right for you? To help you with your decision,
let's consider various types of colleges and schools in some detail.

BIBLE COLLEGES

If you are interested in the ministry, you may want to consider attending a bible college. Don't overlook, however, religious programs
in other types of colleges and universities. You may or may not get
credit for some or all of the courses taken at a bible college if you
later wish to transfer them to a degree program at some other type of
higher education institution, so if you intend to use them later for
such purpose, check the matter out before enrolling. The American
Association of Bible Colleges is the accrediting source for member
colleges that offer instruction, certification or degrees in affiliation
with churches of many denominations. AABC is recognized by both
the U.S. Department of Education and the Council on Postsecondary
Accreditation (COPA). You can get information on bible colleges by
writing to AABC, Box 1523, 130-F North College Street, Fayetteville,
AR 72701.

SCHOOLS WITH OCCUPATIONAL PROGRAMS

By "occupational program" we are referring to a certain type of
program that is normally the equivalent of two years or less of full-
time study leading to a certificate, diploma, or associate degree.
Normally these programs are very technical in nature and include few,
if any, liberal arts components. Many of these programs, but not all,
are ends in themselves—that is, they would probably not provide any
credit toward a four-year degree if you chose later to get one. You
might think that a person with credentials from an occupational program earns only a modest income. However, in many fields the average income can be as high as or even higher than in some fields where
a bachelor's or more advanced degree is required.

There is no single classification of schools with occupational programs. In fact, many colleges and universities offer certificate or associate degree programs in occupational fields, so do not count them out in your search for an occupational program. The largest concentration of such programs, though, will be found in the next three types of institutions.

TRADE AND TECHNICAL SCHOOLS

The Accrediting Commission of the National Association of Trade and Technical Schools (NATTS) provides institutional accreditation for private schools offering programs leading to occupational objectives. NATTS is recognized by the U.S. Department of Education and by the Council on Postsecondary Accreditation (COPA) as a national accrediting agency. NATTS' *Handbook of Trade and Technical Careers and Training* discusses the importance of accreditation. You can get a free copy from NATTS, 2021 K Street, N.W., Washington, DC 20006-1077. The *Handbook* also provides a considerable amount of information on careers, programs, and where you can find them. NATTS also publishes free brochures on choosing a career. Two of the most interesting are "What's a Nice Girl like You Doing in a Man's World?" and "College Plus: Put Your Degree to Work with Trade and Technical Skills." Also, for $1.50 you can receive *Getting Skilled,* a 145-page guide to private trade and technical schools.

NATTS' *Handbook* describes 98 careers you can prepare for in two years or less, beginning with Actor and continuing through such jobs as Blueprint Reader, Cosmetologist, Data Processor, Emergency Medical Technician, Legal Secretary, Operating Room Technician, Surveyor, and, finally, X-Ray Technician. Hundreds of schools with such programs are listed in most states and in territories under the jurisdiction of the United States.

BUSINESS AND SPECIALIZED SCHOOLS

The Association of Independent Colleges and Schools (AICS) has a membership of 570 business and specialized schools, junior colleges (two-year), and senior colleges (four-year). Their Accrediting Commission is recognized by the Department of Education and COPA, and it accredits institutions that are predominantly organized to train students at the postsecondary level for business careers in industry, government, or the professions. If you are interested, you may request a free copy of their annual *Directory of Educational Institutions* from AICS, Suite 600, 1730 M Street, N.W., Washington, DC 20036. The *Directory* states, "A business or specialized school usually offers educational activities with only an occupational objective. . . . A business or specialized school is not precluded from offering college-level programs and may also offer adult and continuing education programs." The *Directory* lists schools offering such programs as Accounting, Broadcasting, Business Administration, Culinary Arts, Golf Course Management, Travel and Tourism, and Welding. These schools are located in virtually all of the states and in several U.S. territories.

Remember, although AICS and NATTS members are occupational schools, these two associations are not the only ones that accredit schools with occupational programs. Some of these schools are instead accredited by COPA, and you will have to look in COPA's directory also in order to be sure you have covered the full range of accredited institutions with occupational programs.

TWO-YEAR COLLEGES

Our degree-granting higher-education system is largely composed of two-year colleges, four-year colleges, and universities. We caution the reader that generalizations about types of institutions can be seriously misleading. You can make a wise choice only by studying the nature of a specific institution as it will affect you in your degree program, not as it may affect someone else in his or her program. Myths about types of institutions have guided far too many students and parents of students to choose college or university X over Y when Y (or A or B or C) actually would have been the better choice.

What are these myths? Here's just one: "Two-year colleges are all small and, therefore, offer close faculty-to-student relationships (which is good), but the faculty is not of high quality (which, of course, is bad)." If this kind of myth were to guide your thinking, you might be shocked to discover that some two-year colleges are huge, many times the size of some universities. Also, the faculty at a two-year college might even be of better quality than that of a nearby university—better at teaching, better at advising, and perhaps even more successful in research and publication. So, having cautioned you about myths, we will proceed, adding further cautions as we go.

Two-year colleges are often called junior colleges or community colleges—the name varies with mission, locality, and custom. These colleges grant certificates, associate degrees, or diplomas (in Canada). Junior colleges tend to be small and private whereas community colleges may be small or large, and public.

Junior colleges have been in existence for decades, often affiliated with religious organizations. In the past their policies tended to be conservative and directed mostly toward liberal arts studies and younger students. Many junior colleges are still oriented that way, but others have adopted career and technical programs and have actively sought to serve adult students. At most junior colleges the student will find small classes and close relationships with professors.

For a time, many community colleges grew so fast that receiving a quality education was questionable at some institutions. Today many fine programs and professors are found on community college campuses. Usually supported partly by state funds, partly by tuition income primarily from local students, and partly by local public funds, community colleges generally are more responsive than most other colleges to local career needs.

Degree programs at junior and community colleges may be called either terminal or transfer. Transfer programs are designed to allow the student who is awarded an associate degree to move without loss of credit into an upper-division program, that is, one consisting of the last two years of a baccalaureate degree. However, to be certain of full transfer credit, you should check with the admissions office or registrar both of the two-year college and of the four-year colleges to which you might later transfer.

Terminal programs are those in which no higher-level degree is contemplated or planned for. Credit for most courses in such programs would probably not be granted toward another program at a higher degree level. If you intend to take a terminal degree at a two-year college, be certain you have your long-range goals well defined. You will want to avoid possible loss of credit later if you should decide to continue your education.

There are a number of accrediting agencies for two-year colleges, so you would not get a comprehensive listing by writing to any one of them. Your best bet is to use a computer-assisted college selection system or a college guide such as Peterson's Annual Guides/Undergraduate Study, *Guide to Two-Year Colleges.* The majors index of this guide is particularly helpful, showing you quickly which colleges have the program you want. Community colleges especially are popular among adults. They are inexpensive and they often have arrangements with four-year colleges to allow easy transfer of credits into a baccalaureate program. Further, since transfer programs are designed to mirror the first two years of a bachelor's degree, adults who want a degree from a private college with high tuition often begin their program at a community college and then transfer to complete their degree, thereby gaining the degree they want and avoiding two years of greater expenses while doing it. (But see chapter 7 for a caution—sometimes the "higher-cost" college actually is the better bargain.)

FOUR-YEAR COLLEGES AND UNIVERSITIES

Four-year colleges award baccalaureate degrees primarily, but some of them also offer associate degrees and certificates. Some even grant graduate degrees, but the number of their graduate degree programs is likely to be small compared to their undergraduate degree programs. Many four-year colleges allow talented students to complete the degree in less than four years. Some have three-year degree programs in which a waiver of certain credit-hour requirements is granted. You may also find that you can accelerate your program by taking courses during the summer session, or by taking an overload during the academic year. Certain four-year colleges have combination programs that begin with your first three years of work at the college. Then when you are able to gain entry to a professional school, such as one in medicine or dentistry, you can receive your baccalaureate degree from your original college by substituting the first year of professional study for the last year of undergraduate work.

A college with its own campus (that is, not located with other colleges of a university) often states in its catalog that its students can enjoy a close personal relationship with faculty and staff. The emphasis at such a college is more likely to be on teaching students than on conducting research or publishing. Don't depend on it, though. The unofficial motto of the college might be "publish or perish," and the amount of concern shown to students may be minimal despite all the natural advantages afforded by a highly favorable student-to-faculty ratio.

Universities are composed of two or more colleges or schools, and they customarily offer a variety of graduate degree programs. Research and publishing are major aspects of their educational activities. Judged on the basis of the emphasis that most colleges place on teaching and advising students, some universities may be behind. But of course many universities are concerned about both classroom teaching and treatment of students as individuals. Fortunately, some of the finest scholars on a university campus can also be among the best teachers. If your interest, say, is in English literature, and you would like to come into contact with as many renowned scholars as possible, then you might wish to seek out a major university with a fine English department. Do not depend, though, on having those professors as classroom teachers at the undergraduate level. Sometimes you might, but at other times your contact with them could be limited to occasional lectures in a large auditorium.

A major university could be a fantastic place for you. Quite surely you would find there the potential for high-quality learning plus cultural, social, and athletic experiences. You would find dozens and dozens of groups and activities to stimulate your mind and body. But you might also feel lost in the labyrinths of university life. Largeness and smallness are relative, of course. Gulliver in the land of Lilliputians was huge; in the land of Brobdingnagians he was tiny. The University of Vermont has about 10,000 undergraduate and graduate students.

To some people that university would seem impossibly megalithic, a place where the individual student would get lost in the crowd. To others, it would represent a folksy kind of place where people get to know one another and spread out on the grass to chat and study in the welcome springtime sun. It is not so much the size, or perhaps even the type, of the institution that is important but the size and type of its total effect on you as related to your needs.

PUBLIC OR PRIVATE?

Adult readers of this book who come from certain parts of the country may remember from their early days an intellectual snobbery that tended to separate private from public institutions. For instance, according to one popular conception of education, public colleges were thought to *train* teachers and farmers, not *educate* young men and women. Those colleges, and other state schools, were not intellectually rigorous enough to suit the tastes of a segment of our society that was conditioned to send their children all the way across the country if necessary to enter an Ivy League school.

Some of that snobbery still exists. Unfortunately, some of the public colleges seem to have given ammunition to their critics from the private sector. They have defended themselves against charges of low academic standards not by seriously attempting to elevate those standards but by using the excuse that their mission is to provide the greatest possible access to higher education.

Of the more than 3,000 colleges and universities in the United States, slightly more than half are privately controlled. However, four out of every five students attend public institutions. Of the 60 largest institutions, only five are private. The largest 25 are all public, with enrollments to over 50,000.

At the two-year-college level, the difference in numbers of institutions and enrollments is even more striking. Of over 1,445 two-year colleges, about 900 are public. Only about 3 of every 100 students attend a private as compared to public two-year institution.

The average tuition and fees at public institutions are about one-fifth of those at their private counterparts. (As you will see in chapter 7, the average actual cost difference to you, though, may not be as great as you think it might be.)

If you are considering large universities, the question of public or private as related to quality does not make much sense. (Is the University of Southern California, a private institution, better or worse than the University of California at Berkeley, a public institution? Would anyone really care to spend time on such an inquiry?) Even in the case of small colleges we would urge that considerations other

than public or private control should determine your choice. Whereas   **37**
some states have not done as good a job as others in ensuring appropriate quality in their public institutions, the administrations of some
private institutions have also been remiss. The quality of education
attainable in an institution does not depend so much on the nature
of control, public or private, as it does on the long-term quality of
that control.

REPUTATION AND ACCREDITATION

Reputation is an elusive thing. It defies precise definition, enumera-
tion of its components, and prediction of its effects. Yet it exists, and
it is powerful. It may draw a new student through a school's gates
without any previous direct contact being initiated by that institution.
We are convinced that good schools and colleges, as well as good res-
taurants and good books, are most often marketed more effectively by
casual word than by forms of deliberate advertising. A single student
who feels good about what he or she is getting or has gotten at a school
can be worth far more to the school than the classiest advertisement.

The reputation of a school's certificate, diploma, or degree can have
great financial, social, and personal significance for its holder. For
example, a degree from college A may be worth more in the marketplace than one from college B. Your standing in certain social circles
may relate to the credentials you hold. Also, the way you feel about
your school may affect the way you feel about yourself, which in turn
may affect important aspects of your life not directly related to your
schooling.

Loss of reputation by a school is a sad thing to see. In the late 1960s
and early 1970s, some schools responded to pressures for greater access
to higher education by suddenly initiating an open-admission policy.
Virtually any student who wished to enroll could do so. Not past level
of achievement but level of performance once enrolled was supposed to
be the standard by which the student would be measured. Predictably,
the level of performance in thousands of cases turned out not to be
satisfactory, Yet students were allowed to advance until an outcry
from concerned students, faculty, administrators, legislators, and the
public itself forced some improvement. Tens of thousands of alumni
of those institutions, graduated in the days when high standards pre-
vailed, understandably, are upset about what happened. They believe
that the credentials they earned in a better day were seriously degraded
and that they were cheated by their alma mater.

Reputation derives from the degree of quality maintained through
the years. Obviously you would like to choose the best-quality school

38   at which you can be successful. But do you have any way of making
an informed choice, since quality and reputation are such nebulous
matters?

For those of you considering programs at occupational schools we
can only suggest that you talk to as many people as possible who are,
or have been, associated with the school. Are the graduates readily
accepted in their chosen field, and do they go on to get promotions
and advances in income? As a group, are they well thought of in the
profession?

For you who are considering other types of programs, especially
from institutions that offer degrees and require standardized entrance
examinations such as the Scholastic Aptitude Test (SAT) or American
College Testing Program Assessment (ACT), we suggest a method. We
think that one indicator of reputation for an institution as a whole
may be available to the person who has no other indicator, although
we emphasize that it cannot be used precisely. That indicator is the
quality of the student applicant pool as reflected in SAT or ACT scores.
If you find two institutions that are reasonably comparable in size,
type, and program offerings, but there are significant differences in
their applicants' entrance examination scores, the institution with the
higher scores may be of better quality. This is because either a school
gradually tends to adjust its admissions and teaching standards to
meet its students' capabilities, or it sets standards and expects its
students to meet them. Either way, entrance examination scores may
be at least a rough measure of expectation of student performance
and, hence, the quality of the system. You will find information on
SATs and ACTs in some of the college guides in your library, most
notably Peterson's, which shows the percentage of each applicant
group scoring in each testing range. If you remember that even apparently similar institutions can vary a great deal from one another in
mission and programs, you may find that comparison of entrance examination scores could be of some worth.

In earlier sections we have discussed accreditation. If you are considering a *nondegree* occupational program, it probably is important
that at least the institution, if not the particular program, be accredited
by one of the authorities recognized by the Department of Education
or COPA. If you are seeking a *degree*, you should be especially concerned about accreditation. Your goals and intended use of your credentials will have a great bearing on the importance of accreditation to
you. Most people never think to investigate the accreditation status
of the school they are considering. But don't trust to luck. Take the
steps we have suggested. You wouldn't want to discover someday that
your educational credentials are a source of pain and embarrassment
rather than of pride.

Could any factor be more important to you in choosing the right school than quality of instruction? Yet, of all the elements we discuss in this chapter, this is among the most difficult for you to judge. Quality of instruction may vary enormously even within departments, so how can anyone make meaningful comparisons between departments, much less institutions? Educators may be able to get a reasonably good idea of levels of quality within their institution and may even be able to make some meaningful comparisons with other institutions. But how can you, the prospective student, do the same?

In comparing schools, make some phone calls or visits and ask about faculty quality. Usually near the end of a school's catalog you will find a list of faculty and credentials. How do the credentials you find there compare with those of faculty at the other schools you are considering? If you note a discrepancy among schools, ask why this is so. Especially if you are considering a university, inquire about the amount of emphasis by the faculty on their teaching and advising as compared to scholarship.

The student-faculty ratio will give you a quantitative measure of how much attention you can expect as an individual. If, for example, you find that lower-level courses (often listed as 100- and 200-level courses) habitually carry an enrollment of more than about 30 students, this is an indicator that you ought to question how serious the college is about providing individual attention to its students. Large lecture courses are all right if they will constitute a small portion of your total curriculum, but if they appear to be numerous, question why this is so.

In assessing the answers you get to these inquiries on quality of instruction, you will recognize that people associated with institutions of higher education usually present their institution favorably. Sometimes, though, a staff or faculty member or a student will tell a different kind of story, one that comes from honesty, perhaps, or maybe from bitterness, and you have to take this attitude into consideration.

CURRICULUM

Curriculum variety and flexibility are especially important to the adult student, yet these are often areas of weakness in adult evening and weekend programs. Ask about the total number of fields of study leading to a certificate, diploma, or degree that are offered in these programs as compared to the total number in the day divisions. Then compare the percentages among the schools you are evaluating. The higher the percentage, the greater the curriculum variety and flexibility you are likely to find. This is so because courses, especially at the

40   lower levels, often service more than one major. The more majors you find, the more choice you will probably have in selecting courses that fit your schedule. Don't assume that a university is naturally going to offer you more curriculum variety and flexibility than a small college. The university might give relatively scant attention to the needs of adults whereas the college might try hard to serve its adult students.

WEEKEND AND EVENING SCHOOL PROGRAMS

Should you give special consideration to programs designed particularly for adults? "STOP WASTING THOSE WEEKENDS!" reads the glaring headline of the brochure received in response to a *New York Times* advertisement. "Invest them in Marymount's Weekend College in Tarrytown, New York, 45 minutes from midtown Manhattan. In one to four years you can earn a bachelor of arts degree by attending classes every third weekend."

The program at Marymount enables students to complete 30 credits per year by taking 9 credits each trimester plus one independent study or tutorial course in an area of special interest. Classes meet every third weekend from Friday evening at 7:30 to Sunday at 4 P.M. This schedule permits a student to make the same progress as a student enrolled full-time in a conventional college, while attending classes only six weekends each trimester. The program is "designed for highly motivated students, capable of independent work." Marymount's weekend college is one of a large number of such programs offered throughout the United States.

There may have been a time when students attending classes at night found few courses to choose from and little hope of studying under the best instructors. Today the situation in many places is changed where administrators, recognizing the growing importance of adult students, have expanded course offerings and improved faculty quality and student services during evenings and weekends.

Most programs for adults offer evening courses between 6 and 10 P.M. on weeknights with the majority of classes offered from Monday through Thursday. In some locations Saturday classes as an extension of the evening schedule are also popular. Sunday classes are still rare except at schools offering structured weekend programs.

A major advantage of evening and weekend courses is that they often require just one 3-hour class meeting per week. Some courses, though, such as languages, may not be conducive to one meeting a week and may necessitate attendance twice a week. But this is still less demanding than the traditional daytime regimen of two or three or four classes per course each week.

If you are taking two courses during the semester, it may be possible   **41**
to select courses that meet on the same nights. Evening schedules
often are planned to enable students to take a natural sequence of
courses on a consecutive time schedule. For many such reasons, evening and weekend programs are popular among adults.

SUMMER SCHOOL PROGRAMS

Can you arrange job and family commitments to allow you summers
free for study? If so, you may be able to have a wonderful time yet
take grand strides toward your educational goals. "Summer by the Sea"
says one college advertisement. "Combine a great vacation with an
exciting educational experience." If you prefer the mountains, several
colleges throughout the country will give you the opportunity of
combining summer study and fun in fresh mountain air. Or consider
these offerings by the University of California, Santa Cruz, as listed
in *Learning Vacations* by Gerson G. Eisenberg (Peterson's Guides,
Inc., P.O. Box 2123, Princeton, NJ 08540, 1982, paperback, $7.95):
"International study tours for adults, two to four weeks, usually in
the summer. Recent examples include a calligraphy workshop and
tour in London (three weeks) and a pottery tour of Japan (17 days)."

Just name your summer sport—sailing, backpacking, horseback rid-
ing—and you are sure to find a college to accommodate you and your
family while you study. Colleges have become increasingly eager to
make better use of their facilities in summer, so fun and study programs
have proliferated. You may happily discover that you can simultaneously get college credit and have a great vacation for less money than
you would spend for a similar vacation not attached to college study.
You may be able to live in a college dorm room or efficiency apart-
ment, take your meals in the cafeteria, and enjoy cultural and social
events for a reasonable price. A woman of our acquaintance, a widow
with two children, works in an elementary school cafeteria from September through the third week of June. Then she and the children
pack up and go to a college, or sometimes two colleges, for the summer.
Some of her most interesting college work has taken place outside the
classroom. She has studied Shakespeare's nature imagery in a cabin in
the Adirondack Mountains (while the children swam, played tennis,
fished); she has painted the Pacific Ocean for credit and surfed after
class just for the fun of it; she has studied the therapeutic aspects of
figure skating in a breathtaking setting in the Canadian Rockies. She
has played and learned her way almost to an associate degree, entirely
through summer school programs.

You may enroll in virtually any summer course at any school unless you are matriculating there. Other than for prerequisite courses
in some instances, usually there are no admission requirements for

42   summer school programs. If you are already matriculated, however, and are planning on attending some other school's summer program, be sure beforehand that your school will accept the credits you will earn.

If your interests lead you to consider trade and technical schools, business institutes, or two-year colleges rather than four-year colleges and universities, you might find that you can participate in a great learning experience through a summer internship, working in the field of your choice, earning money while doing it, and making progress toward your certificate, diploma, or associate degree. For example, Blair Ruller, as a student at the Culinary Institute of America in Hyde Park, NY, had a summer internship as a chef in a restaurant on the West Coast. An Easterner, Blair had never been west of Buffalo. In his summer internship, not only did he get to practice his trade while progressing toward his associate degree, but he spent his leisure hours in fantastically beautiful settings on the Pacific Ocean. It was an unforgettable summer for him.

EXTENSION CENTERS

Remember the days when the only place you could take a course was on a campus? If you were fortunate enough to live within a reasonable distance of the campus, you might have been able to squeeze out enough time from your busy schedule to sit in on a class two or three times a week. But if you had to commute 45 minutes to an hour or more each way, forget it!

Fortunately for many adults today, that situation has changed. If you live in a medium-sized or large metropolitan area and are not fortunate enough to live near a campus, there is almost certain to be an off-campus center or satellite within reach. Waning enrollments on campus have encouraged many colleges and universities and other types of institutions to reach out to the adult market and establish programs in community centers, libraries, and unused school buildings.

While most campuses offer reasonably good facilities and services, those at extension centers should be checked out. Will you be sitting for up to three hours in chairs intended for children? Are the classrooms well lighted and air conditioned? Will necessary instructional aids (chalkboards, projectors, screens) be on hand? Is parking convenient and adequate? Will required course books be sold at the off-campus location? Will you have easy access to library services? Is there a snack bar or at least a vending service provided? Each of such factors affects your comfort, convenience, or ability to learn. If you do encounter problems while attending classes at an off-campus location, don't hesitate to complain, and encourage your classmates to do the same.

Be especially cautious when considering extension centers operated
by other than local institutions. Horror stories are abundant. For
example, students have been promised a full program only to find
later that the center in fact has been giving them inferior instruction
and a partial curriculum, the rest of which must be taken on the main
campus that is several states away. Many states have begun to crack
down on the abuses of extension centers. The process of gaining
quality control, though, probably will take years. In the meantime,
you should recognize that extension centers can be a real boon for
you when well operated by a high-quality institution. Investigate the
circumstances carefully when you consider an extension center.

GOING AWAY TO SCHOOL OR STAYING WHERE YOU ARE

Which is right for you? Nontraditional programs make this a non-
question. But in considering traditional programs, most adults would
say they have no choice; they have to attend a school near home.
What they may really mean is that they choose not to take the risks:
perhaps quitting a job, moving a family, leaving friends and relatives,
resettling in a community where a school offers the program they
want, and then after getting their credentials, seeking a new job. We
have heard all kinds of stories about going away to school—enough to
convince us that we ought not try to give advice beyond highlighting
a few of the major considerations.

Does that distant school offer one of the best programs of its kind,
and are you absolutely sure that program is right for you? Have you
talked with a graduate of the school, preferably of the program? Are
you willing to make at least a two-day visit to the campus to check
out the program and living arrangements?

Unless you are more unattached to your current location than most
adults, you should patiently consider such things. You will want to go
with confidence if you make that choice, and your satisfaction when
you are enrolled at that school will be greater if you have carefully examined the matter. An entirely new environment indeed may be just
what is needed for an entirely new you.

If, though, you are like the majority of adults, you will stay where
you are and commute to a school near home. Even if your first impulse
is to think less well of what is in your own backyard, or if the school
near you is not highly regarded generally, remember that certain programs within it might be well respected. Program quality tends to vary
a good deal within schools. Most institutions have at least one or two
very good departments, and a certificate, diploma, or degree in one
of those programs will carry more career weight than the name of the
school itself.

Academic Credit Policies

This matter of importance in choosing a college will be treated in detail in chapter 5.

Costs and Financial Aid

Money is almost always a major factor in an adult's choice of a school. When they are faced with a choice between a school costing, say, $25 a credit and one where tuition is $100 per credit or more, the decision for many adults may seem cut and dried. When the selection of a school is based simply on a comparison of tuition and fees, though, the result is often a poor decision. You should check with the financial aid office of each school you are considering in order to determine what assistance, if any, is available from the school. Depending upon policies for transfer and experiential credit awards, coupled with the amount of financial aid available, your credentials could cost less at a school where the tuition is high than at a school where tuition is lower. Much more on financing your degree will be covered in chapter 7.

Facilities, Services, and Attitudes

In many ways throughout this book we treat the question of facilities, services, and attitudes as related to you, the adult student. We suggest that you deliberately draft a checklist of concerns. If child care is important to you, for instance, put it high on your list. Add your library concerns and anything else that may trouble you. Then as you make your calls or visits, your list of questions will grow, just as will the answers, as you speak with students, faculty, and administrators. And soon the picture will become clearer: School B offers more of what you need in regard to facilities, services, and manner of treating you than does school A.

Cultural, Social, and Fraternal Activities

Higher education institutions often are the hub of community cultural life, especially in small cities and towns. The school you choose, especially if it is a large college or university, might very well have an art gallery, a museum of natural history, classic and avant-garde film series, and music and theater series. Social and fraternal possibilities are endless, from small groups with specific interests to large gatherings with diverse interests. Fraternities and sororities exist on some campuses specifically for adult students. If cultural, social, and

fraternal activities are important in your choice of school, the dean   **45**
of students, director of continuing education, or head of the student
government should be able to give you the information you need for
seeking out groups for further investigation.

CONCERNS RELATIVE TO CERTAIN STUDENTS

Special Programs for Minorities

If you feel you might benefit from a special program, you should
be aware that there are programs that could meet your needs. For
example, many colleges in New York State participate in the Higher
Educational Opportunity Program (HEOP). Although this program is
not exclusively designed for racial minorities, it has a large percentage
enrolled. The program provides special remedial courses, counseling,
financial aid, and other kinds of assistance. If you are interested in a
special program, check with your state's education department to determine what might be available. Also note the financial aid references
in chapter 7. Some of them are of interest particularly to minorities
and may provide insight into special programs as well as information
on financial aid sources.

Special Programs for Women

Contributed by Nancy Lampen, *Assistant Professor, Speech Communication,*
Monroe Community College, Rochester, NY, **and Jeanne Crane,** *Educational*
Consultant, Canandaigua, NY

A woman in Pittsburgh hears about a program for women in her
area and is able to pursue the science degree she always wanted. In
Oregon a woman who received a bachelor's degree in liberal arts 15
years ago discovers she can take a women-in-management program
that she views as her ticket to reentering the work force. These are
examples of "special programs for women."

The possibilities are exciting yet confusing. There is no one definition of special programs for women and no one single place to look
for information. Because federal and state funds were available to
start many programs, these programs are often found in places where
you might not expect to find them. What exists in your area may or
may not meet your goals or fit your circumstances. The offerings can
range in length from a two-hour information session for reentry women
at one school to a full degree program at another. Most of these programs have been designed in a painstaking way to address the needs of
women from a variety of backgrounds or at least the in-depth needs

of one group of women. A few are little more than marketing techniques for increasing the number of enrollees. This section will acquaint you with types of programs and offer suggestions of things to consider before committing yourself to a specific program.

Many institutions recognize that the decision to go to school may be a difficult one, so they have developed programs to provide information and support for making the transition. Such programs include women's orientation programs that cover many of the issues in this chapter as specifically applicable to that school; special counseling for returning women by personnel trained to understand adult development needs, family stresses, and the anxieties faced by someone who has been away from education for a number of years; peer-support groups or women's groups that offer women an opportunity to explore feelings and problems with others who have had or are having similar experiences; and individual and/or group career counseling to explore nontraditional fields, examine marketplace potential for job placement, and facilitate the setting of realistic short- and long-range goals.

Some offerings have been designed to give women opportunities that were not open to them earlier. Past sex stereotyping, particularly in high school, has led to many women not having had the proper preparation (especially in science and math) for beginning the higher education program of their choice. Both noncredit courses (such as those to reduce math anxiety) and credit courses (such as introduction to college chemistry and algebra) may be necessary before admission to a specific certificate, diploma, or degree program is granted.

The whole area of women's studies originated to compensate for the lack of serious attention given women. Some institutions have separate departments in women's studies that may offer a major or such elective courses as The History of the Women's Movement, or Women in Literature. Some institutions have not created a separate department but rather have integrated women's issues into already existing courses, such as Sociology of the Family, perhaps including a unit on women's roles or on sex equality.

There are many kinds of women's centers to serve you. Ann Diehl, a past president of the United States Association of Evening Students, says:

> An example would be the Women's Educational and Counseling Center at the State University of New York at Farmingdale, which offers a complete range of support services for women. At the Women's Center women find that their "unique" problems are shared by many, and also that there are answers to questions about themselves, their educations, and their careers.

With all the possible options, how do you choose the program of study you want, that's affordable, that's within a reasonable commuting distance, that doesn't stereotype you but has an environment that allows you to be all you're capable of being, and that offers assistance when you need it? Perhaps we can help somewhat by providing a checklist of items you might keep in mind when making your decision. No one institution is likely to provide all of these features as applicable particularly to women, but probably only a few of them are of special significance in meeting your specific needs. You might check off those items that are most important to you and then go back and rank them according to your needs.

Checklist

1. Are women now present in that institution's programs which traditionally have enrolled only men?
2. Do these women consider their higher education experience as basically positive?
3. Does the school give credit for what you have learned as a homemaker, a volunteer, or a job-holder?
4. Are adult women depicted in publications of the school?
5. Is there a support group for returning women?
6. What is the percentage of women faculty and administrators? If it seems to be low, is there a satisfactory explanation?
7. Is there a child-care center?
8. Does the financial aid office have information on special sources of financial aid for women?
9. Are there any special programs for women?
10. Are there cooperative education (combined work and study) options for reentering women so that you can gain experience and build a résumé to improve your status in the labor market?
11. Can the placement office tell you about the employment success of other reentry women?

By now you should have a sense of the range of programs for women and some approaches for deciding which program is best for you. If you need further help, you may be able to get both guidance and publications that address your needs from the following organizations:

Displaced Homemakers Network, Inc.
1010 Vermont Avenue, N.W., Suite 817
Washington, DC 20005

Project on Equal Education Rights (PEER)
9th Floor, 1413 K Street, N.W.
Washington, DC 20005

Women's Educational Equity Act (WEEA)
Education Development Center
55 Chapel Street
Newton, MA 02160

48   ACCOMMODATION TO THE NEEDS OF THE DISABLED

Contributed by S. Tapper Bragg, *a graduate of Hofstra University, Hempstead, NY, at the undergraduate, graduate, and law school levels, and himself a disabled person*

In addition to all the other factors involved in choosing a school, physically disabled individuals must consider whether institutions in which they are interested can accommodate their special needs. Before making a final choice, a disabled applicant should visit the school to determine whether he or she can function properly in the physical environment of the campus. A personal interview with an appropriate administrator is highly desirable, if not essential, to allow the official to become familiar with any special needs that the applicant may have and to allow the potential student to sense the attitude of the administration to the disabled.

The twin goals of a program for physically disabled students should be to make the campus accessible to them and to make it possible for them to complete an academic curriculum. Handicapped individuals are expected to meet the same admissions and retention standards as any other students. The sole reason for providing special facilities and services is to compensate for or remove any barriers beyond the student's control that may unfairly hinder academic performance. Physical facilities should be modified as necessary to accommodate the disabled. Attention must be given to ramps and elevators, restrooms, public telephones, drinking fountains, parking places, and the marking of locations in Braille.

If note-taking is a problem, one possible solution is to ask a fellow student to provide carbon or photo copies of his or her notes. With permission of the instructor, a student might be allowed to record lectures on tape.

Disabled students may need additional time and/or the use of an electric typewriter to complete examinations. It may be possible for the institution to arrange for volunteer writers, provided by local service organizations, to whom examination answers may be dictated. Adult students, however, should be aware that these volunteers are generally not available in the evening or on weekends when many of them take courses. It may, therefore, be necessary to reschedule examinations at a mutually convenient time. Will the institution be receptive to such special arrangements?

Adult students for whom transportation is a problem may wish to live on campus. Those who do should be certain that residence halls meet their needs. If the institution permits, severely disabled students may hire private attendants to assist them. Some schools hire other students to provide their disabled colleagues with limited assistance in activities of daily living.

Leonard DuBoff, a sightless Hofstra University graduate who now   **49**
teaches law, has suggested that blind students can acquire texts in
Braille or talking-book form from the school library's interlibrary loan
program or the National Council of Jewish Women. The American
Foundation for the Blind can supply a drawing kit that converts illustrations into raised-line drawings. (See your library's copy of *Encyclopedia of Associations* to get the address of the association that provides services to meet your specific needs.) An entire afternoon or
evening may be set aside to work in the library with a reader when
preparing a research project, and papers may be written with the aid
of tape recorders.

Unfortunately, higher education programs for the deaf and hard of
hearing are in their infancy. Among the services provided by some
institutions are note-takers, classroom sign-language interpreters, special counseling, and sign-language classes for staff members.

Disability is no barrier to successful participation in cocurricular
activities. Physically handicapped students frequently assume leading
roles in student government, campus media, institutional governance,
and academic and social organizations. Some schools provide outlets
for the athletic interests of their disabled students through such activities as wheelchair basketball, wheelchair football, archery, swim-
ming, track and field, table tennis, and square dancing.

The first contact of many able-bodied persons with the disabled
often takes place on a campus. While some adjustments may be needed
on both sides, interaction between the disabled and able tends to
develop easily, and discrimination is not a significant problem. A fellow
student should not feel hurt when assistance offered to a disabled
individual is refused. Most disabled persons prefer to act independently
whenever possible. On the other hand, they usually recognize when
assistance is needed and in those cases may gladly accept aid or even
request it. The general campus population should neither fear nor feel
awkward in encounters with their disabled counterparts. With a little
experience, people will soon find that contact with a physically handicapped person need not be a source of trauma.

In choosing a school, a disabled student should carefully assess each
campus in terms of its ability to meet both educational and physical
needs. The following publications should be useful both to disabled
persons who are choosing a school and to administrators charged
with developing and supervising programs for the disabled:

Accessibility Modifications (with Appendix) by Ronald L. Mace,
available for $3.00 from the North Carolina Department of Insur-
ance, Special Office of the Handicapped, P.O. Box 26387, Raleigh,
NC 27611.

Campus Advocacy: How to Start an OPIDS, a guide that describes
the steps for campuses to take in order to activate service programs

for disabled students. Available from the Office to Promote Independence of Disabled Students, Activities Center, Memorial Hall, The University of Georgia, Athens, GA 30602. Single copy free.

VISITING CAMPUSES

Catalogs, brochures, and bulletins provide valuable sources of information about programs, course offerings, and student services, and they should be examined. But a truer picture of what a school has to offer you might be obtained through a well-planned visit to the campus.

Be sure to visit at a time when classes are in full session. The only advantage of visiting a campus during intersession is the ease with which you will find a parking space. It is best to set aside two full days if possible (or at least one day) since you will need ample time to visit various campus facilities and talk to some key people. The following are among the places you might want to include in your tour:

- Admissions office
- Financial aid office
- Office of the dean of continuing education or adult student programs
- Office of the academic department head in the field of your interest
- Office of the evening or adult students' organization
- Career placement and counseling office
- Offices of program coordinators responsible for awarding credit for life experience, noncollegiate courses, and proficiency examinations
- Library and other research facilities
- Computer center (if applicable)
- Bookstore
- Student center
- Child-care facilities (if applicable)
- Dormitories (if applicable)
- Cafeteria
- Athletic and recreational facilities
- Classrooms, lecture halls, and laboratories

You would be wise to list all of the places you would like to visit in the order of their importance to you and to follow this sequence as closely as possible during your tour. Then if you run out of time, you will at least have visited the most important places. You might also be prepared to take notes, and you should collect as much relevant printed literature as possible. This information will enable you to reflect upon your visit later and make a more objective comparison with other schools. Finally, if you wish to meet with a specific person, you **51** should call a week or two in advance and make an appointment.

Some schools will permit a visitor to sit in on a class as an observer. While this might provide some insight, it may consume too much valuable time, and observing a class is a hit-or-miss proposition. No school has all good or all bad instructors, and all instructors have good and bad days. You might use your time more effectively by questioning several adult students who have spent some time in the program you are considering.

The most important objective of your visit should be to acquire a sense of how well the school fits your particular needs and interests—both personal and academic. Factors you should consider carefully are the general attitude toward adult students and the programs and facilities available to accommodate their special needs. These could make a big difference in your potential success as an adult student.

WHAT IF YOUR LOCAL SCHOOL DOES NOT MEET YOUR NEEDS?

What can you do if you simply cannot find a local school that offers a program of the type you are certain you want? You still have options. First, let's think about degree programs.

Suppose you want a program in accounting, but your local college only has a business administration program. You might decide to take the business program in its entirety because it's the local program that is closest to meeting your needs. At least it could lead to a job in which you would deal with accounting problems in a general way, and that might prove to be satisfying enough.

Or you might consider using local college courses to advance you well along the path toward a particular degree that you can later complete, either through transfer to another college or through means we will explore in the next two chapters. In any case you will want to examine carefully the course requirements leading to the degree. And don't rely on your own examination, but check out the matter with the advisers for the program that you will ultimately be completing. Be certain you know which courses you will need, and which ones from your local college they will accept. At that local college you will probably find many of the components of the program you eventually will be completing. For example, if you are determined to be an accountant and your local college offers only the business administration degree, you will certainly find that some basic accounting courses are a part of that business program. You will be able to take them and get them credited later toward your accounting degree. Also at the college near home you might be able to take the economics, mathematics, and core liberal arts and sciences courses that would be required in your eventual accounting program. Thus, even though your local

52   college does not offer a degree in the program you want, a significant
portion of that program may be completed there through proper
selection of courses.

What about vocational programs that do not award a degree? Although there might be some transfer capability from a local program
in, say, drafting to a program for architectural engineering technicians in some other city, this is not very likely or even practical. Most
vocational schools prefer to give all of the courses themselves rather
than accept parts from some other school. Also, moving to another
city to complete your program right away so your credentials can be
used might not be practical for you.

For the person who is stymied locally in seeking a degree or pursuing some other kind of credentials there is still another hope. In
earlier sections we introduced nontraditional study as a means to
higher education, and in the next chapter we will take a more detailed look at it.

Student Profile

DAVID MCROBERTS of Louisville, Colorado

*My certificate program as an airframe and
powerplant maintenance technician broadens
my career options.*

I'm not so old (twenty-seven), but sometimes it seems I've been
practicing my profession of flying for a long time. I flew gliders at
age fourteen and got my commercial pilot's license while I was still in
high school. I anticipated some dead ends, though, in the profession
unless I got some more education and training, which led me to a
certificate program at Colorado Aero Tech in Broomfield, Colorado.

Many of my classmates are younger and have not had any college.
Some, though, like me, have had some college and have specific
reasons for also wanting the program this school offers in airframe
and powerplant maintenance.

I had spent two years at Pacific Union College in Angwin,
California. The college is affiliated with the Seventh-day Adventist
Church, and I felt the urge to combine my flying experience with
church work. Through a combination of circumstances I ended up as
a missionary pilot, flying for one year in the Solomon Islands and
New Guinea. After a year back in the states, I was called back to the

islands to fly for one more year. My wife, Jan, accompanied me, and
much of our work was complementary. She also is a pilot and has a
master's degree in public health services (and she also flew gliders at
age fourteen, although I didn't know her at the time).

After we returned from this second missionary tour I got a job
flying Twin Otters and Dehaviland Dash 7s, and Jan became a real
estate broker. As a step in becoming an airline or corporate pilot I
decided to finish my degree, a B.S. in Aerospace Science, at
Metropolitan State College in Denver. The college would accept my
work at Colorado Aero Tech toward my degree requirements, so no
time would be lost, and there were other advantages to taking the
certificate course. For one thing, I have been involved with the
Antique Airplane Association, and can use my training to help
rebuild and restore antique aircraft (I have my own 1947 Luscombe
and am in the process of restoring a 1947 Aeronca Chief). And, even
more important, my program as an airframe and powerplant
maintenance technician broadens my career options. If something
should go wrong with pursuing a career primarily as a pilot, there are
many things I could do with my training at Colorado Aero Tech.

At school we get lots of practical experience, working on both
radial and jet engines, and hydraulic and electrical systems. We do
dope and fabric work, sheet metal work, and much more. I had long
known about the school because I grew up near it, and a high school
teacher encouraged me to enroll several years ago. The facilities are
great, and I'm well pleased that I entered the program. Although
full-time schoolwork and my part-time work as a flight instructor
keep me busy, I'm sure that Jan and I will survive, and the future
looks bright indeed.

4.

Considering Nontraditional Higher Education

Which nontraditional program or course of action would best fit my needs?

EXTERNAL DEGREES

Suppose, after evaluating local institutions, you decide that you cannot complete the program you really want. Or suppose that a degree program that regularly takes you out of your home and interferes with your work presents insurmountable barriers for you as a would-be adult student. Or suppose you want the opportunity to work on a college degree at your own pace, not the one set for you by a fixed class schedule. Or suppose you want to start right now, but the semester has already begun at your local college. Or suppose you simply cannot afford the cost of a college degree at a local institution. Or suppose that you would like to have the degree in a year or two or three instead of in the several years it might take you working away, one or two courses at a time, in a traditional setting. Or suppose that over a period of years you have acquired the equivalent of a good deal of college learning and perhaps some college credit, but not a degree. You may have taken a smattering of college courses, some on various campuses, some by correspondence. In addition, you may have taken military service courses and company in-service courses and had a variety of learning experiences that were not the result of any formal instruction. These are a lot of suppose's and may-have's, and we could add more. If one or more apply to you, then you should consider enrolling in an external degree program.

What is an external degree program? It is one that has no require-   **55**
ments, or minimal ones, for on-campus attendance. It relies largely
on independent learning, and most often can be entered at any time
of the year. It usually grants significant credit for documented learning you have already acquired, and will grant credit for other forms
of learning as you go along and submit new accomplishments to be
judged for credit. The various sources of credit in external programs
include:

1. Previous college work, even if it comprises miscellaneous courses
   rather than an integrated program. Such work is usually accepted
   at full value regardless of how long ago it was taken.
2. Current college work, taken at a local college, to be transferred
   to the external degree program.
3. Correspondence courses, from accredited colleges or universities.
   You may have taken such courses already, or you can easily take
   them at home, selecting your courses from thousands of offerings at more than 70 institutions.
4. Proficiency examinations, such as CLEP, ACT PEP, AP, CPE,
   RCE, GRE, or TECEP, which you have already completed or
   can pass, sometimes with minimal preparation.
5. Military service. Courses, examinations, and on-the-job experience you may have had, or are now getting, in the military can
   all lead to credit.
6. Noncollegiate courses you may have taken, or can take, offered
   by businesses, industries, government agencies, labor unions,
   police academies, and other organizations.
7. Experiential learning (experience credit), for appropriate jobs,
   volunteer work, travel, reading, creative work, or other kinds of
   experiences.
8. Cooperative education, apprenticeships, and internships, for the
   work/learning experience that the degree-granting institution
   may arrange specifically with your current employer, or with
   another employer.
9. Possession of professional licenses (such as LPN, RN, CPA,
   CLU, FAA) that may be evaluated to be the equivalent of college courses.

In many cases adults have already acquired the knowledge and
need only to take the correspondence courses, proficiency examinations, or experiential learning assessment to gain the credits, often
with little or no further study. The significant number of credits that
are frequently derived from the sources listed above, and others, will
usually enable you to attain your college degree externally in much
less time than it would take you to get that same degree on campus.

56   You can be a full- or part-time worker in your home or at a job, far from a campus, and yet pursue college studies. In short, you can earn a living while you earn your college degree.

An external degree program does not preclude you from participating in on-campus experiences, if that is your wish. If you prefer to attend some college classes, and you have an accredited campus nearby, you will usually be able to integrate your courses into your external degree program, even if it is administered by a distant college.

Over 75 accredited colleges and universities offer external degree programs. One of the most popular programs is Regents College Degrees (formerly called Regents External Degree Program) of the University of the State of New York. This program will allow you to apply past accomplishments toward the following degrees: in liberal arts—Associate in Arts, Associate in Science, Bachelor of Arts, Bachelor of Science; in business—Bachelor of Science; in technology—Associate in Science (Nuclear Technology), Bachelor of Science (Nuclear Technology), Associate in Science (Computer Software), Bachelor of Science (Computer Software), Bachelor of Science (Computer Technology), Associate in Science (Electronics Technology), Bachelor of Science (Electronics Technology); in nursing—Associate in Science (Nursing), Associate in Applied Science (Nursing), and Bachelor of Science (Nursing). Candidates for Regents College Degrees may meet degree requirements through any combination of the following educational experiences:

- College courses taken for credit through a regionally accredited institution, whether taken in residence or by correspondence
- Scores earned on proficiency exams (most of those discussed in chapter 5)
- Military service school courses and MOS's
- Experiential learning measured by a Special Assessment Examination
- Noncollegiate instruction (as listed in the guides described in chapter 5)
- Certain Federal Aviation Administration (FAA) pilot certificates

Anyone, anywhere in the world, may enroll in the Regents program. Its administrative fees are modest, and in return for them you receive evaluation, a master transcript, and advising services, as you request. The program is fully accredited by the Middle States Association of Colleges and Schools.

The Regents Credit Bank is a service of Regents College Degrees for people who need to consolidate their educational accomplishments onto a single transcript that is widely acceptable for employment or college enrollment purposes. The same policies on acceptance of credit that govern Regents College Degrees also apply to the Regents Credit Bank.

You may obtain detailed information on either of these services by writing to: Regents College Degrees, Cultural Education Center, Albany, NY 12230.

Associate degrees, baccalaureate degrees, and even graduate degrees (including the Ph.D.) can be earned in many disciplines through a variety of external degree programs. Accredited programs are offered in most states. Several programs are open to anyone in the world regardless of age, previous education, or citizenship.

But are these degrees any "good"? Read the profile of Dawn Logan-Weinberg in this chapter to see just how good an external degree can be.

External degrees can be the only avenue to higher education for some people, among them some handicapped or incarcerated individuals. Marjorie Phillips of New York City was awarded her associate in arts degree by the Regents program on her 80th birthday and then went on to achieve her bachelor's degree soon thereafter. She explains, "I was physically unable to travel by bus or subway to attend classes. I had always been interested in pursuing a college education but had never been able to find a program which would accommodate my physical limitations." Her granddaughters, one in medical school and the other a senior in college, proudly refer to her as their "intellectual grandmother."

Lawrence S. Gaskins got his Regents degree while in prison. He subscribes to the motto, written on a cell-block wall, "Prison is in the mind. If your mind is free, any amount of bodily imprisonment can be overcome. But if once you let the mind become imprisoned, you are truly in hell." Larry says, "Today I am a different man. I have a good job, a loving wife, a new home, and the respect of my fellow workers and my community. Today I feel more alive than at any other time in my life." He is continuing his education with a goal of attaining the Master of Social Work degree and helping others to overcome their problems so they can achieve their full capabilities.

Some external degree schools, such as Thomas A. Edison State College in New Jersey, do not require a student to take any courses through the college in order to receive a degree. In fact, Edison does not offer any courses and it has no faculty in residence; the college is chartered by the state solely for the purpose of guiding and evaluating college-level learning and awarding external degrees. Students have been awarded as many as 90 credits by Edison for life learning (although such large amounts are unusual). The remaining credits required for a bachelor's degree are earned by passing college proficiency exams or by other means.

58   Advantages of external degree programs usually include freedom from classroom attendance, open admissions policies, a flexible curriculum, low cost, and credit for noncollegiate experience. Disadvantages include lack of classroom contact with other students, limited personal contact with course instructors, and the difficulty of maintaining the necessary discipline and motivation needed to pursue a degree independently. Like Dawn Logan-Weinberg, you may also be faced with some skepticism from potential employers and others, however unwarranted, about the legitimacy of an external degree. Probably you won't though, for two reasons. Dawn chose a professional field in which licensing is required; thus, specialized accreditation in addition to institutional accreditation was an issue. Only a few external degree fields of study, like fields pursued in the traditional way on campus, are subject to specialized accreditation. Also, since Dawn first faced that skepticism, external degrees have become much better known, as have the abilities of graduates of those programs. Many employers value the qualities demonstrated in the attainment of an external degree: determination, initiative, and the ability to plan and complete an extended project independently with minimal guidance. Certainly, many graduates have testified that their external degree credentials have helped them to promotions and to greater job and personal satisfaction. Many have also used their credentials to qualify for study at higher degree levels.

You should be aware, though, that some so-called external degree programs are run by unscrupulous profiteers. "Diploma mills" sometimes create an "accrediting authority" just for the purpose of "accrediting" itself. As the United States Department of Education warns, "The liberal chartering laws in some States permit the existence of correspondence schools whose practices amount virtually to the sale of diplomas or degrees. Such degrees have no academic value or recognition and may even discredit the professional and intellectual integrity of the holder." The FBI and U.S. Department of Justice have recently begun to investigate and indict fraudulent operators of some diploma mills. Some states are making their chartering laws more rigorous. We believe that you would benefit by considering programs accredited by authorities recognized by the U.S. Department of Education or the Council on Postsecondary Accreditation. Among the accredited institutions offering external degrees you should be able to find a program that meets most of your needs.

Before investing your time and money in an external degree, you might do well to seek more information or even professional counseling. A source of additional information is *Your College Degree: The External Degree Way*, by William C. Haponski, Sandra G. Haponski, and Charles E. McCabe. This 30-page booklet provides detailed information on the external degree process and gives data on a sample program. (It is available, together with information on external degree counseling, from ETC Associates, 507 Rider Road, Clayville, NY 13322, for $3.00, including postage and handling.) ETC also publishes the 64-page *Directory of External Degrees from Accredited Colleges and Universities* ($12.95 including postage and handling).

CORRESPONDENCE PROGRAMS AND COURSES

If you like to work independently but feel you need some structure and direction, you might consider correspondence study. Correspondence education is offered by a wide variety of institutions and agencies and is designed to meet many educational goals. It can be used oftentimes as a means of credit toward a degree whether external or on campus, and it can be used in many nondegree situations.

A correspondence course normally involves a predesigned series of lessons that must be completed in a prescribed sequence. A text is either provided or purchased locally. As you complete each written assignment (after studying the appropriate section of the text), you mail it to the school. Your instructor grades your work and returns it within a short time with comments and suggestions. You may either wait for this feedback on your assignment or go right on to the next lesson. Anytime you have questions or problems, you can write to your instructor. Some schools also arrange telephone communication or visits with instructors. Instructors are usually conscientious and thorough when providing feedback to students. The individual attention the correspondence student receives from the instructor is often much greater than would normally be received in the classroom. However, the lack of face-to-face interaction with instructor and classmates is a major shortcoming for some people. Also, the correspondence course package does not permit the flexibility that is often possible in conventional classroom courses.

Correspondence study does have certain advantages over the classroom setting. Most noteworthy, you are free to study at times of your choosing, and at your own pace (although a reasonable time limit for completion may be set for some courses). It is possible to finish a correspondence course in a few weeks if you push hard, or, if this is too fast, you may take much longer to complete it. You have a wide range of course offerings, and usually you can start at any time of the year. In addition, if you are taking the courses for credit, the cost of correspondence study generally is less than the tuition you would pay if you took a comparable course in residence. And, of course, you avoid the cost of commuting and related expenses.

Courses for Credit

Many accredited colleges and universities in the United States offer undergraduate correspondence courses, and a few offer graduate courses, for credit. These courses can be used as part of a program at the institution offering them, or at some other school. The majority of these colleges and universities are members of the National University Continuing Education Association (NUCEA). It publishes *The Independent Study Catalog,* available in your library (or from Peterson's Guides, P.O. Box 2123, Princeton, NJ 08540, for $5.95 plus $1.25 postage). You may also want to consult *The Macmillan Guide to Correspondence Study* in your library. Most residential colleges and external degree programs will accept correspondence course credits from accredited sources. However, the number of credits that may be applied toward a degree could be limited to 30. If you need a credit course that is not available at your college or in your external degree program, a home study course from another accredited institution might be the answer. Before you enroll, however, make sure the course will be accepted for credit by your school. If you want to apply the credits of a non-NUCEA-member college or university to a degree, we suggest you make sure that the institution is accredited by an authority recognized by the U.S. Department of Education or the Council on Postsecondary Accreditation.

Noncredit Courses for Learning New Skills

If you are not interested in credit but want skills that will enable you to get promoted in your present career, change careers, set up your own business, learn the rudiments of a trade so you can save money by doing things yourself, or just learn a new skill for the enjoyment of using it, then you can consider noncredit correspondence courses and programs. The National Home Study Council (NHSC) is the accrediting authority for noncredit home study courses, and is recognized by the U.S. Department of Education and the Council on Postsecondary Accreditation. Send for NHSC's free annual *Directory of Accredited Home Study Schools,* National Home Study Council, 1601 Eighteenth Street, N.W., Washington, DC 20009. Perhaps you would like to learn some computer programming languages so you can use your small business computer more effectively. Courses from Heathkit/Zenith Educational Systems in St. Joseph, MI, might help you. Or suppose that you want to start your own income tax preparation and financial planning business. You are not interested in a degree, or perhaps have one already in some other field. National Tax Training School in Monsey, NY, could be your answer for basic and advanced income tax preparation courses, or Insurance Achievement,

Inc., in Baton Rouge, LA, for financial planning. The *Directory* will **61** guide you to the appropriate schools, and they in turn will send you catalogs and other information. The number and variety of courses are amazing.

Not all home study schools are accredited by NHSC and covered by their code of conduct and ethics. This does not mean that an unaccredited school should be avoided, but you should be cautious when considering it. Accreditation for vocational programs through correspondence probably is not as important as it would be for credit courses that you expect to apply toward a degree. If a nonaccredited correspondence school will give you the type of training you want, and you are satisfied with the cost and method of payment, then you should certainly go ahead with the course. If a large amount of money is required before you actually begin a course, though, this should raise a red flag. Before enrolling, you might do well to check out the school with a local Better Business Bureau or Chamber of Commerce.

Other Types of Noncollegiate Courses

We have already referred to the American Management Association's home study courses as an example of what you can get through independent study. Many reputable associations that do not come within the purview of one of the accrediting authorities we have discussed, as well as some government agencies and various nonprofit organizations, have developed correspondence courses for the enrichment of their members or the general public. The Armed Forces, for example, have some of the finest correspondence courses ever developed. Some of them are not just for active duty personnel, but for people connected in other ways with defense work. Your own company may have correspondence courses and you might not know about them. Use the *Encyclopedia of Associations,* read your company newsletters, or visit your company's human resources office for help in locating appropriate courses. If the source of a correspondence course is a reputable, well-established organization, you probably will get excellent results from your home study experience.

TELEVISION, RADIO, AND NEWSPAPER COURSES

While you were watching your way through years of sitcoms, game shows, soap operas, and football games, as most of us have done, no doubt you always hoped that one day the medium of television would offer much more than that. Occasionally we have had reason for optimism; a few programs have been both entertaining and enlightening. But as an educational medium, television largely has been a disappointment. Well, now we have good reason for renewed hope. After decades of struggle since the early 1950s, the infusion of billions of dollars, and the dedication of many researchers, programmers, and broadcasters, educational television seems to have established itself at last. Excellent courses and even parts of degree programs can now be pursued on a regular basis via television, and without doubt, a strong trend for developing more and more distance learning capabilities is with us. This cannot help but benefit working adults, the handicapped, and those people who otherwise are not well served by traditional higher education.

You can take television courses that are aired in segments at fixed times or else you can receive a video cassette or disk for viewing at your convenience. Most often the course comes as a package, with texts or other study material and examinations included. Sometimes you proceed entirely independently, but often you supplement independent work with guided study. For instance, you may call an instructor at the local school sponsoring the course, or even attend some classes to review past material and get direction for future lessons. Well-produced courses have received rave reviews from students. The medium of television allows much more to be done visually than usually is possible in a classroom. For example, you not only get the narrator's description of the Parthenon in an architecture course, but you "visit" it, seeing close-up views under varying light conditions. The learning experience often is more vivid and lasting under these conditions than it would be in a classroom setting.

Some local colleges and universities have developed their own television courses, often as a supplement to degree programs pursued in the traditional way on campus. But the expense is so great that more often the courses are initially developed centrally or funded by a consortium of institutions and television stations and then used individually by members or others who purchase the rights. Three of the major organizations that produce and distribute television courses are similar in that if you are interested in receiving credit or other credentials (rather than just viewing for your enlightenment), you sign up with the sponsoring higher education institution in your area.

The International University Consortium for Telecommunications in Learning (IUC) is an international network of colleges, universities, public broadcasting stations, and cable systems. Through its members, IUC provides complete bachelor's degree programs to adults who cannot, or choose not to, enroll in traditional college courses. Currently there are twenty-four institutions and twenty-one broadcasting stations, located in fourteen states and in Canada, affiliated with IUC. The Consortium offers undergraduate guided-study courses in three areas of study: technology and management, behavioral and social sciences, and humanities. The curriculum includes a variety of courses at appropriate levels to permit member schools to award a bachelor's

degree to students who complete all or most of their work through
IUC courses. One such course is Time's Harvest: Exploring the Future,
which looks at alternative visions of the future and introduces the
underlying philosophies and activities involved in futures studies. It is
an eight-program series including such themes as "Running Out of
Water" (effects of pollution and overuse) and "The Computer Comes
Home" (implications of computers in the home). Each college adopts
IUC courses as part of its curriculum and determines credit value, degree requirements, and tuition fees. For information on the participating school that may be near you, contact IUC, P.O. Box 430,
Owings Mills, MD 21117-0430.

Another consortium that develops television courses is TEP ("To
Educate the People"). It has developed courses in humanities and the
arts, social science, science and technology, and elective subjects. One
course, Work and Society, investigates key issues of work, workers,
economic life, and related matters. Another, Changing Life on Earth,
starts with a definition of life and goes on to the question of where
humans fits into the history of life. Depending upon the sponsoring
institution, some courses may be used to fulfill many of the requirements of a degree program. To find the closest participating institution, write to TEP, Center for Urban Studies, Wayne State University,
5229 Cass Avenue, Detroit, MI 48202.

Nontraditional adult learning was given a big boost when Walter H.
Annenberg recently gave $150-million to the Corporation for Public
Broadcasting for the development of college-level television and radio
courses. Aired by the Public Broadcasting Service (television) and National Public Radio, and used by many colleges and universities, these
courses include a study of the brain, Congress, computer literacy, the
Constitution, writing, and other areas. The courses are close-captioned
for those with hearing impairments. Forthcoming courses include
economics, French language, introductory physics, geophysics, and the
history of art. In addition to the television courses, audio cassettes are
available to radio stations or individuals. Fields of study on cassette
are Contemporary Western Europe, Contemporary China and Japan,
Women and the Family, and Western History. In addition to the Annenberg Project courses, PBS shows many other courses, with over 800
colleges and universities using them. Many more courses are being
programmed for both television and radio, so by the time you read
this they may be completed. You can get information on Annenberg
courses that may be available in your area by calling 1-800-LEARNER
(in Illinois, 312-256-3200), or by writing to Annenberg/CPB Collection, 1213 Wilmette Avenue, Wilmette, IL 60091. Information on all
PBS courses can be obtained from PBS, Adult Learning Service, 475
L'enfant Plaza, S.W., Washington, DC 20024, or by telephone: 202-
488-5360.

In addition to the television and radio courses, you might be able to take newspaper courses that are sponsored by some newspapers in affiliation with colleges and universities. Contact major metropolitan newspapers that serve your area to determine whether they offer such courses.

USING YOUR COMPUTER TO TAKE COURSES AND GET DEGREES

Happily, the computer has applications for nontraditional learners. First, you can take a variety of correspondence courses that will be greatly facilitated if you use your computer in completing many of the requirements. Areas you can study are: applications in computer science and data processing, computer operations and operations control, computer hardware, information and database systems, numerical computations, programming languages, programming systems, theory of computation, and educational, societal, and cultural considerations. (See "Index to Subject-Matter Areas," *The Independent Study Catalog,* referred to in the discussion of correspondence courses.)

Also, you should realize that you may be able to get college credit for expertise you gain on your computer at home or at work. You may also be exempted from some of the requirements in a certificate program at a trade or technical school or a business school. What you have learned independently may be equal to or greater than what you would have learned in a classroom or correspondence course. See the next chapter for methods of converting your expertise into credit or advanced standing.

Finally, you may be able to use your computer as the device for taking a course, improving your career skills, or even getting a degree. TeleLearning Systems, Inc., has developed what they call an Electronic University. The courses vary from those you might find at trade and technical schools, such as Construction Cost Estimating, and Starting and Managing Your Own Business, to courses that might be offered by colleges for credit, such as College Composition, and American History I. Some courses are for hobbyists, such as Container Gardening for the City Dweller. According to TeleLearning Systems, the method is simple. The student signs up for a course and, with a modem (that's computer talk for a telephone linking device), is able to receive lectures and exercises from the instructor, and also can communicate directly with the instructor at specified times, all through the telephone via the keyboard and screen of the computer. TeleLearning also has made arrangements with some schools to enable people to work on degree programs through computer linkage to courses. TeleLearning's system is so new that we have not been able to get sufficient feedback to form an opinion of the usefulness of the system (it cer-

tainly sounds good). You may get information by calling 1-800-
22LEARN (in California, 1-800-44LEARN), or writing to TeleLearning Systems, Inc., 505 Beach Street, San Francisco, CA 94133.

OTHER ALTERNATIVES TO ON-CAMPUS PROGRAMS

Dr. K. Patricia Cross, the author of several studies on adult education, has found that colleges and universities represent only 40% of
organized learning opportunities. If, for whatever reason, you think
that an on-campus program may not be for you, you can choose
from a vast smorgasbord of higher learning opportunities other than
those already treated.

Going to School Where You Work

Some major companies have in-house training programs that are the
equivalent of programs at some of the best educational institutions.
General Electric, for instance, not only offers courses in its local
plants but also has a 30-acre campus overlooking the Hudson River at
Crotonville, NY. The campus has living accommodations for 135
students. Courses are taken there by G.E. employees and students
from other companies and agencies around the world. Many of these
courses can later be accepted for college credit. (More on this avenue
to credit later.)

In addition to offering their own programs, some companies have
invited local higher education institutions to offer classes for company employees right on company premises. Several newspaper and
magazine articles recently have featured these on-site programs, noting,
for example, that undergraduate programs were being offered at the
locations of such major corporations as Burroughs Corporation, Aetna
Life & Casualty Company, and Grumman Data Systems Corporation,
while graduate programs were available at TRW, Fluor, Digital Equipment, Bechtel, and Ford Motor Company. According to one educator
who was cited, "This is the trend of the future." Less than 4% of the
employees who are eligible for educational assistance from their employer take advantage of it—an astounding statistic. In fact, your own
employer, if it is a major corporation, may even be bringing school to
you at your work site, and you may not know it. Check with your
company's human resources office to see what might be available.

Community Programs

Educational programs are available for you through local public
schools, religious institutions, museums, libraries, and civic and
community agencies. Theater groups, local dance companies, and arts

66   councils exist partly to serve your needs. Programs from sources such
as these may be your passport to a new lifestyle, higher earnings, or the
sheer enjoyment that comes from participating in some new learning
activity.

Independent Study

If you aren't interested in academic credentials and just want to
study for your self-improvement or for some other reason, read *The
Independent Scholar's Handbook: How to Turn Your Interest in Any
Subject into Expertise,* by Ronald Gross. It presents many ways that
creative people can expand their horizons with or without the structure that is imposed by a prescribed program. See the book in your
library (or order it from Addison-Wesley Publishing Company, Inc.,
One Jacob Way, Reading, MA 08167, for $8.95).

ELDERHOSTEL: A SPECIAL PROGRAM FOR OLDER ADULTS

For older adults, the Elderhostel program may provide exciting learning experiences in a variety of locations. Elderhostel is a network of
over 700 colleges/universities/independent schools/folk schools and
other educational institutions in the U.S., Canada, Bermuda, Mexico,
Great Britain, Scandinavia, Holland, France, Germany, Israel, and
Italy offering special low-cost, short-term, residential, noncredit academic programs for older adults. Elderhostel is open to people over
60 or those whose participating spouse or companion qualifies. Most
of Elderhostel's programs begin on Sunday evening and end on the
following Saturday morning and are limited to 35 to 45 people. Tens
of thousands of people have already enjoyed this unique experience.
Would you like to take an Alaskan photography expedition at Prince
William Sound Community College or study the Roman Army and
Hadrian's Wall at the University of Durham in Northumbria on England's eastern coast? You may find out about this year's programs by
writing to Elderhostel, 100 Boylston Street, Boston, MA 02116.

Student Profile
DAWN LOGAN-WEINBERG of Glen Oaks, New York

*The time it took to get from housewife with no
marketable skills to professional status was
greatly shortened by my external degree program.*

When I considered earning an associate degree in nursing through
the Regents External Degree Program (now named Regents College
Degrees) of the University of the State of New York, I asked myself:
Would it be honored professionally? I spoke to my hospital in-service
education director, and although she was enthusiastic, I met with
some skepticism in other corners. "Would it be recognized
academically?" was their question. "By the Board of Regents, the
University of the State of New York!" I replied. I decided I would
try. Within a little more than a year and a half I had racked up 146
credits and still had never attended a college class.

Shortly after completing my associate degree I applied to three
hospitals for a job as an RN. I was accepted at one almost
immediately and was called for interviews by the other two, a good
indication that they were seriously considering hiring me. The
independent study degree that was somewhat questionable less than
two years before was now being accepted as valid without question.
The attitude of my fellow staff members had changed from "Do you
think it's any good?" to "Oh, you're a brain; you're one of the smart
ones who could do it on your own." Whether this is so is a moot
point.

I went on to finish my bachelor's degree in nursing through the
Regents program, getting my degree about a year and a half after I
had completed the associate degree. I received a raise in pay and
turned down an opportunity to become Head Nurse because by now
I had begun applying to all three graduate schools in the area.

Adelphi University was my preference because of its excellence in
clinical component and its location. I was accepted there on a trial
basis since they were a bit skeptical about the independent study
degree. (The Regents program at that time was being evaluated for
specialized accreditation by the National League for Nursing. Since
then it has been granted full accreditation, and if I were applying
today, quite certainly I wouldn't have had to deal with that
skepticism.) I was told frankly by Adelphi that I would be a "guinea

68 pig" as well as a pioneer and would be under constant scrutiny. I replied that I was accustomed to that by this time.

I did well in my first course and was accepted on a full-time basis, later receiving a Graduate Achievement Award and a full-tuition traineeship with a stipend from what was no longer a skeptical admissions committee. I graduated with a Master of Science in Nursing and was selected to be a member of nursing's national honor society, Sigma Theta Tau. I was a qualified psychiatric clinical nursing specialist and so able to fulfill my lifelong dream of working as a psychotherapist.

I am now working as a nurse-therapist at the Inwood Mental Health Clinic, a satellite of the New York State Psychiatric Institute in Manhattan, and I love it! The time taken to get from housewife with no marketable skills to professional status was greatly shortened by my external degree program. I am now a woman who has been able to see all my dreams come true. Well, perhaps there is just one more—*Dr*. Dawn Logan-Weinberg. Sounds good. I've sent for some Ph.D. program catalogs.

5.

Getting Credit for What You Already Know

How can I achieve my educational goals in the shortest possible time?

YOU MAY BE CLOSER TO ACHIEVING YOUR GOALS THAN YOU REALIZE

Regardless of whether you are considering a traditional or nontraditional program, as an adult with a variety of experiences in your background, you have an advantage you should exploit. The matter of getting all the credit you can for what you have already accomplished will be so important to you that we are devoting a full chapter to it. Let's consider first the case of enrollment in an on-campus degree program.

Traditionally, earning a bachelor's degree required four years of full-time college attendance. An adult carrying a typical part-time load of two 3-credit courses each semester was able to earn only 12 credits a year. At that rate, a conventional four-year bachelor's degree took *ten years* to complete! Many adults have earned degrees the slow way; perhaps you know or have heard of someone who has struggled through years of night school in order to earn a degree. Yet many of these people had already acquired considerable knowledge of their academic discipline through life experience. Stories have been told of business executives sitting through basic management courses that they would probably be able to teach as effectively as the professor. Imagine an accomplished professional artist taking Drawing 1, a journalist taking English Composition 1, or a musician taking Introduction to Music! At one time, such absurd requirements were not unheard of for adults.

69

Fortunately, most institutions now provide means for individuals to demonstrate and document college-level knowledge and receive equivalent course credit. By taking advantage of means for gaining credit for prior knowledge adults with no previous credits may be able to earn an associate degree in as little as 18 months and a bachelor's degree in as little as three years. Coauthor Charles McCabe completed all of the requirements for his bachelor's degree in less than two and a half years by taking advantage of the credit policies outlined in this chapter.

Some external degrees may be earned in even less time. These programs rely heavily on crediting your prior knowledge, as already discussed. Thus it is especially important when applying to such programs to be thorough in presenting your potentially credit-worthy background.

Enrollment in an on-campus program at a business or specialized school, or trade or technical school where certificates or diplomas rather than degrees are presented may be a different situation. The courses might be so skills-oriented that the theoretical knowledge you have gained through experience might not be relevant, hence you would get no credit for demonstrated conceptual learning. However, skills that you have mastered may indeed be considered in advancing you to a higher level than that of others beginning the program. Thus you could save time and money by ensuring that the admissions office at such a school is fully aware of your experiential background.

Regardless of the type of program you are considering, there are four major sources of credit you should not overlook: prior credit-bearing courses, certain prior noncollegiate courses and training programs, proficiency examinations, and documented experiential learning.

TRANSFER CREDITS FOR PRIOR COURSES

If you have completed credit-bearing courses at an accredited institution, whether on campus or by correspondence, you should have them evaluated for credit by the institution in which you are considering enrolling. Transfer policies vary, and different policies may apply for different programs at a single school. Transfer credit for previous postsecondary course work is generally handled as follows:

1. Courses must have been completed at an accredited institution (with rare exceptions).
2. Credit will not ordinarily be granted for courses passed with a grade of less than C or C-; however, some institutions will accept a D if it is offset by an A or a B in another course.

3. Most institutions have a residence requirement of at least 30   **71**
   semester hour credits; that is, 30 credits must be earned at that
   institution. Usually those credits must also be the final credits
   earned toward the degree. Since many baccalaureate degrees
   require 120 credits, course work accepted for transfer usually
   will not exceed 90 credits.
4. Full credit (usually not exceeding 64 semester hours) is ordinarily transferable if you have an associate degree, regardless of
   how long ago it was earned. State universities often guarantee
   admission to transfer students from public two-year colleges in
   the same state. The guarantee does not, however, ensure admission to a specified college or curriculum.
5. Course work completed more than a specified number of years
   prior to admission is often nontransferable; however, special
   degree programs for adults usually do not impose a time limit.
6. For advanced standing to be granted, courses must usually be
   deemed "appropriate" or "suitable" to fulfill a requirement or
   elective of the degree program to which the student is being
   admitted.
7. A limitation, often 30 hours, may be placed on the number of
   credits that may be accepted for correspondence courses, noncollegiate instruction, standardized proficiency examinations,
   and documented experiential learning. External degree programs, though, usually allow most, or all, credits earned in these
   ways to count toward fulfilling degree requirements.
8. Official transcripts from all institutions that have been previously
   attended are required for evaluation of proposed transfer credits.
9. Some colleges and universities with regional accreditation (often
   considered the highest level) do not accept some or any of the
   credits earned at an institution which does not have regional
   accreditation. Thus credits earned at a trade or technical school,
   or business or specialized school in a certificate program might
   not be accepted by a regionally accredited college or university.

CREDIT FOR NONCOLLEGIATE INSTRUCTION

Several types of activities may result in credit even though the activities were not associated with accredited colleges and universities.

Military Training

Most institutions will award credit for certain in-service course work
completed by service personnel and veterans. Credit for military service training courses and work experiences, when granted, is usually

72 based on the recommendations outlined in *Guide to the Evaluation of Educational Experiences in the Armed Services,* a publication of the American Council on Education. Many institutions will also grant some credit for physical education to matriculated students who are service members or veterans of active military service.

The Defense Activity for Non-Traditional Education Support (DANTES—formerly known as the United States Armed Forces Institute, or USAFI) is an educational service that provides support to the voluntary educational programs of all the military services. Over 7,000 independent study courses from regionally accredited colleges and universities are available to service personnel through the DANTES Independent Study Support System. While the majority of the courses available through this system are applicable to undergraduate degree programs, some of the participating colleges offer courses at the high school level, and some offer graduate-level courses. The *DANTES Independent Study Catalog,* available at education offices of military installations, is the key to the independent study system. The catalog lists the participating colleges, the available courses, and the necessary course information.

Most of the proficiency examinations offered by other testing services as described later in this chapter are available through DANTES. In addition, DANTES administers its own DANTES Subject Standardized Tests (DSSTs) (see pages 77-78 for details). The DSSTs have been evaluated by the American Council on Education for academic credit recommendations.

DANTES also administers the professional certification examinations of the following groups:

- American Association of Medical Assistants
- American Medical Technologists
- Institute for the Certification of Engineering Technicians
- National Institute for Automotive Service Excellence
- Institute for Certification of Computer Professionals
- International Society for Clinical Laboratory Technology
- National Registry of Emergency Medical Technicians
- Institute for Certified Professional Managers
- American Society for Quality Control
- National Association of Social Workers
- Administrative Management Society
- American Speech, Language and Hearing Association
- American Nurses' Association
- Association of Operating Room Nurses
- Electronics Technicians Association, International
- Dental Assisting National Board
- National Board for Respiratory Therapy

A transcript of the grades and scores you may have earned through
courses and examinations formerly offered by the United States
Armed Forces Institute (USAFI), as well as scores earned through
examinations offered by DANTES, is available through the DANTES
Transcript Service, maintained by the Educational Testing Service
(ETS) in Princeton, NJ. Both active-duty service members and veterans
who took courses and tests through USAFI may apply to have their
transcripts sent from ETS to the higher education institutions of their
choice. For grades and scores earned prior to July 1, 1974, write to:
ETS, Box 2879, Princeton, NJ 08541; no charge. For examinations
completed after that date, send $4.00 to ETS, Box 2819, Princeton,
NJ 08541. If you have any problems, the National Military Personnel
Records Center, 9700 Page Boulevard, St. Louis, MO 63132, is able
to verify a discharged veteran's MOS as well as military schooling. It
is imperative that the request be in writing and signed by the veteran.
The name of the course, the course number, the location where the
course was taken, and the dates of the course should be included in
the request. In addition, the veteran's name, service and/or social
security number, and branch of the military should be furnished.

Training by Industries, Businesses, and Governmental and Other Agencies

An increasing number of postsecondary institutions, particularly
those offering special adult programs, have adopted policies to permit
credit for certain "in-house" training given by your employer. The
usual criteria for determining if such non-college-sponsored instruction qualifies for credit are: (1) college-level conceptual knowledge
and/or specialized skills must have been taught; (2) the instructor
must have been qualified to teach the course; (3) requirements must
have been imposed for successful completion; and (4) classroom attendance must usually have been involved, although specialized independent study followed by a proctored exam may qualify. Basically,
the course must have content equivalent to that which might also be
found in a course offered by an accredited postsecondary institution.

Examples of employer-sponsored instruction that might qualify
for college credit are company in-house management seminars, police
academy training, technical training provided in various industries,
and hospital laboratory courses.

Other Continuing Education Programs

Many courses in continuing education, besides those given by your
employer, could also qualify for credit. A few examples are courses in
effective speaking and human relations from Dale Carnegie & Asso-

74   ciates, Inc.; income tax preparation courses offered by H & R Block, Inc.; real estate courses sponsored by a local board of realtors; finance courses offered by a local chapter of the American Institute of Banking; and various computer courses conducted by the Xerox Corporation.

Successful completion of such courses must be documented by a certificate of attendance or a letter from the sponsoring organization. You might also be asked to submit your course books and notes, if available, to further substantiate the course content. A syllabus, or course outline, prepared by the sponsoring organization will probably be required. Faculty members are usually called upon to evaluate noncollegiate courses and make recommendations as to how much, if any, credit should be granted.

You do not necessarily have to attend classes in order to get credit. Correspondence courses may also be evaluated for degree credit even if they were not taken through an accredited college. TV, radio, and newspaper courses also might qualify.

Basic reference books on credit for noncollegiate instruction are *The National Guide to Credit Recommendations for Noncollegiate Courses* (published by the American Council on Education), and *A Guide to Educational Programs in Noncollegiate Organizations* (published by the University of the State of New York). Taken together, these two guides document the ever-increasing sources of credit available to you for certain courses taken in noncollegiate settings. Libraries and admissions offices of higher education institutions are likely to have copies of these basic resources. If you believe you have participated in credit-worthy activities but they are not listed in any of the standard references, ask to have them evaluated for credit nonetheless. The references provide guidance, not all-inclusive prescriptions, for credit.

PROFICIENCY EXAMINATIONS

Proficiency examinations can enable you to accelerate significantly your progress toward your educational goals. For instance, 30 credits earned by examination may represent one year of full-time college attendance plus thousands of dollars saved in college costs. When you consider the potential benefits, proficiency examinations are often well worth the effort. Knowledge you have acquired through life experience or independent study in some subject commonly taught in college can often be documented by taking a test and achieving a score equal to or better than the average (based on scores achieved by college students who have completed a course in that subject). You may even receive credit equivalent to that college course. Although your practical knowledge may be limited, if you have an aptitude for

the subject you can probably learn enough by studying a college text   75
or review book to pass the exam. A wide variety of qualifying exams
is available through several nationally recognized programs.

Caution should be exercised to avoid duplication of credits when
taking proficiency exams. If you already have a course on your transcript or plan to take a course entitled Accounting I, for example,
you would not also be granted credit for an introductory accounting
subject exam. Duplication of credits through proficiency examination,
life-learning assessment, noncollegiate course evaluation, and regular
course work is a common dilemma encountered by adults in college.
For this reason it is important early in your adult college career to
determine the examinations for which you may be able to receive
credit. You would be wise to begin preparing for and taking these
tests as soon as possible so you can plan your remaining courses without risk of duplication.

Preparation for any of the standard proficiency tests is important.
Study guides are available either through the testing service or at your
local library or bookstore. Another kind of preparation may be equally
important. Rosemarie Sunderland, who reduced the time for a B.A.
from eight years to less than half that time by taking proficiency
exams, gives some practical advice: "While it is most important to
know the test subject well, getting to know the location of the testing
facility beforehand is also extremely important. On a pretest visit,
looking for parking facilities, the building, and the rooms to be used
for the exams will later save time and nerves. Arriving at the testing
center without extra tension helps you to keep a clear head."

Advanced Placement (AP) Program

The Advanced Placement (AP) Program of the College Board is intended for high school students. After taking certain courses, students
take AP exams and receive advanced standing in the subjects if they
do well. However, anyone can take the exams, even those who have
not taken AP preparation courses and are not in high school; therefore, adults are eligible. Three-hour AP exams are given in May on
several introductory college courses in the humanities, social sciences,
physical sciences, languages, the arts, and mathematics. Arrangements
to take AP exams must be made several months before the test date.
While most colleges recognize the exams, they often disagree as to
what constitutes an acceptable grade for granting credit. Some colleges
will exempt students who pass AP exams from introductory course
requirements, but will not allow credit. Others require that you repeat
a similar exam after admission to validate your grade. Before taking
AP exams it is wise to check out your college's (or prospective col-

lege's) policies. Information on AP exams should be available in the guidance office at your local high school.

Proficiency Examination Program of the American College Testing Program (ACT PEP); Regents College Examinations (RCE) of Regents College Degrees

A variety of ACT PEP exams are offered to test conceptual knowledge in many aspects of business, social, and professional services (such as nursing), as well as in liberal arts, sciences, and technology. Free study guides for ACT PEP tests are available. ACT PEP exams, though, may not be as widely recognized as CLEP exams. If your college will award credit for ACT PEP exams, you should write for a free Candidate Registration Packet to: ACT Proficiency Examination Program, P.O. Box 168, Iowa City, IA 52243. These examinations are the same as those offered in New York State as Regents College Examinations. For information, write to: Regents College Examinations, Cultural Education Center, Albany, NY 12230.

Incidentally, if you took an examination to gain admission to college, you might be eligible for advanced standing or equivalent course credit. The ACT Assessment Program (commonly called the ACT) of the American College Testing Program and the Achievement Tests of the College Board are used by some colleges to assess experiential learning. If you've taken such exams, you should determine if your college will evaluate the results for possible credit.

College-Level Examination Program (CLEP)

The College-Level Examination Program (CLEP) is designed specifically to document college-level knowledge acquired outside the usual educational settings. This program of the College Board was founded on the premise that nontraditional learning is a viable alternative to classroom study—what you know is more important than how you learned it. The acceptance of CLEP is widespread; not only are CLEP exams used by colleges as criteria for granting credit but CLEP exam scores have also been employed by business, industry, and government as a measure of competence for licensing and as a criterion for advancement.

Many adult students with whom we have corresponded have expressed enthusiasm about CLEP. Coauthor Charles McCabe earned 18 CLEP credits. He thought that was quite good, then heard from Dawn Logan-Weinberg, who earned 60 credits from CLEP.

You too may be able to earn CLEP credits and save yourself consid-   77
erable time and money. To find out, you can obtain a free brochure,
"Moving Ahead with CLEP," by writing to: CLEP, Box 1824, Princeton, NJ 08541. As the College Board explains, "The tests are not
easy; ... But don't sell yourself short. If you are within striking distance, you can take steps to get yourself ready."

Two kinds of CLEP tests are administered, the general examinations
and the subject examinations. The CLEP general examinations cover
subjects usually studied by college freshmen and sophomores as a
foundation for upper-division course work. Five general examinations,
each taking 90 minutes, are offered. The exams cover English composition, mathematics, natural science, social science, and humanities.
You may take only one or any combination of the general exams. All
exams are entirely multiple choice; however, the English composition
exam provides for an optional essay in lieu of the second half of the
test. Credit granted by participating institutions for an acceptable
score is usually 6 credits for each general exam or up to 30 credits
for the entire battery of tests. Most CLEP tests are given the third
week of each month, except in December and February. The English
composition with essay examination is given only in October and June.

CLEP subject examinations are achievement tests covering a wide
range of undergraduate courses. They are multiple-choice, 90-minute
tests. In addition, with few exceptions, each has an optional 90-minute
essay that may or may not be required by the college from which
credit is being sought. Credit for each subject exam varies; usually
either 3 or 6 credits are granted for each test on which a passing score
is achieved. The following subject areas are covered: business, education, humanities, mathematics, sciences, and social sciences.

Each college has its own policies as to which exams are accepted,
how many credits are granted, and what constitutes an acceptable
test score. However, the Commission on Educational Credit of the
American Council on Education provides general recommendations
that are followed in many instances.

After reading "Moving Ahead with CLEP," which briefly outlines
the content of exams in the above areas, you may decide to take a
CLEP exam or two. Or you might want to obtain more specific in-
formation by ordering the College Board book, *Guide to the CLEP
Examinations*, $5.00, College Board Publications, Box 886, New
York, NY 10101.

DANTES Subject Standardized Tests (DSSTs)

Until recently, DSSTs were available only to military personnel.
Now they are open to all people who wish to demonstrate knowledge

78 on a postsecondary level. The DANTES program complements CLEP with examinations in applied technology, business, languages, mathematics, science, and social science areas. The applied technology area may be of particular interest to adults entering a technical or trade school. Examinations in that area include forestry, auto mechanics, carpentry, drawing and graphics, electronics, radio servicing, television servicing, air-conditioning, refrigeration and heating. Most of the examinations carry a 3-credit-hour recommendation by the American Council on Education. For free brochures, write to: Educational Testing Service, Box 56-D, Princeton, NJ 08541. For a list of institutions administering the exams and granting credit for them, write to: DANTES Program Office, P-166, ETS, Princeton, NJ 08541.

Thomas A. Edison State College Examination Program (TECEP)

TECEP is Edison's proficiency examination program, offering more than 90 different examinations in several fields. The examinations are used extensively in New York and New Jersey and are gaining national recognition. Fields of examination include humanities, social sciences, natural sciences/mathematics, business, and professional areas. The last category includes subjects as diverse as control techniques of diagnostic histopathology, real estate sales, and vocational rehabilitation. Most of the questions are multiple choice, but some are short answer or essay. Test description booklets providing outlines of test content and some suggested readings can be ordered. Testing times for the examinations range from one and one-half to four hours. It is not necessary to be an Edison student to take the examinations; arrangements may be made to take them at your local college or university. Contact the Director of Testing, Thomas A. Edison State College, 101 West State Street, CN545, Trenton, NJ 08625.

Ohio University Course Credit by Examination Program (OUCCEP)

Ohio University's proficiency examination program offers more than 100 courses in which you may choose to demonstrate your proficiency, such as accounting, business law, electronics technology, health and sport sciences, journalism, and philosophy. If you have special interests that are not covered by existing proficiency exams, the university will try to arrange a special examination for you. It is not necessary to be an Ohio University student to take examinations. Request Ohio University Bulletin *Independent Study,* from Independent Study, Tupper Hall 302, Ohio University, Athens, OH 45701.

Graduate Record Examinations (GRE)

Graduate Record Examinations were developed by Educational Testing Service to help the admissions offices of graduate schools assess students' undergraduate knowledge. Some external degree programs, though, use the tests to award substantial blocks of undergraduate credit in major subject areas.

Two types of tests are offered: a General Test and Subject Tests in 17 disciplines. Because the General Test is basically a measure of developed abilities and the Subject Tests are measures of achievement in particular fields of study, the two types of tests are often used to complement each other in admission decisions. The General Test measures skills acquired over a long period of time and not related to any specific field of study; each Subject Test assumes either an undergraduate major or extensive background in the specific subject.

Any accredited graduate or professional school, or any department or division within a school, may require or recommend that its applicants take the General Test, a Subject Test, or both.

Test dates, registration deadlines, locations of test centers, and other information are published each year in the GRE *Information Bulletin*. Free copies of the *Information Bulletin* are made available to students at most undergraduate and graduate institutions throughout the country or may be ordered directly from ETS by writing to Graduate Record Examinations, CN 6000, Princeton, NJ 08541-6000.

Departmental Exams

Many colleges permit students to take exams specially prepared by faculty members and receive credit for, and/or exemption from, specific courses offered by the college. Sometimes standard waiver examinations have already been developed for certain courses, and suggested study guides are provided for interested students. Some colleges may allow a matriculated student to take an advanced credit examination in any course offered by the school. However, the college might stipulate that other course requirements, such as term papers and special projects, also be fulfilled to receive equivalent course credit. Departmental exams are often discouraged by faculty members who may view them as an unwarranted concession, or a threat to their livelihood, or simply an undesirable extra burden. Consequently, such exams are often unreasonably difficult. However, this is not always the case; if you have a good understanding of the subject matter, you have nothing to lose by asking the department chairman or a faculty member for permission to take an exam to demonstrate that you have already mastered the course content. This is often referred to as "challenging" a course.

80   CREDIT FOR EXPERIENTIAL LEARNING

Special assessment of experiential learning is another way you might get degree credit from your college. It can be tailored by your college to your specific circumstances and designed to measure the degree of college-level knowledge you have acquired from your life experiences in several categories.

Career

An executive secretary earned 23 credits in business law, communications, economics, finance, advertising, and personnel administration, all because of her previous work experience.

Volunteer Work

A woman devoted much of her time to volunteer work for a hospital and several civic and religious organizations in her community (serving in responsible leadership positions). She earned a total of 21 credits in business, economics, political studies, psychology, and religion.

Travel

A woman loved to travel. Whether she was visiting the pyramids or some town not too far from her home, she looked for unusual things to see and do, and people to meet. She always kept notes and, upon her return from a trip, wrote a short travel column for her church's monthly newsletter. She received 16 credits for sociology and journalism based on the excellence of her columns across the years, supplemented by her detailed notes on lifestyles of people.

Unsponsored Independent Study

A handicapped woman, unable to travel, nevertheless "visited" many countries. Concentrating her efforts on one country at a time, with the special aid of her public library, she ordered books, movies, and filmstrips. With language tapes and tutoring she learned the language of the country she was "visiting," and she invited a foreign student from that country to live in her home while he or she was attending a university in the city. Her only "charges" to the student were conversations in the student's language. When she decided to get a degree, she was awarded substantial credit in the areas of language, literature, art history, political science, history, and several other disciplines.

Stephanie Phillips of Milford, CT, was active in community theater. **81** She says: "Prior to a careful reading of my college catalog, I never realized categorizing those experiences could eventually earn me three college credits."

These are typical examples of the innumerable forms of experiential learning for which colleges and universities throughout the United States have awarded credit. You, as an adult, have probably acquired knowledge equivalent to college-level learning through your life experiences. Some of this knowledge probably can be rewarded with college credit. The Council for the Advancement of Experiential Learning (CAEL) will help you locate colleges that will give such credit. Write to CAEL, 10598 Marble Faun Court, Columbia, MD 21044, or call 301-997-3535.

DOCUMENTING EXPERIENTIAL LEARNING

Understandably, you will not automatically get college credit for life experiences. You must be able to document what you have accomplished.

Varying procedures are designated by colleges to allow adult students to demonstrate the nature and extent of their life learning. Typically, the student prepares a portfolio for each academic area or subject in which life-learning credit is sought.

One student prepared nine life-experience portfolios because he wanted to be sure of receiving maximum credit. Each portfolio highlighted a different aspect of his ten-year career as a business executive and related that experience to specific academic areas. Each portfolio consisted of four sections:

- A concise cumulative life-learning outline listing positions held, special assignments, and appointments that related to the academic category
- A specific life-learning outline detailing the relevant duties and responsibilities involved in each of the posts listed in section one
- A brief objective summary of the nature of the life experience
- A subjective essay demonstrating personal growth and conceptual knowledge gained as a result of the life experience

Documentation accompanying the portfolios included:

- Letters from a former superior and a business associate verifying positions held and dates of employment, duties and activities, achievements, and expertise developed
- Copies of professional certificates and awards of recognition
- Copies of intracompany and outside correspondence (including a number of complimentary letters received from superiors)

- Samples of reports prepared, in-house newsletters edited, and training materials and company policies developed

This student's final award totaled 66 credits. Although the university's policy allowed for a maximum of only 30 life-experience credits toward its B.A. degree requirement, all 66 credits were posted on his college transcript, which would later be reviewed by potential employers and graduate schools. Perhaps most significantly, though, 30 credits represented one year of full-time study for him, and savings in tuition alone of more than $3,000.

Most colleges use alternative methods of demonstrating life learning in lieu of, or in addition to, written portfolios. Regents College Degrees uses a special assessment process—an individually designed examination (usually oral) that can be accompanied by a portfolio of the candidate's written or artistic products. The College of Public and Community Service at the University of Massachusetts at Boston accepts a variety of methods, including written portfolios, oral examinations, analysis of a project, and on-site evaluation. Thomas A. Edison State College in New Jersey requires a student to demonstrate proficiency through oral or written reports, submission of a portfolio, performances, or "other appropriate means." In any case, it probably would be a good idea to review your college's undergraduate catalog and identify any courses related to your life experience.

You may want to submit additional supportive material, such as copies of correspondence, samples of your literary or technical work, or examples of your artwork. In the case of foreign languages, music, or the performing arts, you will probably be asked to demonstrate your proficiency. Colleges normally require documentation of work experience and accomplishments. This usually means that you must submit letters from present and past employers, detailing dates of employment and positions held and verifying specific achievements. Documentation might also take other forms such as articles in newspapers or periodicals, copies of theater or concert programs, tape recordings, videotapes, and official records or documents. In addition, you might be interviewed by the evaluator.

The key to relating life experience to college learning is to establish that the experience resulted in your acquiring conceptual knowledge. Conceptual knowledge should not be confused with skill, which is the ability to carry out some function or activity, although there is sometimes a fine line separating the two. For example, the ability of an experienced tax-return preparer to complete accurate tax returns may not demonstrate knowledge of the fundamental concepts of our tax structure (an integral part of most college tax courses).

For gaining credit at trade and technical schools, and business and specialized schools, you may have to demonstrate skills rather

than conceptual learning. Survey the skills-oriented tests, such as **83**
some offered by DANTES, for areas in which you can demonstrate
competence.

How do you get specific guidance on documenting your experiential
knowledge? First, see if the institution in which you are interested
has a policy and a set of guidelines. External degree programs are
more likely to have a written guide than are traditional institutions.
For example, both the Regents College Degrees and Thomas A. Edison
State College have workbooks to assist the applicant in defining goals
and directions, and in documenting prior learning. CAEL has several
publications that will be of help. Ask them for their publications list
and their brochure, *A CAEL Service to Learners.* Of particular interest
is their workbook, *Assessing Prior Learning—A CAEL Student Guide*
($5.00), a step-by-step guide for portfolio preparation. They also have
a pre-assessment service called Comp-Activity Inventory. It helps you
decide if the assessment of your educational experiences and accomplishments by a college or university is likely to result in a large enough
credit award to be worth your time, effort, and expense. Comp-Act
costs $22 and can be taken at home. After successfully completing
the inventory, you would follow the school's procedures for documenting your noncollege learning. Write to CAEL at 10598 Marble
Faun Court, Columbia, MD 21044.

Some institutions will give you a pre-assessment free of charge or
at low cost, but many will not. Check this point with the admissions
office. If you cannot get a pre-enrollment assessment of your experiential learning, yet you decide to enroll anyhow, it is best to undertake
the evaluation process as soon after matriculation as possible because
your life-learning credit award could duplicate courses you've already
taken. And it might also have a bearing on which courses you should
take to satisfy specific degree requirements. One student at an Arkan-
sas college put off his life experience evaluation until he was 6 credits
short of his B.A. degree, only to discover in dismay that his life experience award for education totaled 18 credits. (He had developed
and taught a course for businessmen.) Had he not procrastinated, he
would have avoided two semesters of part-time study and saved over
$1,200 in tuition. As a college dean, William Haponski found that
few adults enrolled at his college had bothered to get credit for what
they already knew. Most were not even aware that this was possible
despite the specific guidance given in the college catalog. These illustrations highlight an important point: The credit you may receive
from life learning equals time and money—often, a lot of both.

In this chapter we have tried to show you that your educational goals
may be reached sooner than you realize. As an adult you have a significant advantage over younger students. Because you have lived

84 longer and have already had credit-worthy courses or experiences, you should be getting at least some credit for what you already know.

6.

Getting Accepted at the Institution of Your Choice

How do I apply, and how can I improve my chances of being accepted?

ADMISSION PROSPECTS

Adults sometimes confuse enrolling in a course with "admission," or "matriculation." If you just want to take some courses, whether for credit or not, in most cases you will just have to sign up for them. At the end of the instructional period you will receive a grade and an entry on a transcript. This in itself may be valuable for career or other reasons. But if you want some sort of certification such as a diploma or degree at the end of a comprehensive program of instruction, then probably you will have to apply for admission (or matriculation) to the program and meet certain criteria.

If a certificate, diploma, or degree program at a trade or technical school, or at a business or specialized school, is your goal, you may be assured that the admissions office will be receptive to your application. Or, if you are worried about getting accepted at a two- or four-year college or at a university in a traditional or external degree program, you shouldn't be. In these days, admissions officers are accustomed to having adult students in their programs.

Don't be apprehensive about the detailed admissions criteria outlined in most catalogs, such as high school course prerequisites, recommendations, or college entrance examination scores. The chances are good that some of the requirements may not apply to you as an adult. If they do, alternate ways to be admitted are probably available.

For example, the *New York Times* published an article about Harry Gersh, who was admitted to Harvard as a freshman at age 63. Mr.

86	Gersh explained, "I bothered the admissions office until they agreed to let me in." Then the *Times* provided a follow-up three years later when Mr. Gersh graduated—magna cum laude. If you are as qualified as the young graduating high school senior (and many adults are), you stand a good chance of being admitted to the school of your choice, whether it is local or distant. In fact, you should apply to more than one school if it is convenient for you to do so, perhaps two or three. Acceptance by at least one is then more likely. Also remember that, although external degree programs sometimes admit students under age 25, they were designed for adults. Admission is therefore more than likely; after looking into admissions criteria you may very well discover that the external degree program you have chosen was designed to admit people just like you.

BUT WHAT IF YOU DON'T HAVE A HIGH SCHOOL DIPLOMA OR ITS EQUIVALENT?

The high school diploma is the traditional basic requirement for admission to colleges and other types of postsecondary institutions. But today you do not have to be a high school graduate in order to enroll at many schools. You may qualify by passing a high school equivalency examination, by securing a Competency-Based or External High School Diploma, or, if you are seeking admission to college, by taking college courses to demonstrate your capacity for college-level work.

Nationally, the General Educational Development test (GED) is administered to allow adults to meet state requirements for high school graduation. If satisfactory scores are attained, the adult receives a certificate that is the legal equivalent of a regular high school diploma. In many locales, classes to prepare you for the GED are available during the regular school year. Details may be obtained from your community high school or your state education department. Also you may want to look in your library for the book *Passing the GED* or order it from Scott, Foresman Lifelong Learning, Order Dept., 1900 East Lake Avenue, Glenview, IL 60025, 722 pages, $8.95.

For people who have served in the armed forces, GED test scores are available from various sources depending upon the date and place you took the test. Be sure to include the following information: complete name, service number, branch of service, dates of active service (years), and place where tested (military base, unit, etc.). The various addresses and applicable dates are as follows:

1. GED tests taken on or prior to *May 31, 1974;* write to:

    DANTES
    P.O. Box 2879
    Princeton, NJ 08541

2. GED tests taken *overseas after May 31, 1974;* write to: **87**

> GED Testing Service
> One Dupont Circle
> Washington, DC 20036

3. GED tests taken *within the United States after May 31, 1974;* write to:

> the Department of Education (in the state in which the test was taken)

4. GED tests taken *through Job Corps;* write to:

> Manpower Administration
> 601 D Street, N.W.
> Washington, DC 20013

The Competency-Based High School Diploma (CBHSD) has an instructional system based primarily on adult-performance-level life skills that is open-ended and self-paced. Entering students go through an assessment phase and receive an individualized prescription for obtaining a diploma. The system is structured to allow credit for competencies the student is able to demonstrate at the time of entry, so nobody has to learn subject matter already mastered. Successful participants earn a regular diploma from a local high school. Contact the director of adult education at your local high school or your state director of adult education for information about the availability of this program. Additional information may be obtained from

> Director
> APL Project
> Education Annex S 21
> The University of Texas
> Austin, TX 78712

The New York State External High School Diploma helps adults in eight states. A diagnostic phase includes advice on learning resources that can be used to prepare for entry into the program. For information on taking this program in Connecticut, Maryland, Massachusetts, Michigan, Montana, New York, Rhode Island, and Virginia contact the education department in your state or send a self-addressed stamped envelope to

> Assistant Commissioner for
>   Occupational and Continuing Education
> New York State Education Department
> Albany, NY 12234

88   Also recall from Charles McCabe's experience (related earlier) that several state education departments award high school equivalency diplomas to residents who complete 24 credits of college course work. Your state may have such a provision, so contact your education department.

Even if the school you wish to attend will not grant you regular admission without a high school diploma, you might be able to enroll as a nonmatriculated (not enrolled for a certificate, diploma, or degree) or "special" student and take courses for credit or other formal recognition. As you progress, the school will assess how well you are doing, and then, if you are qualified for matriculation based on your performance, it will apply the credits or other credentials you earn toward your degree. (One note of caution. Nonmatriculated students are generally ineligible for most sources of financial aid.) If you are considering college, and the college of your choice will not allow you to take courses without being matriculated, you might be able to take your first 24 credits at another local college to get your high school equivalency diploma, and then transfer the college credits, thereby wasting no time in getting your degree.

PRESENTING YOUR CREDENTIALS EFFECTIVELY

Undergraduate admission applications for most postsecondary schools are short and straightforward. Be sure to fill out the forms exactly as directed. On the form or an addendum sheet, list any significant continuing education courses you have completed, including employer and armed forces training programs. Also list any professional certifications earned, such as teaching, nursing, or real estate licenses. You might also consider attaching a copy of your résumé or a short autobiography accompanied by copies of awards or letters of commendation. Admissions officers usually want to know how you have spent your time since you left formal education.

If you have any doubt as to the strength of your academic credentials, you might consider enclosing an essay written to demonstrate your strong motivation to pursue higher education at this stage in your life. In the essay you could comment on your previous academic, employment, or personal experiences and the ways they relate to your current desire to attend school. If you submit an essay it should be grammatically correct and carefully written and rewritten to be clear and concise. Otherwise, the essay might be detrimental rather than helpful to your admission chances. Ask someone who is a good writer to critique your essay, then have it typed and proofread. Keep a copy for possible later use.

Letters of recommendation are not usually required for admission, except to graduate programs. However, some schools, particularly the most selective ones, may request them. Since it is probably not possible or practical for you to look up former teachers, the school will probably allow you to submit letters from other individuals who know you. Present or past superiors at work, or professional acquaintances, can usually comment on your potential ability to work at the postsecondary level. (If you happen to know a professor or instructor at a higher education institution, his or her recommendation might be ideal.) Normally, you should ask someone who is a graduate of that school to recommend you since that person would know from experience what qualities are required to succeed there. Obviously, it is especially desirable to find someone who has achieved a high professional station in life, such as a doctor, lawyer, business executive, or legislator. Naturally, the person you choose should know you fairly well and respect you.

Composing a good letter of recommendation can be a difficult and time-consuming task. You should do whatever you can to lessen the effort required of the writer. Be specific about what the letter should include, such as how long the person has known you, in what capacity, why the person is qualified to comment on your ability to work at that level, and statements attesting to your ability, motivation, and discipline. Some schools may eliminate this problem by providing a form with specific questions to be answered by the person recommending you.

COLLEGE ENTRANCE EXAMINATIONS: SAT AND ACHIEVEMENT TESTS AND THE ACT

Trade and technical schools normally will not require entrance examinations (although they may require demonstration of certain basic skills). Some business and specialized schools might, especially if they offer degrees. Most external degree programs also will not require these tests.

Although many colleges do not require standard admissions tests for adults, some will want to see your scores on one of the two nationally recognized college entrance examinations: the College Board's Scholastic Aptitude Test (SAT) or the American College Testing Program's examination (ACT). Some colleges give applicants the option of submitting scores from either the SAT or the ACT, while others specify one test or the other. Some of the more selective schools also require College Board Achievement Tests, which measure reasoning ability and proficiency in specific subjects.

The SAT is designed to measure developed academic ability in verbal and mathematical areas. All the questions are multiple choice, and you are given 30 minutes to complete each of five sections. In addition, a half-hour Test of Standard Written English (TSWE) helps place you at the appropriate level in a freshman English course. This test does not affect your SAT score. Information and registration forms for both the SAT and College Board Achievement Tests can be obtained from high school guidance counselors or from

> The College Board
> Admissions Testing Program
> Box 592
> Princeton, NJ 08541

The ACT assessment consists of four tests of 35 to 50 minutes each. The multiple-choice questions focus on analytical and problem-solving skills and also require some general subject knowledge. ACT information and registration forms are available from high school counselors or from

> ACT Registration
> Box 414
> Iowa City, IA 52234

Barbara Dunn of George Mason University, Fairfax, VA, describes her experience in taking the SAT:

> A visit to the local university yielded a week's worth of reading in the form of literature, catalogs, and application blanks, and started the process of reentry after I had been out of school for 25 years. Because I wanted to be a regular day student, I would have to take the SAT at the local high school. Fortunately, my son was a student at the same school and also was taking his SAT, so I was familiar with the application procedure. He was relieved when we were assigned separate dates for the test, but I wasn't. I would have been glad to have had someone to lean on, even my own unfriendly, embarrassed teenager. On a Saturday morning, I arrived at the school cafeteria with my sharpened pencils and settled into a folding chair. Luckily for me, my son's calculus teacher was there, and she was good moral support. Whenever I would start to get numb, my attention would drift and I'd look up, and she would wink at me and smile. Finally, it was over and there was nothing to do but go home and wait for the grades to be mailed. It was all worthwhile—my scores allowed me to enter George Mason University.

Can you prepare yourself to score higher on college entrance examinations? This is a hotly debated issue among agencies involved in preparing and supervising such tests. You can find preparation courses advertised in many large cities. Some people praise the courses, while others say that such courses can merely acquaint you with the test format and that you could get similar aid at less cost if you study one of the practice books that contain sample questions. Certainly, as a minimum preparation, you should familiarize yourself with the format, and practice answering some sample questions. The College

Board offers a booklet, *Taking the SAT, A Guide for Students*, which   **91**
includes sample tests and answer sheets. To get a copy, write to the
College Board at the address above. Other College Board publications
which might help you are *10 SATs* (actual recent tests), $8.95, and *The
College Board Achievement Tests* (14 actual recent tests), $9.95.
Also see *SAT Success*, published by Peterson's Guides, P.O. Box
2123, Princeton, NJ 08540, $8.95 plus $1.25 shipping and handling.
The ACT booklet *Taking the ACT Assessment* provides a section of
sample ACT questions. Write to ACT using the address above.

Both ACT and the College Board have procedures for revealing
details of how you did in your entrance examination, and these
procedures are explained in the material you will receive. If you are
unhappy with your scores on college entrance examinations, you
may take the tests again. The College Board will present scores of all
examinations to the college admissions office, but ACT does not.
Colleges have different procedures when presented with more than
one set of scores; some consider only the highest, while others may
also take the lower scores into consideration.

Remember, though, that many schools have special admissions
criteria for adults. Even if the admissions policy clearly stipulates
that the SAT or ACT examinations are required, you might want to
request an exception. As an adult, your aptitude for work in a higher
education program can probably be determined by an evaluation of
your experience and achievements.

DEADLINES IN THE ADMISSIONS CALENDAR

Timing may be important to you in gaining admission. Many colleges accept enrollments twice a year, in the fall and spring. Colleges
on trimester or quarter systems often admit students three or four
times a year, before the beginning of each period of instruction. Some
colleges accept applications after their stated deadline. Also, a large
percentage of colleges have a "rolling" admissions policy, which
means that applications are considered as soon as they are received
and decisions on admission are rendered soon thereafter. Trade and
technical schools, and business and specialized schools, may or may
not have terms which correspond to those of colleges and universities.
You will have to inquire.

You should note any admissions deadlines as soon as you decide
to apply. This is especially important if you want to attend a selective
school, since they usually have firm deadlines. Also, you will need
sufficient time to complete your application and have your transcripts
and any other necessary documents mailed to the school.

Most schools charge a nonrefundable fee for applying for admission.
It can range from $10 to $25 or more. If you cannot afford this fee,

and some students cannot, write to the director of admissions and ask whether or not the school will waive the fee. It is important to check this well in advance of the application deadline.

INTERVIEWS

Interviews are not always a part of the selection process but may be an important part of the screening process for certain adult programs. If you are asked to come for an interview, be prepared to comment on why you want additional education and why you are interested in that particular institution. Come prepared with specific questions about the programs that interest you. This will demonstrate your thoughtful concern about choosing this school and one of its programs.

FOR THOSE WHO DECIDE AT THE LAST MINUTE

If you have missed admissions deadlines but decide at the last minute you want to go to school, you may have a "walk-on" option. It occurs during the two- or three-week period just before school opens, through registration, to just after registration. Sometimes schools discover quite late that their projections of enrollment are not being met. If you apply during this period you might be accepted.

In summary, your chances of being accepted by the school of your choice are excellent. You can compete successfully, both during the application process and later as a student. Your careful preparation and attention to detail during the application stage will greatly improve your chances for success.

Student Profile
MILDRED TROUPE of Brooklyn, New York

 *Applying was much easier than I expected it would be.*

I grew up in the rural area of southern Georgia. Actually, woods is a better characterization of the area where I was reared. Our nearest neighbor was two miles away. However, I had plenty of company. My family was a relatively large one—I had five brothers and seven sisters. I was the sixth child.

As a high school student, it had always been my desire to continue my education by going to college. But I had to forego my desire for a college education after my high school graduation due to a family crisis, and later, as a result of my ever-changing work shift. When I finally got to college, it was a dream come true.

When I was 16 years old my mother died. At that time, there were nine of us still at home, The youngest—my baby brother—was three months old. I was the second oldest at home. My mother had taught every member of the family who could understand the importance of accepting responsibility. Her teachings were instrumental in keeping us together.

When I graduated from high school it was my turn to take over the responsibility of managing the household. A year and a half later, my father remarried. Subsequently I moved to Brooklyn, New York, in hopes of pursuing a career and a life of my own. At that time, college was the farthest thing from my mind.

There I was, a naive young girl from Fitzgerald, Georgia— experiencing a culture shock and filled with anxiety—determined to succeed. Less than three weeks after I arrived in Brooklyn, I started work as a long-distance telephone operator. Advancing in my job was now uppermost in my mind, and that is exactly what I did. Within four years, I was promoted to assistant manager.

Advancement in my job was not the only thing I had accomplished. Being out in the business world aided in transforming a taciturn young Southern girl into an assertive woman.

Hungry for a change and a day shift, I accepted a lateral transfer into the sales department as a service adviser. Initially the work was challenging and gave me a great sense of accomplishment. But before I realized it, one of the saddest things that can happen to an individual happened to me: I became complacent.

The encouragement of my supervisor to attend college was unsuccessful. For only a high school graduate, I made an excellent salary. Why should I go to college?

After two years as a service adviser I became bored and discontented. I watched the college graduates in my department being promoted; some had less job knowledge than I. The limited upward mobility for those without college degrees, boredom, and an innate thirst for knowledge rekindled my old desire to attend college.

I selected Pace University's two-and-a-half-year National Council of Negro Women (NCNW) program, which awards an Associate of Arts degree. Several acquaintances had attended this program, and all of them spoke highly of it. Applying was much easier than I expected it would be. I was relieved to learn that no admissions test was required, just an interview. I had visualized much red tape, but my application was completed in one day. Much of the paperwork was handled by the NCNW staff, who were very cooperative and supportive throughout my college experience. I was even allowed to begin classes as an unmatriculated student pending receipt of my high school transcript by the admissions office.

The ten-week cycled program combines liberal arts and business subjects. And the classes are scheduled conveniently—I attend two nights a week and one Saturday a month.

Before I started college, I established scholastic goals. I planned to strive for straight A's, and accept not less than B's. I realized my goals were high, but I have always been a believer in a person's ability to accomplish anything he or she wants to.

When I entered college, I experienced the same anxiety I felt when I applied for my job with the New York Telephone Company. My fears were soon dispelled. Many of the students in my class worked for the same company as I. I had known two of them before entering college, and we developed an instant camaraderie.

Adjusting to college life is not easy, but the rewards are great. The time I spent studying and doing homework has paid off. After almost two years, I am still maintaining my initial scholastic goal of straight A's. A price tag cannot be placed on what I have learned. Deciding to enter college was the turning point of my life. I intend to continue for my Bachelor of Arts degree.

7.

Financing Your
Higher Education

How can I possibly pay for it?

Contributed by **Carol Mackintosh**, *Director of Financial Aid, Utica College of Syracuse University, Utica, NY*

FINANCIAL AID

One aspect of going back to school that concerns adult students greatly is the question of expense. You may find yourself wondering not only how you can afford tuition and books, but also how you can support yourself and your family if you have one. Many adults give up education because they don't know that there is financial aid to help pay for higher education and living expenses or because they simply don't know where to get application forms or how to fill them out. Preventing that waste is what this chapter is all about.

The primary goal of financial aid programs is to provide access and opportunity to those students who could not otherwise attend school. The complexity of financial aid programs, though, has brought with it a great deal of confusion regarding the application processes associated with the many and varied assistance sources that are at a student's disposal. To avail themselves of financial aid programs, students must apply for them amid a maze of forms, acronyms, instructions, and requests for information.

Fortunately, the higher education institution nearest you most likely will have a financial aid office to help you. (All institutions administering federal funds are required to have one.) Even if you are not planning to attend that institution, you probably will find this office willing to advise you. Someone in the office will help you explore options and provide you with information on current government, college, and private sources of aid and how to apply for it. There is

95

no better way to get specific financial aid information than to visit the financial aid office of the schools you are considering attending. However, this chapter and the Financial Aid References at the end of it provide you with sufficient general information about financial aid to enable you to prepare intelligently for such a visit or even to "go it on your own" until you actually register at the school where you have been accepted.

Students in trade, technical, business, or specialized schools or in external degree programs will find that most aid discussed in this chapter is open to them, but eligibility may be different from place to place and field to field. It is best to send away for all the information that appears helpful and check your eligibility carefully.

The most common way to qualify for financial aid is to document your "financial need." Financial need is determined by a financial aid officer using specific procedures as required by law. It is the difference between the cost of going to a particular institution and the money you (and your spouse, if you have one) can provide to cover that cost.

We'll return to the crucial question of need shortly. Meanwhile, we'll explore other types of aid and we will use "college" to refer to all types of higher education programs.

SOURCES OF AID NOT NECESSARILY DEPENDENT ON NEED

Although the preponderance of financial aid is available to meet need, some grants (also called scholarships) are given to students in recognition of academic, athletic, artistic, or other abilities. Some colleges also have special funds to help certain targeted groups. For example, many colleges have opportunity programs for students who have poor or unusual academic backgrounds and who are in extreme financial need. Many also have special returning-student or women's grants designed for older students. Often colleges offer senior citizens free tuition. You should state your special circumstances and ask the colleges in which you have an interest to send you information on such programs to see if you qualify.

Other than the above, there are five general sources of money you may be able to use while you are a student. Each of these categories of funds requires research to see if you qualify. To aid you in the process, here are some facts on these five sources.

Aid from Employers

Many employers make funds available for employees to improve their job skills, usually reimbursing them for courses satisfactorily completed (or sometimes only for those completed with a grade of B

or higher). Lynn Gallagher of Baldwin-Wallace College, Berea, Ohio,   **97**
began taking college courses when she discovered that part of her
employer's benefit program included tuition refunds. The personnel
office should be able to tell you if student aid programs exist at your
place of employment.

Colleges and universities in particular frequently offer their employees tuition remission benefits. This means that if you are employed at
such an institution, you would be able to take courses free or at
reduced tuition at that institution or possibly even at another one.
Benefits may extend also to your spouse and children. Some adults
have taken jobs at educational institutions specifically to qualify for
this aid. Consider the financial impact of having your entire family
educated at no or reduced tuition! That may be of greater value than
your salary for several years.

Aid from Professional Organizations, Businesses, and Other Agencies

Professional organizations, businesses, and other groups sometimes
offer aid to their members, or to families of their members, or to
potential members, or simply to deserving people. For example, a
professional women's organization might make educational funds
available to women who are seeking to enter that professional field.
Sabina Leonard of Trocaire College in Buffalo, New York, says:
"There are a lot of grants that go unused every year simply because
people don't know about them. I found that a letter to a congressman works wonders. My congressman sent me a list of companies
and organizations that make grants available, such as the $300 yearly
grant from Clairol through the Business and Professional Women's
Association."

You should search for such sources. (See Financial Aid References,
at the end of the chapter.) In particular, check with organizations to
which you or your spouse belong.

Aid from Social Agencies

Some social agencies provide funds to students even if the primary
function of the agency has nothing to do with education. It is wise to
investigate carefully your rights with each sort of agency. Unfortunately, counselors in some agencies simply do not know what educational aid they administer. The college's financial aid counselor may
be able to give you advice concerning local interpretations of laws
within the agencies with which you are involved. However, you will

be responsible for actually applying for aid from the agency. Below are some major agency sources of aid to students:

Veterans Administration

Benefits are available to veterans with other than dishonorable discharges. The benefits for which a veteran may be eligible depend on when he or she was in the service and if he or she incurred any disability. In certain cases, spouses of veterans with service-connected death or permanent disability are eligible for veterans' educational benefits. Your local Veterans Administration office can help you find out exactly which programs are available to you.

Vocational Rehabilitation

Funds are available for students who have a physical or mental impairment that will put a limitation on employment. If you have such an impairment, you should make arrangements to meet with a vocational rehabilitation counselor who can usually be found through your state or territory government. You will be required to have a medical examination and may also be asked for financial information.

Aid to Native Americans

Aid is available through the U.S. Bureau of Indian Affairs for both four-year college programs and vocational training. Application forms are available from the Bureau of Indian Affairs Office in the Department of the Interior. If you are at least one-fourth Indian, Eskimo, or Aleut, are enrolled as a member of a tribe, band, or group, and have financial need, you should pursue this aid. Many states also have aid programs for Native Americans, and you should contact your state government for information.

Social Security

Programs that may be helpful to older students are widow or widower benefits for parents. If you are a widow or widower with children, you should see your local Social Security office.

Social Services

Funds may be available to help you support your children, particularly if you are single parent. In many social service agencies, there is a work incentive program. Under this program, it is possible to receive vocational training from a postsecondary school for about one year. If you are considering a program such as licensed practical nurse studies or secretarial science, and you receive welfare, you should ask about work training.

Food Stamps

Often students can qualify under the Food Stamp Program. Check with your local social service agency.

Aid Available to Students in Specialized Fields   99

Some money is available to students who intend to pursue certain professions immediately after graduation. On the national level, these programs include nursing programs and Reserve Officers' Training Corps. Details of eligibility are given in Major Sources of Financial Aid at the end of this chapter.

Some states and colleges have specialized aid for students taking certain academic majors. Ask either the college you are considering or your state education department to inform you if such aid is available.

Aid from Lending Institutions

Two kinds of loan programs are available to students who are enrolled at least half-time in a participating postsecondary school. The Guaranteed Student Loan (GSL), which generally comes from a commercial bank, credit union, savings and loan association, or other lender, is available to all students with financial need, as determined by the appropriate needs-analysis formula. Students may qualify under formulas that financial aid officers are qualified to interpret for you.

An independent student (one not dependent on parents for financial aid) who fails to qualify for the GSL under the formulas may apply for a loan under PLUS, which does not require a demonstration of need. This loan carries higher interest and a more immediate payback period. It should be considered only after the possibility of getting a GSL has been thoroughly explored.

Having outlined several ways you may qualify for aid, we want to remind you that most students qualify for aid by demonstrating financial need. Therefore, the remainder of this chapter will be devoted to an explanation of how you apply, how the need system works, and what kinds of aid are available.

APPLYING FOR NEED-BASED FINANCIAL AID

To document financial need, most colleges request a statement of a family's financial strength. Factors such as income, assets, size of a family, number of family members in college, and indebtedness play a role in determining a given student's ability to pay for college expenses. Many students typically apply to more than one college, particularly new students. Consequently, for the convenience of student and college alike, most institutions ask that prospective students use the Financial Aid Form (FAF), published and processed by the College Scholarship Service, Princeton, NJ 08541, the Family Financial

Statement (FFS), published and processed by the American College Testing Program, Iowa City, IA 52243, or the Application for Federal Student Aid, processed under the auspices of the federal government. Any of these services will provide your financial information to the colleges you designate, eliminating the necessity for you to file numerous financial aid applications. In addition, you will need to submit one of these forms for any kind of federal aid. Because of processing time, you should complete one of these forms as soon as you know you are going to enroll, even if you have not been accepted at a college. Forms can be obtained from a high school guidance office, a college financial aid office, or the services at the addresses given.

ESTABLISHING NEED

The vast majority of financial aid given by colleges and the federal and state governments in this country is granted only to meet documented financial need. Financial need, you may recall, is defined as the difference between your cost of going to a particular college and the money you (and your spouse, if you have one) can provide.

As the first step in establishing need, the college that intends to offer you admission will establish your cost of going to that school. This cost itemization for each incoming student who applies for aid is called the student's budget. The budget will include the cost of tuition and books, and living expenses such as food, housing, transportation, and child care. These budgets vary from college to college according to the student's tuition, and even within colleges according to the student's living situation.

Consider the case of Julia, a divorced woman with two children to support, living expenses of $6,000, a $3,200 tuition expense, and a $300 cost for books at college X. Her total budget at college X would be $9,500. Julia's budget would be different at college Y where the tuition is $700, and she needs $300 additional transportation money because college Y is farther from her home. Her total budget at college Y would be $7,300: $700 for tuition, $300 for books, and $6,300 for living expenses.

	College X	College Y
Tuition	$3,200	$ 700
Books	300	300
Living Expenses	6,000	6,300
Budget	$9,500	$7,300

As the second step in establishing need, after the budget is set, a college will decide what money is available from you (and your spouse) to meet college expenses, according to the information you have **101** provided on an FAF, FFS, or federal form. In Julia's case, colleges X and Y would consider her net income of $1,000 and the $2,400 she receives in child support as money available to meet her expenses. Since she has no major assets, owns no home, and has no major indebtedness, these factors are not considered. At both colleges X and Y, Julia would have a family contribution of $3,400 (net income of $1,000 plus child support of $2,400).

Only after a budget is established and your contribution has been figured can the college determine if you have financial need. If your contribution is less than the budget, you are eligible for aid. The higher the budget, the more likely you are to have need. In Julia's case, she has different needs at the different colleges due to the difference in the budgets.

	College X	College Y
Budget	$9,500	$7,300
Family Contribution	3,400	3,400
Documented need, or eligibility for aid	$6,100	$3,900

It is important to note a few things here. Budgets vary from school to school, but, generally, family contribution does not change. Since the amount of financial aid that you can receive is a function of the college's cost and your ability to contribute monies toward that cost, you may qualify for more aid at a college with high tuition than at a college with low tuition, but you will still in all likelihood be expected to contribute about the same amount of your own. In Julia's case, she qualifies for $6,100 in aid at the high-cost school and $3,900 at the low-cost school, assuming a family contribution in each case of $3,400. It could actually cost Julia about the same to go to an expensive college or a less expensive one. This indicates that it is probably not wise to choose your college on the basis of cost alone.

SOURCES OF AID BASED ON NEED

Financial aid to meet need takes the form of a grant, a loan, a part-time job, or some combination of these three. Grants (or scholarships) are direct awards, and repayment is not required. Loans are funds that must be repaid. Loans are usually guaranteed by some agency and offered at low interest; repayment is usually due after you leave college. Part-time employment provides an opportunity to earn money. The college decides whether to give a grant, a loan, part-time employment, or a "package" that consists of a combination of types of aid.

102 Pell Grant

The largest source of financial aid is the federal student-based grant called the Pell Grant. It is currently authorized in amounts up to $2,100 per year. The maximum amount that actually is available in any one year, though, may vary with congressional appropriations. Part-time students have their awards proportionately reduced from the maximum yearly entitlement. You may apply for the Pell Grant using the FAF or FFS described above or by using the Application for Federal Student Aid.

State Student Incentive Grant (SSIG)

State student-based grant programs vary from state to state according to constitutional, legislative, or policy restrictions. For example, the most generous state aid programs exist in California (through the California Aid Commission Programs), Pennsylvania (the Pennsylvania Higher Education Grant Program), and New York (the Tuition Assistance Program). Because of the wide variations in state programs, as well as in application procedures, you should direct your inquiries to the financial aid officer at your local college or to your local state scholarship agency. Your state education department will give you the agency's address.

After helping a student apply for student-based aid from the federal and state governments, the financial aid office will refer the student to agencies from which she or he may receive funds. The agencies most often referred to were described earlier: the Veterans Administration, Vocational Rehabilitation, Bureau of Indian Affairs, Social Security, and social services.

Once all the sources from outside the college are exhausted, the financial aid office will begin to consider giving the student aid that is administered by the college. The most common forms of aid follow.

Supplemental Educational Opportunity Grant (SEOG)

The Supplemental Educational Opportunity Grant is for colleges to give to students who they feel would be unable to pursue or continue their higher education without the grant. This program is funded by the federal government and administered by the colleges. This means that, within the federal guidelines, the college decides who gets the money and how much.

College Grants   103

These grants are funded and administered by the colleges. They are usually described in the college catalog or in the college's financial aid brochure.

National Direct Student Loan (NDSL)

This is a federal program administered by the colleges. There is no interest on the loan while a student is in school. Repayment with low interest begins six months after the student leaves school. If you enter certain fields of teaching or teach in designated schools, some or all of your loan may be forgiven.

College Work-Study (CWS)

This employment program is jointly funded by the federal government and the college. It provides part-time jobs for eligible students in private or public nonprofit organizations such as the college's campus library, a local hospital, or a youth agency. CWS is designed to provide a flow of income to assist students in meeting everyday educational expenses. Usually the salary received will be based on the current minimum wage, but it may also be a function of the type of work that is assigned and the ability of the student to perform that work.

FINANCIAL AID PACKAGES

The financial aid packages that students receive vary greatly depending on the resources of a given student and the types of aid funds available to a college. Our friend Julia, for example, might have received two different packages from colleges X and Y.

	School X	School Y
Budget	$9,500	$7,300
Family Contribution	3,400	3,400
Need	$6,100	$3,900
Grant	$3,700	$1,500
Loan	1,400	1,200
Employment	1,000	1,200
Package	$6,100	$3,900

Following are three student packages that demonstrate the sort of differences that are possible within a single school. These three students each have a $7,000 budget:

		Student A	Student B	Student C
Budget		$7,000	$7,000	$7,000
Family Contribution		1,000	2,000	4,000
Documented Need		$6,000	$5,000	$3,000
Federal and State	Pell Grant	$1,800	$1,300	$ 800
Aid	State Grant	200	100	0
Agencies and	Social Security	$ 0	$ 0	$ 0
Programs	Veterans' Benefits	0	2,400	0
	Social Services	0	0	0
	Vocational Rehabilitation	500	0	2,000
	Work Incentive	0	0	0
	Indian Affairs	0	0	0
College-	SEOG	$ 500	$ 0	$ 0
Administered	College Grant	1,000	200	200
Funds	NDSL	1,000	500	0
	CWS	1,000	0	0
	Campus Employment	0	500	0

After the financial aid office has exhausted its resources or if a student is unable to establish need but feels a financial crunch, the office will refer the student to the Guaranteed Student Loan or PLUS loan programs. These loans are the ones described above that come from a lending institution. In many instances, even if need is met by various sources, a student or his or her family will be able to obtain these loans to supplement financial aid.

IF YOU CANNOT ESTABLISH NEED

If you cannot establish your financial need according to the prescribed procedures, yet you know you have need, you should be aware that you can discuss your situation with the staff of the financial aid

office and they will help you find alternatives. There are several points **105**
you should talk over if you find yourself in this situation:

1. Was the budget used by the financial aid office realistic? If you can justify a higher budget, you may qualify for aid or additional aid.
2. Was the contribution expected of you (and your spouse) too high? Should it be adjusted due to some unusual noncollege expense you are facing?
3. Many colleges have payment plans that allow students to make their tuition payments over the entire semester rather than in one large payment at registration. The interest or bookkeeping charges are usually minimal. The plans are worth exploring if you don't receive aid or if you receive less aid than necessary to pay your tuition at registration.

SOME OTHER POINTS ON FINANCIAL AID

If you decide to continue your education and if you decide to pursue financial aid, the list of reminders below will help you through the complex world of financial aid. Most of these pointers apply whether you choose to attend part-time or full-time.

1. Make an appointment to meet a financial aid counselor at the college you are interested in attending if you can travel to it; otherwise ask a counselor at a nearby college for assistance. As Sabina Leonard of Trocaire College puts it: "The main thing to remember is that no one can help unless you are willing to swallow your pride and let them know you need help."

   You may not be eligible to receive financial aid from every source that you consider, but you most decidedly will not get aid from those programs that you do not know exist, or for which you don't apply.
2. Read the college catalogs for financial aid deadlines and make sure that you meet them.
3. Complete the Financial Aid Form, the Family Financial Statement, or the Application for Federal Student Aid described earlier. Complete any other forms you may be given by the financial aid office.
4. Provide the college with all the documents it requests. Tax forms, letters from social agencies, and separation or divorce papers are among the forms often requested.
5. See any people outside the college in agencies or organizations that may be of help to you.
6. Reply to all mail you receive and keep copies. Never change an address without letting the financial aid office know.

7. If you decide you will need a Guaranteed Student Loan or PLUS loan, apply at least six to eight weeks before you start college.
8. Once enrolled, you must reapply for financial aid each academic year since funding levels, eligibility criteria, and family circumstances invariably change from one year to the next.
9. If you are offered aid in a package that you cannot take advantage of—for example, part-time employment that is not possible because you would have to pay a baby-sitter—you should discuss changing types of aid in your package.
10. The details of the major financial aid programs offered nationally are outlined at the end of this chapter but of course are subject to legislative changes. Although the data were current at the time this book was published, and no legislation is being proposed to change the financial aid picture, you may want to check with a financial aid officer for any subsequent changes.

The process of filing for financial aid is by no means a simple one, but the task is not as arduous and confusing as it seems at first glance. The methods of paying for your college education demand just as much of your time and attention as the choice of a college itself and the prospective field of study.

Fortunately, you need not struggle with paying for your education without the guidance of a financial aid official. Whether you attend a public or a private college, live on campus or are a commuter, financial aid officers are committed to meeting your financial requirements to attend their institution.

INCOME TAX DEDUCTIONS

As an employed or self-employed individual you may, under certain circumstances, claim an income tax deduction for qualifying educational expenses. However, if you are not currently engaged in a business or profession, even though you may be going to school to become qualified for employment, your educational expense is *not* deductible, according to the Internal Revenue Service (IRS).

To qualify, your curriculum must comply with one of the following two conditions listed in *Your Federal Income Tax*, a taxpayer's guide published annually by the IRS and obtainable free from your local IRS office. You may deduct expenses that:

1. meet the express requirements of your employer, or the requirements of law or regulations, for keeping your salary, status, or employment; or

2. maintain or improve skills required in performing the duties of **107**
your present employment, trade, or business.

The IRS points out that qualifying expenses may be deducted
even though you may be pursuing a degree. But only those courses
that directly relate to your occupation qualify, regardless of whether
or not they are part of your degree requirements.

Assuming you meet the above requirements, allowable educational
expenses include tuition, books, supplies, and course-related fees and
expenses. In addition, if you go to school during the same day that
you go to work, you may deduct the cost that you incur in traveling
between your school and work locations. (Commuting between your
school or work location and your home is not deductible.) This transportation expense is allowable even if you make an incidental side
trip home or elsewhere, but the distance must be computed as if
you had gone directly between your job and school locations.

Allowable transportation expenses include the cost of operating
your car, or the current standard mileage rate allowed by the IRS,
plus parking fees and tolls. If you use public transportation, you may
deduct your actual fares. The entire cost of a trip away from home
for qualifying educational purposes may also be deducted as explained
by the IRS (*Your Federal Income Tax*):

> If you travel away from home primarily to obtain education, the expenses
> of which are deductible, you may deduct your expenditures for travel, meals,
> and lodging while away from home. However, if you engage in incidental per-
> sonal activities, you may not deduct the part of your expenses used for per-
> sonal activities.

In addition to educational and travel expenses, you may be eligible
for a tax credit for child care or disabled-dependent care. To qualify,
you must meet the following conditions outlined in *Your Federal Income Tax*:

1. You must be married and must file a joint tax return (using
   form 1040) with your spouse.
2. You must be a full-time student for each of any five months
   during the tax year.
3. You must pay someone (other than your spouse or a person
   you can claim as your dependent) to care for your dependent
   who is disabled or under age 15.
4. Your qualifying dependent must live with you in a home that
   you maintain.
5. Your child-care and disabled-dependent-care expenses must be
   incurred to allow your spouse to work.
6. Your spouse must have income from work during the year.

Name	Type of Aid	Amount Available	Available for Part-Time Study (6 hours or more)
Pell Grant	G	Up to $2,100 per year.* Total varies by appropriation and also from college to college.	Yes
Supplemental Educational Opportunity Grant (SEOG)	G	Up to $2,000 per year.	Yes**
National Direct Student Loan (NDSL)	L	Undergraduate student: $3,000 per year; $6,000 total. Graduate student, including undergraduate borrowing: $12,000 total.	Yes
College Work-Study (CWS)	J	Open.	Yes**
State Student Incentive Grant	G	Varies from state to state.	Varies from state to state.
Guaranteed Student Loan (GSL)	L	Dependent student: $2,500 per year; $12,500 total. Independent student: $2,500 per year; $12,500 total. Graduate student: $5,000 per year; $25,000 total, including undergraduate borrowing.	Yes

Terms	Source of Funds	Application Sent to
Enrolled in eligible institution/making satisfactory progress.	Federal Government	Federal Government or its contractor
Enrolled in eligible institution/making satisfactory progress.	Federal Government	Included in College Aid Application
Enrolled in eligible institution/making satisfactory progress. No interest charged during school or for 6-month grace period afterward or during military service; 5% interest on unpaid balance once repayment begins.	Federal Government and College	Included in College Aid Application
Enrolled in eligible institution/making satisfactory progress.	Federal Government and College	Included in College Aid Application
Varies from state to state.	State and Federal Governments	Varies from state to state.
Enrolled in eligible institution/making satisfactory progress. No interest charged during school or for 6-month grace period afterward; 8% interest on unpaid balance once repayment begins; an insurance premium is deducted from the original loan. An origination fee of at least 5% of the loan is payable to the lending institution at the time the loan is disbursed.	Lending Institutions	Lending Institution and College

MAJOR SOURCES OF FINANCIAL AID (Continued)

Name	Type of Aid	Amount Available	Available for Part-Time Study (6 hours or more)
PLUS Loans	L	Independent undergraduate student: up to $2,500 per year; $12,500 total (in combination with GSL). Graduate student: $3,000 per year; $15,000 total (in addition to GSL).	Yes
Nursing Student Loan	L	$2,500 per year; $10,000 total.	Yes
Reserve Officers' Training Corps (ROTC)***	G	For 4-, 3-, 2-, 1-year scholarship students: full tuition, fees, books. $100 per month subsistence for last two years of study. All students: approximately $600 for summer camp in junior year.	No

   *Actual amount of award varies according to congressional appropriation, year by year.

   **Also available for less than 6 semester hours of study.

   ***Facts given are for Army ROTC. Data for Navy and Air Force somewhat different. Details on these programs and Marine Corps Platoon Leaders Course available from nearest recruiter or campus ROTC office.

Terms	Source of Funds	Application Sent to
12-14% interest payment begins within 60 days after the loan is granted, but full-time students are eligible for a deferment. PLUS is available to independent students and also to parents of dependent students.	Lending Institutions	Lending Institution and College
Enrolled in eligible institution/making satisfactory progress. No interest charged during nursing school or for 6-month grace period afterward; 6% interest on unpaid balance once repayment begins.	Federal Government and College	College
Scholarship students must be under 26 years of age upon graduation; nonscholarship under 28 with waiver possible for prior service. 4 years of active duty for scholarship students upon graduation; for other students, active duty for training for 3-6 months or 3 years of active duty.	Federal Government	College ROTC Unit

Note: Data were current as book went to press. Program details may change as a result of legislation or executive action. Check with a financial aid officer for the most up-to-date information.

CODE: L = LOAN
        G = GRANT
        J = JOB

112   If you meet these requirements, you may claim a tax credit equal to up to 30% of your work-related expenses. The yearly work-related expenses, however, are limited to $2,400 for one qualifying dependent or $4,800 for the care of two or more qualifying persons. Therefore, you may reduce your tax liability in any year by up to $720 for one dependent or $1,440 if the expenses are for the care of two or more people. This credit is not merely a deduction from taxable income but, rather, a *direct credit* that reduces your taxes dollar for dollar.

Additional information on educational and related travel deductions, and child-care and disabled-dependent-care credit, as well as single copies of *Your Federal Income Tax*, may be obtained free from your local IRS office. Be aware that changes constantly affect income tax laws. Whereas the information given above was current at press time, deductible categories and amounts may change, so check with your local IRS office or income tax adviser for any changes made since publication.

FINANCIAL AID REFERENCES

Free Brochures and Pamphlets

Applying for Financial Aid. ACT, P.O. Box 168, Iowa City, IA 52243. Explains how to figure family contribution to college costs.

Educational Financial Aid Sources for Women, and *Scholarships, BPW Foundation.* Send a self-addressed, stamped business envelope to Clairol Loving Care Scholarship Program, 345 Park Avenue, New York, NY 10154. These pamphlets also list additional sources of aid for women.

Federal Financial Aid for Men and Women Resuming Their Education or Training, and *The Student Guide: Five Federal Financial Aid Programs.* Federal Financial Aid, P.O. Box 84, Washington, DC 20044.

A Selected List of Fellowship Opportunities and Aids to Advanced Education for United States Citizens and Foreign Nationals. National Science Foundation Publications, Room 235, 1800 G Street, N.W., Washington, DC 20550.

Undergraduate Programs of Cooperative Education in the United States and Canada. National Commission for Cooperative Education, 360 Huntington Avenue, Boston, MA 02115.

Booklets and Books

Directory of Special Programs for Minority Group Members. Garrett Park Press, Garrett Park, MD 20896. $20 prepaid. Sources of aid for black, Hispanic, American Indian groups.

Need a Lift? The American Legion Education Program, Indianapolis, IN 46206. $1 prepaid. Revised annually, a comprehensive source of educational opportunities, careers, loans, scholarships, employment for veterans and families.

Part II:

SUCCEEDING

8.
Managing During Those First Several Weeks

What courses should I consider? How much can I handle? What can I expect in those first weeks?

Most adult students will be enrolled in evening courses at a local institution on a part-time basis. Some will enroll full-time, like most of the younger students on a campus, and they will attend classes during the daytime. Still others will be utilizing one of the many other educational paths we have discussed: taking weekend seminars, perhaps, or independent study courses at a local school, television courses, correspondence courses, or external degree programs from a distant institution. In this chapter we will first address the most common circumstance, that of the part-time student taking evening classes. However, you should be aware that whatever your particular situation, most of the concerns you will face are common to all adult students regardless of their program or instructional mode. We will mention concerns of particular interest to students in some nontraditional programs, and we will conclude with a section specifically for such students.

OPENING OF THE ACADEMIC YEAR

Those first days in your program will be among the most intensive and memorable (or perhaps we should say unforgettable) days of your life. On that first evening or day of the fall term, you will probably experience excitement, anxiety, confusion, exhaustion, frustration—many things—and all in a jumble. Faculty are moving offices, advising students, trying to get the bookstore to perform the miracle of making

117

118 all the course texts appear on the shelves on time. Students are scrambling to do all things at once. If you find yourself befuddled, you are not at fault. It's the system.

Should you enter school at a period other than the beginning of the academic year, you will avoid some of the hustle and bustle. Those openings after intersession come easier. Faculty have settled into the year's routine of teaching and committee duties, and students have taken care of many registration matters by preregistering in the previous term. Don't worry that you may have missed something; just be patient. The opening of the next new year will soon be upon you, and there will be sufficient confusion on campus for you to share in it.

CONSIDERING TYPES OF INSTRUCTIONAL MODES

Even in these experimental times, traditional class settings are still the most common: Students come face to face with an instructor in a lecture hall, classroom, seminar room, laboratory, or studio.

Lectures

Students in a university often are shocked by the lecture hall when they first encounter it. In registering for Physics 101 they have no idea that in going to class they will be plunged into a horde of jostling people seeking the same goal, room 303. This destination was merely a piece of miscellaneous information that looked innocuous enough on their course schedule, but it now turns out to be a cavern capable of swallowing 500 people. The student who struggles to a seat and sees a few seats vacant will be little comforted to discover she has only 347 others to compete against instead of the capacity crowd of 500.

If you face a similar circumstance, do not lose heart. The professor will probably lecture and you will take notes. And then you will go to a classroom and meet with a teaching assistant who will probably be a graduate student. The lecturer may allow some questions in the lecture hall, but most of your dialog will be with the teaching assistant in class. And except for the few common tests given in the course you will not be competing against the 347 but against those in the classroom.

The disadvantages of the lecture hall are evident. As part of a mass you get little, if any, attention to your needs. The professor is basically a conveyor of information, often less stimulating than a good book on the subject. Yet, for various reasons, some of them valid, the lecture-hall method persists.

Your real advantage in the lecture-hall course is studying with others and comparing lecture notes. Since the professor in the lecture hall is primarily an information disseminator, notes are particularly important. If common tests are given to the whole class of 348 students,

the questions quite certainly will be centered primarily on major **119**
points covered in the lectures. The questions will probably be objective
(so they can be graded by key) and not too difficult (if, in fact, you
have the basics well in mind). The large-lecture-hall experience is most
often an exercise in intensive listening, careful comparing of notes
with others, and precise relation of the lecture material to what is in
the course textbook. Do not get behind, be diligent, and get an A.

Class Sections

The classroom of 15 to 40 or so people is probably going to be
your most common type of learning experience in school. In registering for a course that has several sections (common for lower-level
courses), sometimes you will have a choice of a course section with a
relatively small number of students in it, or one that is almost closed
out with the maximum enrollment. If registrations are nearly complete, class sizes might tell you something. Is the smaller class at a less
desirable hour—say, late in the evening? If so, and you can stand the
inconvenience, register with confidence. If, however, the smaller class
is given during prime time, watch out. Students who didn't register
for this small section may know something you don't about the instructor. If, before registering, you can take time to investigate reasons
for the difference in section sizes, do so. If not, your safest choice
might well be the larger section.

Seminars

Seminars, normally enrolling 6 to 15 people, are expensive for the
institution, so they are usually reserved for upper-level courses where
attrition and specialization make the seminar more common. But
there may be some lower-level seminars. If you know the instructor
and you are confident you can operate effectively under the pressure
of performance among a small number of students, fine. You will
probably get a lot out of the experience. But if grades are important
to you, and neither of those other conditions applies, you would do
well to pass up the seminar and register instead for a course in some
other type of class setting.

Labs

Labs can be fun, and this is fortunate because they can also be a
lot of work. Whether your lab is for science, engineering, computer
science, psychology, or some other subject, you may get a lot of satisfaction from your hands-on experience—testing classroom theory
against physical realities.

120   If you have had no experience with labs or have had bad experiences, you should wait a semester, if you can, to take a lab course. This will give you time to investigate the nature of the lab and learn some of the tricks of the trade from other students before you have to commit yourself.

Someone might advise you to split your lecture and lab; that is, take the lecture during this session, and the lab next session. The problem with this solution is that in the next session you will probably have to restudy lecture material, and this is not the most efficient utilization of your time.

Studio and Physical Education Courses

Studio courses in fine arts, graphic arts, and other subjects can be "guts"—easy courses. We apologize to the instructors who make studios a real challenge. But the facts often are these: Instructors of studio courses usually are performance, not theory, oriented. They are often nontraditional and distrustful of a grading system, *any* grading system. (How do you grade a painting? What would you give the *Mona Lisa*?) It is easier for these instructors to give A's and B's than to chance the stifling of creativity and to try to explain the vague distinctions that may separate the higher from the lower grades. You may have a good time, meet some fine people, and discover latent talent, which is all for the best. An easy studio course could be just what you need for a change of pace and an assured "pass" in an otherwise difficult schedule.

You ought not to neglect considering, too, another possible gut, the physical education course. Attend almost every period, have a good game of volleyball or badminton, get an A and one credit. And don't feel guilty about it. The intellectual work you are doing in other courses more than makes up for the lack of it in P.E. Keen mind, healthy body. You owe it to yourself.

Television, Radio, and Newspaper Courses

As noted earlier, your institution may cooperate with local broadcast and print media to offer some courses that you may take totally or mostly at home. You might want to inquire specifically about this possibility or look for it in the bulletin that lists courses. You usually have a fixed time, such as a semester, to complete these courses, and some evening or weekend meetings with an instructor may supplement the material that is presented in the media. These courses can be particularly convenient to the adult student, but if you have been away from studies for some time, your better choice might be to take

classroom courses first and reserve the media courses for later when **121**
you have gotten more fully into the swing of study and exams.

Self-paced Study

All of the foregoing programs are based on the institution's setting
the pace for progress: you must attend classes or complete certain
requirements at prescribed times. But you may be offered the chance
to do self-paced study. This can be easy for some individuals and impossible for others. Although you may plan your study to fit into
your schedule, and this is certainly convenient, you will have to organize very well and discipline yourself to ensure that you are progressing at a reasonable rate. You will not be happy with yourself if
you wake up one morning to discover that you have accomplished
little and the bulk of your work is still ahead of you.

Programmed Instruction

This type of instruction can be in the form of a packet of written
materials, a videotape, a cassette, or a computer program. The student
studies material that usually includes self-testing at specific stages to
determine if the necessary levels of competence have been achieved.
If so, the student may go on to the next stage; if not, the student goes
back and repeats as necessary or seeks the help of an instructor. At
the end there may be a graded assessment to determine the degree of
mastery of the subject. Programmed instruction is highly effective in
some fields and with some students. As with any self-paced instruction, it requires discipline for the best results.

Correspondence Courses

As noted earlier, these courses usually come as a package with study
and testing materials included. Often the student must complete one
segment, send in a completed examination or paper for grading, and
receive the results before being allowed to progress to the next segment. Time limits usually are liberal, but the institution probably
will want to see reasonable progress as a condition of continued enrollment. In choosing these courses, look for the amount of interaction
the institution will provide. Is an instructor available for consultation
by telephone or letter? Will the examinations be graded and returned
promptly? A well-managed correspondence course can be a boon for
a student; a poorly handled one can result in endless frustration.

Independent Study

Basically there are two types of independent study. One is an alternative to classroom work or an extension of that work. It takes
place on a campus under the direction of an instructor. This type of
independent study usually is reserved for above-average students.

However, some institutions offer standard courses on an independent-study basis to any student who, for some valid reason, cannot complete requirements in the usual manner. Or, after a student completes a standard course, he or she may be allowed to do in-depth work in some aspect of the course on an independent-study basis. Credit also may be allowed for assisting an instructor in a project, such as a survey or scientific experiment. Charles McCabe and some contributing authors earned independent study credit for work on this book. Independent study courses often can be found in a school's bulletin, but if no such courses are listed, do not assume that independent study is not available. Inquire at the departmental or dean's office.

The other type of independent study is that associated with external degree programs. Several of these programs encourage projects that are designed by the student in consultation with an adviser. Your work setting can provide the focus for your study, and you may be able to do some things for your employer that will be helpful to the company as well as provide credit in your external degree program. Your home or community can also be the setting for independent study. You may be able to relate an independent study project with an objective you had wanted to achieve anyway, such as learning how to paint, or composing music, or looking into items of concern to the community as a whole. Thus, you may be able to kill two birds with one stone.

Remember, though, that any self-paced course of study is going to require self-discipline. If you can meet the challenge, this mode of instruction can be just right, conveniently meshing with other aspects of your busy life.

ASSESSING HOW MUCH TO TAKE

Anne Seavey of Bentley College in Waltham, MA, says:

> A working adult student has to be highly motivated or he wouldn't be going to school. Even so, each person should take only the number of courses he can handle, considering the amount of time he has available to spend on those courses. Attending class is the easy part. It is the hours of homework—the reading, the writing, the research, and the studying for exams—that takes the most time. Difficult, too, is sacrificing social activities or having to be satisfied with a messy house because time is needed for studying.

A natural tendency for an adult student is to want to get through a course, or a certificate, diploma, or degree program as quickly as possible. Perhaps you have a promotion waiting or a career change impending. Perhaps you have taken a leave of absence from work for a predetermined period of time and feel you must finish your program on schedule. Or your school may allow one or two tuition-free over-

load credits per semester, and your program will cost less if you take   **123**
an overload and finish early. Many other reasons might be impelling
you to assume a large course load. Before you hoist this burden on
your back, though, consider very carefully whether you will be able
to carry it well to the end of the journey.

If this is your first experience in continuing your education and
you elected to go part-time at the beginning even though full-time
was a viable option, you probably made a wise choice. If you believe
you can manage three courses in three nights per week, you might be
better off taking two. Most adults find two courses to be a challenge
when balanced with career, family, and other demands. Satisfaction
and good grades in one or two courses at the start of part-time study
will be more beneficial to you than barely passing while carrying a
full-time credit load. You may need time to build your confidence.
Take it if you can.

CHOOSING COURSES (AND INSTRUCTORS)

Choosing courses wisely (and instructors, too, in the case of on-
campus programs) is important to your success. A good place to start
is to make sure you need a particular course. Both first-time and
returning adult students sometimes take courses for which they
could later qualify to receive equivalent credit. Before registering, you
should review the chapter on Getting Credit for What You Already
Know, and make a personal assessment of your potential noncollegiate
credit awards.

If you are enrolled in a certificate, diploma, or degree program,
you probably will be required to take specified courses. However,
you may also be allowed to earn credits or other credentials by taking
other courses as electives. You should be aware that while two courses
given at different times may carry the same title, no two courses will
ever be exactly alike. In the instance of on-campus courses, the material you will cover, the way it will be presented, the knowledge you
will acquire, and the enjoyment (or lack of it) you will derive from
the course will be determined largely by your classmates and, particularly, by the instructor.

The kind, not just the quantity, of courses you choose is important.
One combination of courses may be impossible for you and another
combination easy. The difference could be the inclusion or exclusion
of a single course.

Ideally, before registration, you have already investigated the kinds
of courses that will make up your quarter, session, or semester load.
You have consulted with your adviser, talked to adult students who
have taken these courses, and conferred with as many of the course
instructors as possible. You know at least by reputation which courses

are the guts and which are the backbreakers. Even armed with this kind of preparation, though, you are never assured of having selected the best combination. The gut course you chose to pad your program, Film as a Subversive Art taught by Professor Thompson, might become a real problem when at the last moment Professor Cut-'em-up Klondike is substituted for good old Thompson. Don't panic, though. Registration procedure (which we'll come to shortly) should allow you to make adjustments in your schedule.

Beware, too, of the syndrome called "getting the required courses out of the way." Programs of study usually are designed to space required courses reasonably across the full amount of time needed for completion. It is difficult for students even to schedule required courses before the natural time for such courses has arrived. Yet, by straining, some students manage to do this, and many of them later regret it.

Required courses can be among the more challenging courses. If they are required, especially core courses at an introductory level, a clientele is probably assured for the instructors. They may not have to compete with their colleagues in attracting students to these courses, so they can be more demanding in their expectations of the students in them. To take a chance on putting too many difficult courses too early in your program, before you have developed the capability to handle them, does not make good sense.

You should utilize counselors, of course, but your best advice in planning your schedule may come from other students. Try to draw unbiased conclusions by looking for consistencies in what they tell you. Their impression of an instructor often represents your most valuable information for making a decision about taking a course. A given instructor might be considered easy when it comes to grades, but he might also be so boring that you will learn very little. The best instructors will be interesting, reasonably demanding, and fair in determining grades. If you are going to invest several weeks of your time and your money in a course, it makes good sense to find out as much as possible about the instructor before you make the commitment.

SAMPLING COURSES

But what do you do if the instructor's name is not announced in advance? A tactic employed by some students to decide among courses is to screen the teachers after the semester begins. This can sometimes be accomplished by the students' registering for more courses than they plan to complete. (We will add some notes of caution, though, in a moment.) After sitting in on every class for the first week, the students determine which courses and teachers are most beneficial for them, then they drop the courses they believe would be to their

disadvantage to continue. (To drop a course means to discontinue it **125**
in the first few days or weeks of classes; no record of it appears on
your transcript. However, some schools require that you forfeit part
of the tuition, so check this out.) Remember Professor Cut-'em-up
Klondike, the professor you got by mistake when you thought you
were signing up for a gut with good old Thompson? You might be
able to drop Klondike and add someone else.

We should quickly add, however, that not all institutions will allow
a student to sit in class without proper registration, even for a night
or two at the beginning of a session. If an instructor is conscientious
and realizes an unregistered student is in the classroom, the instructor
could be quite forceful in requesting the student to leave. This could
be embarrassing. So, check out the policy before employing this tactic.
In any case, as soon as you have decided on the courses you will take,
be sure that you are properly registered. This will avoid potentially
serious problems with receiving proper recognition for your work.

Another possibility for choosing instructors is to sit in on a class
or two this session for courses you are considering taking in the future.
Remember, a teacher will have a great impact on your success and
enjoyment in a course.

AVOIDING CLOSEOUTS

The best way to avoid being closed out of an on-campus course is
to plan ahead. (You may also have to do this in some correspondence
programs.) Word of a particularly good course or instructor spreads
quickly in student circles. If you want to get into a popular course,
you should register as soon as registration opens. Even if you are un-
decided, you may still want to register for the course provided that
your school has a withdrawal and refund policy. Admission to some
courses may require that you obtain the instructor's signature prior
to registration.

After registering for your first session, you should begin formu-
lating plans for the next session. Each session thereafter you should
make it a point to know well before registration opens exactly which
courses will be offered and which courses you plan to take the following term. If the course schedule has not been published, the department office or an individual teacher may be able to tell you which
courses are likely to be scheduled.

If your official status is that of an underclassman, you may be given
low priority for admission to certain courses required for completion
of your program. The registrar's office may feel that you still have
plenty of time to take such required courses prior to graduation; preference may, therefore, be given to upperclassmen. Should you find
yourself closed out of a course, don't give up right away—there are

ways to get admitted to closed classes. One possibility is to get permission directly from the course instructor. If you can convince the instructor that you absolutely must take *his* course *this* semester, he will probably make room for you. Another possibility is to find out from the registrar's office what "ceiling" was placed on enrollment, then attend the first session and count the students in the class. If someone is absent, you may be able to take his or her place.

CLASS LOCATIONS: AVOIDING CONFLICTS

Be sure to pay attention to the locations of the classes when scheduling more than one class in a given evening. University campuses especially can cover a lot of real estate. Unless in all kinds of weather you enjoy running between distant buildings during the ten minutes that may separate class periods, take the time to check your tentative schedule against a campus map. With some prior planning and without detriment to your overall plan to complete your program, classes can often be grouped by location, deferring the one in a far-off building until a future semester. By then the class location itself may change to be more convenient for you, or your schedule may be more conducive to including it.

THAT FIRST CLASS!

Now that we've covered possibilities for types of course encounters during both your first and your somewhat later school experiences, we come back to the thing itself—that first class! Rosemarie Sunderland of the College of New Rochelle reports: "I arrived for my first class in a state of fear that bordered on numbness. I was in, yet I had no idea what I had gotten myself *into.*"

Rosemarie weathered that first class experience and went on to succeed. Some adults—who knows how many?—undoubtedly do not survive that shock and drop out. Be prepared for anxiety. It may or may not come. If it does, remember that it is a natural element of life as an adult student, it lasts a very short time, and later you can joke about it as so many other students have done.

MANAGING DURING THE EARLY STAGES OF NONTRADITIONAL PROGRAMS

As we said at the beginning of the chapter, most of what applies to students in the traditional programs applies as well to those of you who have chosen other modes of study. We are going to offer some additional suggestions which, in turn, should also be of value to students in traditional programs.

We have probably said enough about some aspects of the need for **127** careful planning and self-discipline in self-paced programs. But we want to come back to the point of an earlier chapter: how important it is for you to get all the credit you can for what you already know. After all, most nontraditional programs were established with that specifically in mind, and you should take full advantage of the unique nature of your program. So if you have not already done so, review Getting Credit for What You Already Know, and make your assessment of potential credit awards before you have progressed much farther in your program.

In the early stages of your nontraditional study you might be concerned that completing your program can be a complex, awesome task, and you may feel very lonesome. You will encounter many new concepts that are unfamiliar, and you will have to investigate a variety of options. If you know little about proficiency examinations, for instance, you will have to learn about them in order to take full advantage of nontraditional opportunities. Be patient. Don't expect to understand everything about your program right away. Unfortunately, you don't have the support structure right at hand that is readily available to a student taking courses in a more traditional manner. But you will have materials from your institution, and you will have an adviser. Use these resources. In a short period of time your bewilderment will be replaced with understanding and you will be proceeding with confidence.

As we noted earlier, correspondence courses and proficiency exams are potentially large sources of credit. Using the *Independent Study Catalog* and your program bulletin, try to match areas of your strength with courses that are offered. In the early stages of your study you should be capitalizing on your strengths instead of breaking entirely new ground. If your program accepts correspondence courses from other institutions, you will have thousands of courses from which to choose, and almost all are from large, prestigious universities. You should be able to find some courses that will be relatively easy to complete and will look great on your transcript. Much the same can be said for proficiency exams as was said for correspondence courses. You already have knowledge and experience in certain areas. Find out what areas are covered by what exams. By first taking exams in areas of relative familiarity, you will gain confidence and the necessary skills to tackle the unknown later in your program. Before taking any correspondence courses or proficiency exams, though, be sure that your program adviser approves of what you are doing. In fact, get the approval in writing so there will be no costly misunderstandings or loss of time, money, or credit over what you have done.

9.

Striving for Good Grades and Satisfaction

How can I get the best grades or most satisfaction (both, I hope) from each course?

GRADING SYSTEMS

Most schools use a letter grading system or a grading scale of 0 to 4.0. However, many incorporate variations into the predominant grading system. Since it is not possible to cover all systems, we will explain only the most common. You should check carefully your own school regulations.

Basic letter grades include A, B, C, D, P, F, I, and W. An A indicates superior performance, B is above average, C means satisfactory, and D indicates marginally acceptable performance (but still passing). However, if you are in a certificate, diploma, or degree program, a grade of D in your area of concentration may not be acceptable. P is passing when the option of pass-fail is elected. The grade P also is commonly used to record credit for proficiency exams and noncollegiate courses. The grade of F is failing. The letter I (incomplete) may be recorded at the instructor's option when you have attended a course but for some reason did not complete all requirements.

The letter W indicates that you officially withdrew from the course before the deadline for withdrawing passed. (This deadline normally comes later in the session than the deadline for dropping a course.) If you feel certain you are going to fail a course, or receive a poor grade which will lower your average, you may wish to use the withdrawal option. At many institutions students are permitted to withdraw from any course during the first two-thirds of the semester. However,

128

more than one or two W's on a student's transcript will probably raise questions in the minds of potential employers or admissions officers of graduate programs.

The pass-fail option can be a valuable alternative if you are taking a difficult course outside your major field. This election usually must be made by formal application prior to a specified deadline; some schools do not permit the pass-fail option to be elected after the first class. The advantage of pass-fail is that you can take a course for which you expect to receive a low passing grade without the risk of the poor grade appearing on your transcript and lowering your average. However, you should be aware that above-average achievement in the course will not be officially recognized, and the course will not count toward meeting requirements for graduation with honors. Other possible disadvantages are that some schools will not accept pass-fail for transfer credit, and a potential employer may frown upon an applicant who has used a pass-fail option more than a few times. Nevertheless, wisely electing pass-fail for just one course might make the difference between graduation and graduation with honors.

QUALITY OR GRADE POINTS, AND HONORS

Quality-point average (QPA), or grade-point average (GPA), is a measure by which students may be compared to determine eligibility for such things as academic honors, scholarships, graduate school admissions, and career opportunities. Each credit hour of completed graded course work is counted in computing the grade-point average. Usually, an A is worth 4.0 quality points per credit, B equals 3.0, C equals 2.0, D equals 1.0, and F equals 0. Pluses and minuses, when used, are given intermediate weights (A- equals 3.7, B+ equals 3.3). The number of credits you've earned for a given course is multiplied by the number of quality points you've earned per credit (determined by your course grade) to arrive at the total quality points earned for the course. Your total quality points for all graded courses completed is divided by your total graded credit hours attempted. The quotient is your current cumulative quality- or grade-point average.

Each term you may have the opportunity to qualify for the dean's list by meeting the criteria of your school. The dean's list is usually open only to matriculated candidates who have completed a certain number of credits during a given session with the required grade-point average (usually at least 3.2). If you aspire to making the dean's list, check your school's catalog or bulletin to determine the requirements.

Graduation with honors should not concern you too early in your school attendance. There will be time to think about honors and honor societies as you move closer to completion of your program

130   requirements. (These topics are covered in chapter 13, Reassessing Your Goals and Performance.) For now, you would be wise to concentrate on the present and simply do your best in each course.

SO YOU WANT TO BE A STRAIGHT-A STUDENT?

Contributed by Dennis Gerard Ellis, *a graduate of Dutchess Community College, Poughkeepsie, NY (A.A.S. in Business; GPA 4.0; rank in class, first out of 754 students); Pace University, Pleasantville, NY (B.B.A.; GPA 4.0; rank in class, first out of 650 students); currently enrolled at Cornell Law School*

Straight A's. Sound impossible? Or at the very least, highly improbable? Well, it need not be either, for this pinnacle of academic success has been reached by many adult students and can be reached by you! Although everyone does not achieve all A's, there is no reason everyone cannot strive for them. This striving is, in itself, the key to academic success.

Many students enter school with a fear of failure. Unfortunately, this fear often leads them into the establishment of passing as their primary goal. Thus, they concentrate their efforts toward obtaining any grade except an F. Aiming for such small goals leads to underachievement. I propose that you settle for nothing less than a straight-A average as your goal. Granted, you may not achieve your goal, but your straight-A motivation and output will be reflected in A's and B's instead of the C's and D's that your short-sighted peers will receive.

I agree with Nancy Hawks, another contributor to this book, who says: "Adult students joke about grades a lot. But I'll let you in on a secret. They were damned important to us. Our high grades were signals of our **Success!**"

Here are some rewards that I consider important enough to justify working toward high grades:

1. **Honors and awards:** They become a permanent part of your school record and are conclusive evidence of your success.
2. **Scholarships:** Nearly every four-year school has funds available for outstanding transferees, as does nearly every graduate school. Educational institutions want exceptional students, and grades are used by virtually every school in awarding scholarships.
3. **Graduate and professional schools:** Almost all good graduate or professional schools require a copy of your undergraduate transcript when considering you for admission. They also have questions on their applications regarding your rank in class and any honors or awards that you may have received. Although graduate studies may seem miles away or not in your plans at all, you may change your mind after a year or two in school. It is wise to prepare for that contingency now.

4. **New jobs or job advancement**: Many employers ask you to list
   your honors and awards or rank in class on their applications.
   Some even require transcripts. An outstanding educational
   record looks good in your employment file.

5. **Yourself**: Even if you can find no other reason to work toward
   good grades, the self-satisfaction that you will derive from top
   performance is sufficient reason in itself. Prove to yourself that
   you can excel. Prove to yourself that you can set high goals and
   work hard to attain them. To those of you who may believe that
   good grades are not an accurate measure of good performance
   and learning, I offer this to think about: Consistently poor
   grades *are* indications of poor performance and *do* imply poor
   learning. Thus, for your own good, prove to yourself that you
   can meet the requirements of the system even if you are opposed to it. Finally, and most important, prove to yourself and
   to others that you are a winner. If you can develop within yourself the ability and motivation that it takes to become a winner,
   they will remain with you throughout your life.

If you motivate yourself toward reaching high goals, establish a
plan of action, and fulfill that plan through hard work and ingenuity,
you will succeed. Good luck!

GRADES AND PERSONAL SATISFACTION

Ideally, a student would earn an A+ in each course and be able to
say, "This was the best course ever." The student would remember
exciting class preparations, invigorating participation in class discussions, fascinating research for papers or reports, and brilliant writing,
and would feel that he or she had not only gotten the best possible
grade but also the highest level of satisfaction from the effort. Unfortunately, such a pleasant circumstance is enjoyed only rarely by
students. Top grades and great satisfaction from courses are not necessarily compatible.

At some early point in your studies you might have to make a conscious and perhaps painful choice between getting a good grade and
deriving the maximum satisfaction from a course. Many avenues can
lead to such a choice. Perhaps you have become fascinated with a
single aspect of the course and you find yourself irresistibly drawn
farther, ever farther in pursuit of it. Then one day you realize you
are not keeping up with assignments that seem dull in comparison to
your explorations.

Or perhaps you often disagree strongly with your instructor and itch
to prove your points in class. You may discover that by disagreeing
you have satisfied your commitment to personal integrity—at the cost

of a good grade. Has the system been unfair to you in both circumstances? Shouldn't you be allowed to explore a subject and not just keep up with assignments? Alas, when you chose to go to school you were given no guarantee that you would be treated fairly in every instance. Nor did anyone say that you could set the standards for what would constitute acceptable work in your courses.

If you find yourself having to make a choice between grades and satisfaction, and you are seriously disturbed by it, you need to review both your reasons for study and your life goals. If, for instance, your primary reason originally was to expand your intellectual horizons, or to learn new skills, and this reason remains valid, then you may wish to commit yourself to achieving personal satisfaction even at the potential cost of receiving a lower grade than you could otherwise attain. But if your original reason, for example, was to enable you to go on for a higher degree, and your acceptance at graduate or professional school is dependent on high grades, then probably you are going to have to swallow hard and subordinate that urge for personal satisfaction to the demands of getting that A.

To be most successful in school, you should consider making your first course of study your instructor, you, and the relationship that exists between the two of you. The rest of this chapter deals with interaction of instructors and students, and some of the possible results and implications of that interaction.

INTERACTION OF STUDENTS AND INSTRUCTORS

Contributed by Philip M. Backlund, Ph.D., *Associate Professor of Communication, Central Washington University, Ellensburg, WA*

You are seated in your first class of the school session and the instructor walks in. What do you know about this person right away? After 30 minutes of class? At the end of the class period? After two periods? Ten? Do you know this person at the end of the session?

How does the student sitting next to you interact with the instructor? After several weeks does she enjoy the class and get good grades whereas you hate it and do poorly? If so, it is possible she has no more capability for enjoyment and good grades than you, that her I.Q. is no better, her background for taking the course is no better, her desire to do well no greater than yours. What, then, may account for the difference in success?

Possibly you and the student next to you look at the instructor differently. Perhaps she sees in the teacher a person who can be understood and appreciated as considerably more than a teaching resource such as a textbook or filmstrip.

Michelle entered a southern university as an 18-year-old freshman **133** and dropped out a year later. Sixteen years later she was back, taking again the second semester of her sophomore year. On the first day of her return to school she was seated in the same classroom, retaking a course she had failed earlier, listening to the same professor deliver the same litany: "If this is a typical class, as I imagine it will be, I can expect from you only one A, a few B's, several C's, and far too many D's and F's."

"You creep," Michelle uttered to herself, just as she had probably done 16 years earlier. Then she immediately retracted the silent reproach. She recalled that several of her earlier classmates had also believed that this woman, Professor Sutpen, was impossible, and they had not done well in her class. But some had succeeded in getting those few A's and B's from this grade-stingy professor. And this time, having learned some useful coping methods as an adult, Michelle decided she would be in the latter category.

Michelle found some students who had gotten those higher grades and asked them about the professor. Michelle also asked her adviser, and she even asked a librarian and a janitor about the woman. Carefully listening in class, Michelle tried to determine just what it was that Professor Sutpen expected from her students. She visited the professor during one of her office hours. Then after a few weeks, the woman Michelle was beginning to know seemed different from the professor she remembered from 16 years before.

Michelle's attempt to understand and relate to the professor took a few extra hours during those early weeks in the course, precious hours she could have used in study. But through listening in class, not getting turned off by the professor's austere manner, and trying to meet the professor's expectations, Michelle discovered she actually enjoyed the course, and she got a good grade too.

CLASSROOM CHEMISTRY

For a moment now, assume that you are the instructor, and you walk into your first class of the school session. You wonder if your time with this class is going to be pleasant or painful.

Every class is different. As an instructor, you have noted that even sections of the same course have unique "personalities." Section A might be lively and B dull. These section personalities can last not just for a class meeting or two, but for an entire term.

There is a mysterious "chemistry" at work in classrooms, and at the beginning of a session an instructor hopes that the formula will be a good one for the remainder of the session. If this chemistry is right, most of the students will benefit. If it is not, many can still benefit. But they may have to be more perceptive and work harder at it.

134   Many students don't realize they are the ones who control much of the chemistry in a class. Your behavior helps set class norms. For example, if from the beginning of the session you make an effort to be cooperative, diligent, and friendly, you will probably influence at least a few other students to act the same way. Only a few students are necessary to set a prevailing tone for a class, positive or negative. So rather than merely waiting to see what develops, perhaps you could actively involve yourself in creation of the class norms by behaving in the way you think is best for that class. Quite certainly your role in creating a pleasant class environment will not go unnoticed by the instructor.

Undoubtedly you will have a bad instructor at some time in your school life. You might be inclined to fight such a person. But fighting an instructor throughout a session will bring you no good.

Even a bad instructor will have *something* good to offer. Probably you sincerely appreciate Instructor A's consistently good job. Try to do the same with the good parts of Instructor B's generally bad job. Your positive attitude will be conveyed subtly to the teacher. Every normal human being has need for a sense of self-worth. The student who enhances a teacher's sense of worth will be appreciated by that teacher, whereas the student who diminishes it will not. At the end of the school session the instructor may very well view you as one of the few students who made his efforts seem worthwhile.

Peer Pressure and Classroom Politics

Our attitudes and actions may be entirely different when we are acting alone from what they are when we are part of a peer group. How we perceive information, draw inferences, make judgments, formulate ideas, and respond to stimuli can be, and often is, profoundly influenced by the phenomenon of group peer pressure. This power by which we seem bound is derived from our strong human need for acceptance by others—classmates, for example—with whom we identify, interact, and socialize. If we fail to conform to the norms of the group we risk rejection, and few people want to be treated as outcasts. On the other hand, is rejection always the consequence of nonconformity? And what is the price of conforming?

Students who have emerged as informal leaders through their assertiveness, either in class discussions or informal conversations, may plant seeds that grow into modes of behavior accepted by the group. You may find yourself in a student lounge listening to a dialog among your classmates such as the following:

"What do you think of the instructor?" asks Joe.

"I think he's ridiculous," says Dave. "This course is a joke. All he **135** wants to do is hear himself talk."

"Yes," chimes in Bonnie, "I'm very upset with that man. I have no idea what he is talking about."

"When I asked him the question about the text, he answered to my satisfaction," injects Frank. "He seems to know what he's talking about."

"Oh, he knows his subject," Dave retorts, "but every time someone questions his views he just shoots him down. I'm not going to open my mouth anymore. Let him do all the talking; that makes it easier for us."

"I agree," says Bonnie, "I'm not going to let him make me feel foolish again."

And so the classroom norm becomes silence. Any individual who violates the norm by asking questions risks being shunned or talked about by the other class members.

Obviously, refusal to ask questions in class is counterproductive to the learning process. Perhaps you or another classmate, recognizing the fallacy of this approach, might speak out and bring the others to their senses. Or someone might muster up enough courage to speak to the instructor about the situation.

If peer pressure is contrary to your best interests, and you have been unsuccessful in getting the group to change its attitudes and actions, try to ignore that pressure. Although it is uncomfortable to jeopardize your status as an accepted member of the group, it is best to think and act in accordance with your own standards and beliefs. If you think a classmate is being unjustly critical of the teacher, tactfully say so. If you feel like asking a question and you are convinced it is a good one, ask it. If you want to make an extra effort on an assignment, do it. You are investing your valuable time and money to learn. Don't let negative peer pressure prevent you from achieving your goals.

Another factor in dealing with other students is classroom politics. While the majority of students are forthright and hardworking, some are not, and they practice classroom politics as a substitute for honest effort.

Al, a glib retail department manager, was capable but lazy. His objective at a business institute was the same as his goal at work: to get by with as little effort as possible. Like many astute politicians, what Al lacked in motivation and discipline he made up for with his ability to "talk a good game." Al made it a point to talk with the top performers in the class. In his convincing manner, he continually suggested that the course was a gut, and the reading assignments could be easily skipped. Al told his classmates that he knew several people who had taken this course last semester. The instructor, he explained, was lax about reading assignments and lenient with grades; therefore, it

136   wouldn't pay to put a lot of work into the cases. It wasn't until it was too late that Al's classmates realized their friendly adviser was merely trying to lower the peak of the curve in order to get a better grade himself.

Classroom politics can take several forms: student with student, student with instructor, instructor with student. The possible variations on the basic formats are endless. Be aware of the politics, and you will cope better with classroom circumstances.

Being on Time and Prepared for Class

Inherent to adult academic pursuits is a large measure of freedom to make choices and shape your study around other less malleable aspects of your life. Let us say that you have a job, and your employer expects you to be at it until five o'clock each day. Then you have to enter unforgiving traffic, struggle your way home, fix supper for the family, enter traffic again, and appear at a six-thirty class. Let's further assume that you used to spend your weekends immersed in family life —taking the children to their lessons, taking them to a museum, or to the zoo. They have come to assume that you are theirs, at least until school begins again for them on Monday. These patterns—remaining at your employment until five o'clock, devoting your weekends to your children—previously were no problem. But now you find yourself frequently late for class because of the traffic and your family responsibilities, and often unprepared because of activities during the weekend with your children. Does the teacher understand?

She may not. Students entering class late can be a serious distraction to the instructor and the class, and students unprepared to participate waste the time of teachers and classmates alike. You assume that your instructor will earn the salary that is derived from your tuition by being on time and prepared for class regardless of the normal demands of her personal life. Why should she not assume that you will earn your good grade at least partially through promptness and preparation?

Discuss anticipated problems of this nature with your instructor. She may accept your chronic tardiness if she knows that you absolutely cannot prevent it. And she may accept your occasional unpreparedness because of family situations, again especially if she knows of a specific reason for it. It is quite certainly better to let your instructor know ahead of time that you may have a problem than it is to take your chances she won't notice, or that she won't care because she understands.

When to Open and Shut Your Mouth

Many good politicians have a keen sense of timing. They know when to speak and when to say nothing. Furthermore, when they do speak they have a sense of purpose; they attempt to score points. The student in the classroom or in conference with an instructor should realize that speaking does not necessarily equate with good communication. A student who *communicates* well with the instructor and her classmates is likely to get a great deal of satisfaction from the course as well as a good grade.

In classroom communication, quantity is a poor substitute for quality. Gauging the degree of classroom participation that will allow you to be an effective class member is important to you. Most instructors (and students) don't appreciate "spring butts," the students who cannot restrain themselves, and all too frequently bounce about in their chairs with fervent, though vacuous, answers. On the other hand, neither do teachers have any reason to admire "zombies," those classroom creatures whose only sign of being alive is getting up to go home after class.

The size of the class itself is a factor in a desirable degree of individual student participation. In a large class of 30 or more students, each student's opportunity for participation is quite limited. Consequently, in order to communicate well you have no need to offer an answer to the bulk of the questions the instructor poses to the class. You can afford to let most of them go by and wait to participate until the moment is *right for you*. The same applies to asking questions. An occasional intelligent, articulate question inserted at the right time is often more valuable than an answer. Anne Seavey of Bentley College says: "If a person listens carefully and concentrates on what is being said yet still doesn't understand something, that is the time to ask questions. Chances are, a number of other students have also missed the point."

Ann Girndt, also of Bentley, provides another dimension to asking questions: "One of my most humorous experiences occurred during a literature class. The professor had outlined the course requirements, which included a subjective report. Subjective report! What in the world was the professor talking about? I listened attentively. The professor had finished explaining, but I was still in the dark. When asked if there were any questions, I responded by saying, 'I've heard every word you have said, but I don't understand what is required.' Although the class roared with laughter, the professor understood my predicament. This time the detailed explanation enabled me to grasp what was required. Later, I did successfully comply."

In a small class such as a seminar of six to twelve people, good classroom communication is even more critical for you. An ideal seminar,

138 in terms of communication, might be one in which each student was always well prepared and eager to contribute, but sensitive to the needs of other students to contribute and benefit from the instructor's contributions. You will not likely impress either your teacher or your classmates by wasting their time with rambling discourse, or at the other extreme, by saying nothing when it is clearly your time to add something to the seminar.

When You Think You're in Trouble

Has anyone gone through a certificate, diploma, or degree program and escaped the sick feeling that accompanies the suspicion that one hasn't done one's best? Highly unlikely. Unless you are an unusual student, sooner or later you are going to be in trouble, or at least think you are. What should you do? Try to ignore your feelings in the hope you may be wrong? Launch a crash study program? Pray?

Such solutions might work. But a better approach probably would be first to analyze your performance as objectively as possible in order to define your strengths and weaknesses, then discuss the situation with your instructor.

Psychologically, you have an advantage. The student who asks for help becomes known to the instructor as a *person*, not just a name on a roster or a face in a class. The teacher might be able to put an F beside a name, but to fail a *person* is quite another matter.

Whether you talk with your instructor informally before or after class, or more formally in her office, be concise. Time is an asset in short supply with instructors. Take notes if necessary, and ask for clarification of unclear points. No matter how sincere your desire to improve, unless you understand her and then act on her advice, you are wasting her time and risking further difficulty when she later inquires about your progress.

So, when you're in trouble, or think you are, review matters carefully, then, if warranted, talk to your instructor and follow up with action. In doing so you may find that you have converted yourself from a name on a roster to a person who matters.

10.

Improving Your Educational Skills

How important are: organization of time?
study habits? reading? writing? speaking?
listening? mathematics? computer basics?
use of the library? note-taking? taking exams?
Can I improve?

ORGANIZING YOUR TIME AND CONCENTRATING EFFECTIVELY

Every hour, virtually every minute of your daily life, must be used effectively in order that you may enjoy the greatest possible degree of success as an adult student. In this chapter we will focus on that part of your time devoted to study.

A human being, like an organization, runs better at certain times than at others. With the extra demands of school upon you, you should try to determine what have been the peaks and valleys of your work efficiency in the past. As a student, you will want to make your peaks as high as possible and minimize the depth of your valleys.

When do you do your best, most creative work? In the morning? afternoon? evening? Your past life may provide you with important clues to determine your best study times. As much as possible, you will want to reserve those most productive periods of the day not for the easiest or most pleasant course work, but for your most demanding or creative work.

At the beginning of a school session, you will want to determine as precisely as possible for each course the critical work that will be required of you. The weighting system each individual instructor will use in arriving at a final course grade will be your guide. When you have evaluated the weighting system for each course, the major work for the session will break down into segments, probably three to six or seven blocks per course. Let's assume that you are enrolled for two courses at your community college. For English 101 the critical

139

140 elements might be: first paper (10 percent), second paper (10 percent), midterm exam (20 percent), term paper (30 percent), final exam (30 percent). For Biology 101 the segments might be: class quizzes (10 percent), midterm exam (10 percent), research paper (20 percent), final exam (20 percent), laboratory exercises (40 percent). As you survey the requirements for each course, some blocks may be missing since a professor is fuzzy about his requirements. But you will be able to define enough tasks so that you can sensibly plan your work. Later you will adjust your plan as you move through the semester becoming more familiar with the material and discovering what is easy and what is difficult for you. If English 101 and Biology 101 are of approximately equal importance to you, and the degree of difficulty for you is about the same, you would be foolish to use a large amount of your best study time for writing the second paper for English 101 (10 percent) and a small amount for the Biology 101 research paper (20 percent). You must be selective; you must keep course requirements and their true importance in the grading systems well in mind as you progress.

We asked Dennis Gerard Ellis, who wrote in the preceding chapter about being a straight-A student, to give us some thoughts on the use of time. Here is his advice.

> I'll bet that many of you have never thought of the time you spend shaving, brushing your teeth, cleaning the house, and driving the car, as study time. If you were to add up all of the minutes of these and countless other routine tasks, you would have several hours of extra study time available each day. You will find that a simple device will enable you to learn while engaged in such tasks—the tape recorder.
>
> For example, take your final outline and anything else you need to know for an exam and go over them aloud in front of a portable tape recorder. Be sure to include any thoughts related to the material that may come to mind while reading aloud. This verbal exercise is itself a valuable learning and reinforcement method. If you have a patient family who won't mind hearing what to them will be boring repetition, you are now prepared to study while performing all of your "thoughtless" (not requiring concentration) duties. You may even listen to your tape outside, while gardening or mowing the lawn (listening with an earphone). Indeed, the uses of this time-utilization device are limited solely by the extent of your ingenuity.
>
> Another technique, which is slightly more flexible, is the use of index cards. You can write anything on them that you wish to learn for an exam. One method is to write key terms on one side and their explanations on the other. You can bring index cards to places where you cannot easily bring a tape recorder such as the supermarket, an elevator, or a boring meeting.
>
> You will be required to do a great deal of reading in most of your courses. While the average student who is an average reader can get through school and maintain average grades, the prospective straight-A student must become more than an average reader to maintain his excellence. He must become a speed

reader. I recommend a formal speed-reading course or, at the very least, a survey of books on the topic in your college library. Naturally, speed reading cannot be used all of the time. Your reading speed should be flexible enough to adapt to the type of material that you are reading and your objective in reading it. For example, you will have to slow down for detailed, technical, or extremely difficult material. At least the speed reader has the option of slowing down or speeding up depending on the situation. The slow reader can only read at one speed—slowly!

Well, there you have it, three ways to make optimum use of your study time: tape recorder, index cards, and speed reading. If you are one of those who, when looking for time to study, can literally count the minutes available, these will make those minutes count!

EFFECTIVE STUDY TECHNIQUES

Much of your study time will be with textbooks, and, considering your high school days, by now you have used many of them. But did you use them effectively? Perhaps you should take a fresh look at those objects that are so familiar to you. Do you really know what to look for in a textbook, and how to look for it?

A high-quality textbook is like a road map. It leads the reader who knows how to use it to a destination.

Just as there are traffic signals and signs along the road to guide the traveler, there are indicators within a textbook to guide you. In writing a textbook an author has a main idea for the book and each chapter, supported by several essential parts in the development of those main ideas. Usually he outlines his material before he writes the chapters. It is natural that textbook writers think in terms of structure, and you can use this thinking to your advantage.

A textbook outline becomes converted into headings. The book title presents the topic area and gives as much orientation to the material therein as is feasible. Chapter headings, boldface headings for sections, and subheadings are all reflections of essential points in the outline. Within sections, italics or boldface type highlight crucial points. Also, cue phrases are used much the way headings are. For example, you will see statements such as these: "Three kinds of...." "There were four causes for...." "The major concerns were first... second... and finally...." Such cue phrases are followed by the three, four, or five points that were promised in the phrase itself.

In addition to words and phrases that give you an overview of the material, visual aids are important. (Chinese proverb: "One picture is worth a thousand words.") Charts, maps, diagrams, pictures, and other illustrations do more than relieve the monotony of the printed page. Many writers consider them so essential they create or assemble their visual aids first, then write their text around these aids. Recog-

142   nizing the value of textbook indicators, you are ready to get more out of a textbook than you may have gotten in the past.

In 1941 Francis P. Robinson published *Effective Study,* a useful book based on research by others and the author's experience with helping college students become more successful. His book, now in the fourth edition, is still being used, and variations on his five-step method have been used effectively by writers and teachers to this day. Thomas F. Staton, for instance, outlines a similar method in his book, *How to Study.* (These books are included in the Annotated Bibliography of Study Aids at the end of this chapter.) The methods of these two authors are:

Survey Q3R (Robinson)	PQRST (Staton)
1. Survey	1. Preview
2. Question	2. Question
3. Read	3. Read
4. Recite	4. State
5. Review	5. Test

You can see how similar those two methods are, step by step. We also suggest a five-step approach: (1) get an overview, (2) ask questions, (3) read actively, (4) repeat important points, and (5) review continually.

1. Get an Overview

No matter how conscientious you are about your studies, to begin a textbook at the first page of your reading assignment and proceed to the end of your first assignment, then to the end of your second, then your third, and so on, is a poor way to learn. By proceeding straightforwardly at approximately an even pace, you may not recognize major points, and even if you do, you may give them no more time than minor ones.

When you first get your textbook, familiarize yourself with it as a whole. The table of contents is the outline of the book. Survey this outline. Note the topics for each chapter and the progression of the chapters. In addition, note other material listed in the contents, such as the preface, foreword, introduction, list of diagrams, list of maps. At the end of the table of contents you may find listed a bibliography, a glossary, appendixes, an index. Now take the time to locate and preview all these latter sections of the book. Only by doing so can you get a good idea as to how helpful they will be during your study. Is the bibliography brief or extensive? Is it annotated? What about

the glossary—how detailed does it seem to be? Is the index extensive? **143**
If so, it should be a significant aid for you.

Once you have surveyed the table of contents and previewed each
of the sections of the text to determine the general content and extent of coverage, carefully read the preface, foreword, or introduction.
It is here that the author will tell you what he is doing, his purpose
for doing it, and how he will go about the task. Thus he is providing
you with the major framework for your study during the course.

The first paragraph of the introduction, "To the Student," in *Writing Themes About Literature* (Englewood Cliffs, NJ: Prentice-Hall
Inc., 5th ed., 1983) by Edgar V. Roberts illustrates the point:

> The chapters in this book are theme assignments based on a number of
> analytical approaches important in literary criticism. The assignments are pre-
> sented in the hope of fulfilling two goals of English courses: (1) to write good
> themes, and (2) to assimilate great works of literature into the imagination.
> Negatively, the book aims to avoid themes that are no more than synopses of
> a work, vague statements of like or dislike, or biographies of an author. Posi-
> tively, the book aims to raise your standards of judging literature—and there-
> fore your ability to appreciate good literature—by requiring you to apply, in
> well-prepared themes, the techniques of good reading.

With such excellent guidance, a student should not flounder around in
Roberts's book, trying to discover what it is all about. (Read again the
Preface and Acknowledgments section of this book. Did we give sufficient guidance on the nature of our book? If not, use the address we
gave you and let us know about it so we can improve the next edition.)

When you begin reading a chapter, employ the survey technique
again. Note the chapter heading and subheadings. If there is a summary at the end of the chapter, read it. The summary provides the
core of the material presented, and you will want to have this in
mind before you read the rest of the text. Scan the illustrations and
captions. The descriptive material associated with them in the text will
be more meaningful later when you read it. Just below subheadings,
usually near the beginning of the first paragraph, you may find key
sentences that point the direction for the section. Look for them,
and if you find them quickly, read them. This kind of survey or preview as a first step well equips you to continue your study.

2. Ask Questions

The good student is the curious student. He or she wants to know
not just who and what, but why and how. This student is inquisitive
about relationships between facts and ideas. Curiosity may have killed
the cat, but it is also "one of the permanent and certain characteristics
of a vigorous mind" (Samuel Johnson, *The Rambler,* March 12, 1751).

As you note the chapter title, topic headings, and subheadings, ask yourself what is likely to be included. Study is most effective when it is an active search to find answers to questions. Formulate your own questions from each heading, and let them guide your reading to find the answers.

For example, in Volume 1 of Norman F. Cantor's *Western Civilization: Its Genesis and Destiny,* chapter 7 is entitled "The Rise of Medieval Culture." You might ponder that title and ask questions such as these: "What were some of the important aspects of medieval culture?" "How did these aspects develop and affect the people?" "What is implied by the term 'rise'?"

The first section heading is "The Romanesque World." "What is meant by Romanesque?" you might ask. "What is its relationship to rising medieval culture?" Equipped with this curiosity and these questions, you are ready to seek the answers by reading the sections. It is unlikely that you have asked irrelevant questions, but if you have you will be able to pause and formulate new questions.

You have probably noticed that the author of a textbook will often place questions in the text. Usually these come at the end of the chapter for review purposes. Sometimes they come at or near the beginning of sections of the text. Regardless of their location and whether or not they are intended for review, use them also to guide your reading. You may be sure that these questions are central to the concepts presented. They may also be similar to the exam questions your instructor will use.

Some texts are accompanied by a workbook, study guide, or instructor's manual. Your instructor may not have ordered the study guide or workbook for your use in the course, but you can order it. Check your library or bookstore copy of *Books in Print* to determine what ancillary aids accompany your text. You may even be able to get the instructor's manual by writing to the publisher. A study guide, workbook, or instructor's manual can be a valuable tool in developing curiosity and a questioning attitude toward the course material.

3. Read Actively

How many times have you read several pages of a book only to realize suddenly that you have no idea of what you have read? Dismayed, you have had to turn back to the beginning and read the material again. To be effective, reading a text cannot be a passive plodding down a page, nor can it be done while daydreaming. It must be an active search to find answers to questions you and the author have raised.

Some people are avid readers of fiction and can analyze and relate to what they have read. These same people can be poor readers of texts.

Why is this so? Fiction presents a world in which a cast of players   **145**
sequentially go about their business of living. The reader can relate to
the people and their thoughts and actions in that living world because the reader occupies a living world of his own that presents
many similar experiences. The "world" of a text, though, is often
not of people who are alive, at least during the time we read of them,
as in fiction, but of people who are dead. Or the world of the text is a
world of things: amoebas or Gothic cathedrals; or it is a world of past
events: the Franco-Prussian War or the meeting between Chamberlain
and Hitler. Through analysis and acts of imagination we have to enter
into that world as fully as possible, handicapped initially by not
knowing an amoeba or a Chamberlain as intimately as we can quickly
come to know a character in a novel.

Reading a text well is an active exercise; it is a search for and reac-
tion to material. A text usually does not generate the same kind of
excitement that may be inherent in a well-told story. The excitement
produced by a text may have to come from a different kind of dis-
covery. New worlds exist in amoebas and Chamberlain. They are
different from worlds you know, perhaps, but they can be no less
exciting once discovered.

4. Repeat Important Points

Some of history's most intelligent people have claimed they really
do not know what they think until they have said what they think.
The mind receives countless impressions in short spaces of time. Living
would be impossible for us if each impression were permanently recorded. Fortunately we forget the huge bulk of what stimulates our
mental processes. But unfortunately we also forget much of what we
would like to remember.

The mind has a short-term memory and a long-term memory. Tests
have shown that most impressions that enter the mind are forgotten
rapidly with the passage of time, and most of the forgetting occurs
very soon after the impressions are received. Only those impressions
that are particularly significant, or those that have been consciously
formulated into ideas and selected for recall, become part of our
long-term memory. So take an important step to store these impressions in your long-term memory: recite.

Yes, talk to yourself. Out loud, preferably. (Not just senile, but
brilliant persons talk to themselves. "After all," quipped a renowned
scientist, "who is more interesting to listen to than myself?") If you
can't talk out loud, conduct an internal dialog with yourself. "Why is
the Gothic cathedral so much higher than the Romanesque?" you
ask after having read a section on medieval architecture. "Because,
for one thing, the flying buttress took some stress off the walls and

allowed them to be lighter and higher. For another ... ," you continue to yourself, and in the process ensure that you really know what you have read. If you can't repeat the essence of what you have just read, don't expect some miraculous recall process to assist you on an exam some days or weeks later. If you can't say it, you don't know it.

5. Review Continually

Immediately after reading, you should review your text markings or notes, expand them as necessary, commit to memory the main points, and try to understand relationships among important elements. You can't just "look over your notes"; you should actively try to remember, to reconstruct, to reflect on ideas and their relationships.

Then, periodically during the school session, you should review your learning. Review, to be most effective, must be a continuous process. It does much more than just help you recall a certain amount of material. It allows you to expand your body of learned material by posing new concepts, new questions, new tentative answers.

During your review you should keep a simple record of concepts with which you are having difficulty. To help herself learn a foreign language, one student used small packs of cards containing words and phrases, the translations of which she had written on the backs of the cards. In every spare moment she reviewed the cards, and every time she missed a word or phrase she would put a tick mark on the card. Periodically she culled out cards that gave her no trouble and reviewed them less frequently. As she encountered new words and phrases, she would make a new card and add it to the pack. After a period of time, using a continual adding and culling process, she was left with only those cards to study that had a large number of ticks on them. By reviewing continually those elements of language that caused her the most trouble, she became proficient in that language.

In summary, to be most effective, your review should begin immediately after reading your assignment. Then it should continue at intervals throughout the course. By spacing your review periods, by attempting always to put together a whole from the parts, your textbook study will become more effective.

In one college with both liberal arts and career programs, about 80 percent of the 62 courses of instruction used textbooks to which effective study methods such as those we have outlined could be applied. If you are like most students, you will probably spend about half of your study time using such texts. And that is an excellent reason for you to use effective study methods.

Some courses, though, require study that involves sources other than textbooks. Such sources might be essays, analytical articles,

books of fiction or nonfiction, poetry, drama, and technical reviews.   **147**
Many of the study techniques already discussed will apply to the
reading of such material, but some will not. Certain disciplines require
a highly systematic, progressive, painstaking approach to learning.
For detailed guidance on how to study effectively in such fields as
science, languages, and mathematics, and how to use sources other
than texts, you can refer to any one of many excellent books treating
the subject. See the annotated bibliography at the end of this chapter
and ask your librarian for further references.

READING

Good reading skills and good study skills are so closely related they
are often taught together in developmental reading and study skills
workshops. We use the term "workshops" often throughout our discussion of essential educational skills to emphasize the participative
nature of these courses. In a reading class, students learn and immediately apply skills. Usually, they interact with the teacher and one another in a highly structured manner, and they sometimes use learning
devices such as tachistoscopes and reading acceleration instruments.

Reading specialists agree that the most important factor in effective
reading is motivation. This means that you, as an adult student, have
an advantage. Excellent motivation, however, obviously does not
ensure that a person will be an effective reader. And even if you are
an effective reader, you probably have the capacity for a higher level
of performance. We believe that virtually every adult student would
benefit from a well-taught reading skills workshop.

"Reading efficiency" is a term used by specialists to measure performance. It is the rate of reading combined with the degree of understanding of written materials. Programs for developing reading
efficiency usually are 10 to 30 hours long, spread across 3 to 10 weeks.

Years ago, many respected educators were convinced that a reading
skills course would improve both the rate and comprehension of
most students. Today reading specialists generally agree that for most
students a reading skills course will bring about a dramatic increase in
rate but will not significantly change comprehension. The higher rate,
of course, means a higher reading efficiency. Various studies differ
on the percentage of improvement for the average student, but a
minimum of 200 percent increase in efficiency seems to be a reasonable claim.

Psychological, neurological, or physical problems may have im-
paired your ability to read effectively. Or you may have had unfortunate academic experiences that have contributed to poor reading
efficiency. It is also possible that although you may be reading effectively now you could develop even more of your capacity. For-

148 tunately, many texts and workbooks that can help you are readily available through most libraries. (See the bibliography at the end of this chapter for a starting point.) Better yet, reading skills workshops have become common in colleges and are also available in high schools and libraries. A note of caution, however, is in order. If you are considering enrolling in any course other than one taught within a well-established school or public service facility, check it out carefully. When you do find a good program, the relatively small amount of time you spend in it may very well be one of your best educational investments.

Before we leave the matter of reading we should pause for a moment to consider the importance of vocabulary. Students who have not developed a curiosity about words are depriving themselves of the full value of any learning experience to be gained by reading. Too often we skip over words we don't know, such as "tachistoscopes" in the first paragraph of this section. (Did you look it up?) Even if we pause to look up such a word that is so obviously uncommon, we sometimes assume we know what "common" words mean. And we really don't! We have seen them before, perhaps used them, yet don't recognize that we have been using them wrong for many years. The context of a word can help you, but there is no substitute for the use of a dictionary. Unfortunately, words are sometimes used improperly even by good writers. Curiosity about words—their denotations, connotations, associations—is at the heart of improved reading efficiency.

WRITING

In our schools, emphasis on reading skills begins to wane beyond the primary grades. Writing skills, however, receive continuing attention at least through the freshman year of college. In these times of low enrollments in the humanities, English professors still constitute a large percentage of the total college faculty, partly because of freshman composition requirements. Effective writing is crucial to success in your higher education program and your career. Your study and reading skills may be excellent, but if you cannot express yourself well in writing you have a terrible handicap. Look into the grading systems used by professors in a variety of college courses and you will find most often that a large portion of the course grades will be determined by the students' written material.

You may not be able to get from your school the help you need in some matters, but almost certainly you will find your school well equipped to help you become an effective writer. Basic or developmental writing courses have become common in postsecondary curriculums. Writing centers where you can get tutorial help are often open for much of the day and evening. These courses and centers will usually help you with the basics: sentence and paragraph construction, grammar, technical accuracy. In addition, the staff at a writing center will often provide more sophisticated services that you may want to use right up to completion of your program. Many students have learned to seek help habitually from writing centers in organizing and documenting term papers. The results, in terms of both their writing improvement and their grades, have been satisfying to them.

In a short section such as this, we cannot go into all of the detail some readers may need for their writing improvement. Many excellent texts will give you this kind of assistance. (*Writing with a Purpose* by James M. McCrimmon is one of the best. This book is cited in the bibliography at the end of this chapter.) We do, however, wish to highlight two cardinal points of good writing.

The first relates to unity. To be satisfactory, any theme, technical report, research paper, or term paper must have unity. If the instructor has to puzzle over what you are trying to say in a sentence, or worse, in a paragraph, or far worse, in the whole paper, you have caused him to waste his time. And that, for sure, is not good. You have also created either doubt as to whether you can think and express yourself adequately or certainty that you cannot.

One of the most common forms of writing in any higher education program is the thesis paper. Your other types of writing assignments will be affected positively if you can consistently write a unified thesis paper.

A thesis paper initially draws its unity from a thesis sentence near the beginning of the paper. This sentence is a clear, concise statement of the conclusion you wish your instructor to accept after you have properly developed your topic.

A thesis always contains a subject and your attitude about it. Your subject may be the effect of the passage of time in Wordsworth's poem "Tintern Abbey," and you may write a long paper about your subject. But you have not written a thesis paper unless you have clearly expressed your *attitude* about your subject. That is, you must give the reader your considered judgment about an aspect of your topic. For example: *Thesis sentence*: The passage of time in "Tintern Abbey" enables the poet to "see into the life of things."

Your subject is "the passage of time in 'Tintern Abbey.'" Your attitude is your judgment that this passage enables the poet, as one line of the poem states, to "see into the life of things." Properly combined, your subject and attitude constitute a thesis, or a conclusion. Your whole paper will be built around this thesis.

Know your thesis. Do not forget your thesis. If necessary, print your thesis on a card and tape it up in front of you. Do not let your thesis escape you while you are writing that paper. It is the source of unity, therefore the source of your grade and your satisfaction.

150   An important step toward achieving unity is to develop your thesis properly. Not for one paragraph, not even for one sentence can you drift away from your thesis if your paper is to be unified. If you have a sense of thesis in you, you will understand that organizationally your thesis paper is a simple thing. It is a logical, orderly development of your conclusion about a particular matter.

In schematic form, a thesis paper may look like this:

- First paragraph (introductory sentence(s), thesis sentence, amplification of introduction and/or thesis).
- Second paragraph (topic sentence, development of topic).
- Third paragraph (topic sentence, development of topic).

—and so on through the paragraphs to:

- Last paragraph (topic sentence, development of topic). Summary or conclusion optional.

Somewhere in each paragraph there will be a key statement. This is the topic sentence, and it usually comes at or near the beginning of the paragraph. Sometimes for variety or emphasis it is placed at the end. It is the sentence around which the rest of the paragraph is built.

Each paragraph should have a reason for its existence and its place in the order of paragraphs. The second paragraph, for example, must relate directly to and develop the thesis. Because of this, it cannot be the third, tenth, or last paragraph. Succeeding paragraphs in turn must independently relate to and develop the thesis, and each should logically follow the preceding paragraph. And so on down the paper. A summary or conclusion may not be necessary, but if it is well done, it may add impact to the paper.

A good way to determine whether or not your paper is unified is to check each topic sentence against the thesis sentence. For each topic, ask: "Does it relate directly to the thesis? Does it develop the thesis? Is there a logical reason for its position in relation to the other topic sentences?" If the answer is "yes" to all three questions, you have an adequate framework for your paper.

The second cardinal point of good writing that we wish to emphasize is that writers must always be demanding, objective critics of their own work. After writing your draft, if you try to divorce yourself from your product, to look at your writing as if you were the instructor who will be grading it, you will strengthen your paper. You will look for unity, as discussed above. You will ask yourself about each paragraph, each sentence, each key phrase: "Is it necessary? Is it the best possible expression of the ideas I wish to convey? Does it aid the logical flow of ideas?"

You may find, having asked these questions, that you will have to **151** reorganize your paper. You may have to throw out sentences, paragraphs, sections over which you have labored. You must be able to do so. If something doesn't fit, you must change it or throw it out. Up to this point in your life if you have not truly been an objective critic of your work, and you have not been faced with these difficult decisions, the process can be painful. But your discomfort will diminish with practice, and your satisfaction with your product will grow.

Strive for unity, and be your own most incisive critic. These two points can guide you to better writing.

SPEAKING AND LISTENING

Contributed by Philip M. Backlund, Ph.D., *Associate Professor of Communications, Central Washington University, Ellensburg, WA*

Previous sections have dealt with two other communication skills, reading and writing. This section and the next discuss two equally important aspects of the communication process—speaking and listening.

These two activities occupy much of our waking time (estimates range as high as 73 percent), yet if you are like most students, you received little formal training in speaking and listening. However, a person's ability to communicate orally is being recognized more and more as an essential skill by educators and, of course, by employers. The person who can clearly organize his or her thoughts, speak clearly in most situations, and listen effectively to others has an excellent start toward success at school and work.

Speaking Skills

What are skills in speaking that will help ensure success? We obviously can't cover all of them here, but we can sketch some of the most important ones relating to overcoming nervousness, organizing your material, and actually delivering it. Also, we can refer you to some helpful books (see the bibliography at the end of this chapter).

Virtually everyone is afraid of getting up in front of an audience to speak. In fact, in a recent survey, public speaking was listed as the number one fear of Americans. So, if public speaking makes you nervous, you may take some comfort in knowing you're not alone. For many people, this nervousness extends to less formal speaking situations such as expressing an opinion in a classroom discussion or talking with instructors and other figures of authority on campus. Many people find themselves quite tense in these situations, and that tension prevents them from being effective. Here are some ideas on how to overcome nervousness:

- Set a goal to *manage the tension*, not eliminate it. Even the best public speakers get nervous, but they can reduce tension to a manageable level.
- *Know what you want to say.* The more you know about the point you want to make, the clearer that point is to you, the more confidence you will have, and the more effective you will be.
- *Rehearse.* You would naturally assume that you would practice a public speech (in fact, good public speakers may practice ten to fifteen times for each speech), but you also can "practice" informal speaking by mentally rehearsing the points you wish to make in class or in conference with your instructor. That practice will also build confidence.
- *Take every opportunity to speak.* The more you do it, the better you will get. Set goals like speaking at least once in a group setting every day. Make a point of talking frequently to each of your instructors. These activities will build both your confidence and your skill.
- This is more difficult, but try to *focus on the audience instead of yourself.* The more sensitivity you feel and show for the attitudes within the group, the more the group will respond to you and the less nervous you will probably feel.

Listening to a speech or lecture differs from reading a text in that the listener cannot normally ask the speaker to restate material in the same way that a reader can review a passage. This means that the speaker must pay particular attention to organizing the material for the utmost in clarity. Here are some simple guidelines for organization.

First, give a preview of what you are going to say. For example, you might begin with a statement like this: "In my report today, I'm going to make three basic points. These are...." This preview sets your audience up to listen. They know what to expect and can follow you more easily.

Second, use transitions to mark the movement from one point to another. For example, you might say: "The next point I would like to cover is ...," or, "Now that we've discussed that area, let's move on to...." Such statements help the listener know where you are at all times.

Third, include a summary in your conclusion. For instance, you could say: "In conclusion, let me summarize the points I've been covering. They are...." This helps the listener to remember the major points of your presentation. If you follow this simple organizational pattern, your audience will rarely get lost, and neither will you.

The actual delivery of your presentation both in rehearsal and in **153** front of an audience is another area for consideration. Delivery includes such aspects as the rate of talk, volume, pitch, pronunciation, and grammatical appropriateness. Generally, people judge you against what is known as standard or "network" English. Many people develop language habits that are not "standard" such as using slang, shortened pronunciations, and various dialects. These habits are acceptable as the norm in some situations, but to be assured of success in most situations, you need to develop the skill of using standard English. Classes in voice and diction can help if you think you have a language pattern that may be cause for concern.

You may want to consider taking a basic speech skills course. Such a course would provide information and give you practice in different kinds of speaking, usually in interpersonal communication, small group communication, and perhaps in public speaking. The most important part of this kind of class would be the feedback you would get from the instructor and other students on your speaking performance.

Listening Skills

Your success in your program is greatly dependent on your ability to gather information from a wide variety of sources and then give some form of it back to the teacher in a paper, test, or discussion. The primary mode of gathering information is listening. In fact, we spend more time in listening than in any other mode of communication.

Researchers have classified many types of listening, and of these, the ones most relevant to the educational process include active listening, discriminating listening, and critical listening.

The difference between active and passive listening may seem obvious, but it is often overlooked. Good listeners are active listeners. They put a lot of energy into the listening process; they not only hear, but probe, analyze, and look to the speaker's nonverbal cues. In short, they work at listening. The passive listener, on the other hand, merely receives sound with little recognition or personal involvement; he or she just happens to be present when someone is talking. So the first and most basic point about successful listening is the need to *work* at it.

As a student, you will find a lot of things to listen to, and separating the useful from the useless is called discriminating listening. This is listening for the purpose of understanding and remembering relevant information. This type of listening involves such skills as understanding the meaning of words from the context, listening for details, understanding the relationship of details to the main point, and listening to a question with intent to answer.

154   The third major type of listening behavior you will be engaged in is critical listening. In critical listening you are trying to analyze the ideas or evidence presented by the speaker and to make critical judgments about their value. You are trying to distinguish between fact and opinion or emotional and logical argument, and to detect bias or prejudice. In short, you respond in an evaluative manner, concentrating on specific points and choosing what to discard and what to retain. Good critical listening, used with active and discriminating listening, should assist you greatly in assimilating useful information.

There are many things that can get in the way of effective listening. Here's a list of common barriers to understanding that many people experience. An awareness of them may help you improve your listening skills.

1. The longer the speaker's remarks, the more the listener will tend to shorten, simplify, and eliminate detail from the actual output of the speaker.
2. People forget the middle of a message much more quickly than either the beginning or the end.
3. We tend to hear what we expect to hear and mentally modify messages to conform to what we believe.
4. We sometimes react by criticizing the speaker personally rather than hearing the actual message.
5. People tend to argue mentally with a speaker (especially on controversial subjects) before they fully understand.
6. People tend to listen more to what is easy to understand or to what is familiar. Difficult material requires more effort.
7. People also tend to let other people in the listening group influence their own interpretation.

Now here are some guidelines on how to listen more effectively.

1. Be mentally and physically prepared to listen.
2. Think about the topic or situation in advance when possible.
3. Try to guess the speaker's intent or purpose.
4. Determine the value of the topic for you.
5. Concentrate—do not let your thoughts wander.
6. Listen for main ideas.
7. Become aware of your own biases and attitudes, and try to separate them from the speaker's message.
8. Reflect the message to the speaker; give feedback to determine if you have heard accurately.

That advice is sometimes difficult to follow, but you can try. You can practice by working on one or two points at a time. For example, you might say to yourself, "Today I'm going to work on listening for

main ideas and check to see if my own biases interfere." By doing a **155**
piece at a time, you can gradually build up your skill as a listener.
A good listener is a valued person, as a friend, as a student, and as
a co-worker.

Unfortunately, advice and help with listening skills may not be as
easy to get as help with writing problems. First check with the speech
communication department. While they may not offer a specific course
in listening, most speech courses have a listening component. Also
check with the academic skills or learning center. For further work
on listening, you might find one of the books listed at the end of the
chapter to be helpful.

MATHEMATICS

"Adult students are very concerned about their lack of basic mathematical skills," explained a math instructor. "And they shouldn't be.
Compared to younger students, their insight and ability to reason
mathematically are excellent. They do well in my classes."

Mathematics is central to the curriculum of many programs of
higher learning. And math anxiety is common to many students. It
need not be a problem for you.

You have three recourses for improving your basic mathematical
skills. First, as you encounter difficulty in your courses you can go
back selectively to build your basic skills in order to solve specific
problems. This approach saves time for the person who can keep
himself firmly oriented on the goal of solving those problems. But it
can also be ultimately frustrating since higher-level mathematical skills
often require a broad basic understanding. Second, you can ask an
instructor to recommend a self-help review book. Many good ones
are available. These books often contain diagnostic tests that will
help you concentrate on areas of weakness. Or third, you may be
able to locate an instructor of basic mathematical skills, take a diagnostic test, and if you are found to be deficient, enroll in the course.
For overcoming math anxiety or building basic skills, a mathematics
workshop may be just what you need.

COMPUTER BASICS

The *New York Times* recently carried an article about a computer
show which 7,000 people attended. One woman said, "I'm walking
around here in a fog. I'm so far behind that I'd have to overcome my
computer phobia before I could even sign up for a course on it." Her
14-year-old son said, "I've tried to teach her. She's smart enough.
She's just scared."

156   We hope that by the time the next edition of this book comes out, adults will have gotten over their fear of learning about the computer. There is hardly a career you could consider that in some way will not be affected by the onrushing computer technology. And, as we said earlier, your studies may be made easier by your use of a computer. So, it's best to learn at least the basics as soon as you can.

There are hundreds of books on learning the basics. The bookstore chains have sections devoted exclusively to computer books. We haven't seen all of these books by any means, but the best we have seen for getting started is *The Word Processing Book: A Short Course in Computer Literacy.* Peter McWilliams, the author, says, "This book is written for the absolute novice." And it is. In a light, often hilarious style, McWilliams leads the reader through the basics and makes it all seem simple. No longer need you be mystified by CPUs, RAMs, and ROMs. McWilliams provides a foundation for a most useful skill, word processing, and he includes a buying guide for computers, related equipment, and computer programs. So, you can start with this book, then go on to take a minicourse in computer basics. Surely one is offered somewhere in your vicinity.

USING THE LIBRARY

Effective use of the library can improve your performance markedly and during a year save you hundreds of hours of study time. One of the first things you should do is get your library's guide, usually a small pamphlet of great immediate and continuing value. Also, whether you use a public or college library, you should arrange to take a tour of the facilities. Most school orientations include such a tour, but sometimes the tour is so cursory it amounts to little more than "Here is the circulation desk where you check out books, and here is the reference desk."

Libraries may seem complex to you, but they should not seem mysterious.

If you are basically at ease in the library but know you need to build library use skills, you might get by with a good library use handbook (see the bibliography at the end of the chapter). But if you find yourself in awe, not knowing really which way to turn, you may need a library course.

Most colleges offer introductory courses in general library usage and in bibliographical work. These courses often are mini-courses whereby you may make your studying easier and simultaneously earn a credit or two. The courses will include a description of the holdings, workings, and organization of the library, and the use of general basic bibliographies as well as some special bibliographies.

If a college or public library nearby does not offer a course, ask a   **157**
librarian to spend some time with you. It is unlikely you will be refused
since librarians pride themselves (justly) on their service. A helpful
librarian is a valuable ally against the oppression of too many papers
or projects due all at once.

You should ask your librarian to enumerate the library resources
in your area. Don't assume that public or school and college libraries
are your only assets. You might be surprised to find that the local
Elks club has a fine collection of Welsh literature (a member donated
his extensive holdings), and the Am Vets has a massive collection of
pictures and books on the Italian campaign of World War II (a member
was an Army public information specialist during the fighting). Special
collections may be housed in your local historical society, in your
city or county office building, in the museum on your campus, or in
the chaplain's office. Much to the dismay of librarians, who obviously
would like to control all books for student use, many academic departments persist in maintaining small holdings, and the department
secretary is the key that unlocks those treasures.

Three resources in the library must be used by virtually every student: the card catalog, the serials catalog, and the reference service.

Increasingly, in addition to or instead of a card catalog, there are
now catalogs on microfiche, on microfilm, and in databases, the latter
to be used via a computer terminal. Regardless of whether the catalog
is on cards or is in one of these other forms, its purpose is the same.
It is for locating books and is usually arranged alphabetically in three
categories: author, title, subject (figure 1). Most small and moderate-
sized libraries use the Dewey decimal system, but large research libraries, including those on campuses, most often use the Library of
Congress classification system because it facilitates subdividing categories (figure 2).

To find a book, you locate its call number in the catalog, then locate
the library map, which shows where the book is shelved. If the book
is not there on the shelf, some students will quit in dismay and begin
searching in the catalog for a substitute. Instead, you should look on
the shelf in the area where the book was supposed to be placed, since
books of similar nature will be shelved together. If a satisfactory substitute cannot be found on the shelf, you should not give up but
should ask the librarian to determine where the book you want is
located. The librarian may discover that someone else has the book,
and a "hold" can be placed on it for you when it is returned. If the
book is overdue or lost, steps can be taken to get it for you. If the
book is really important to you, you should find out where it is and
take steps right away to get it quickly. It will not otherwise miracu-
lously appear when you search for it again. If the book is not listed
in the catalog, you can try interlibrary loan. The service is usually

FIGURE 1   CARD CATALOG: TITLE, SUBJECT, AUTHOR

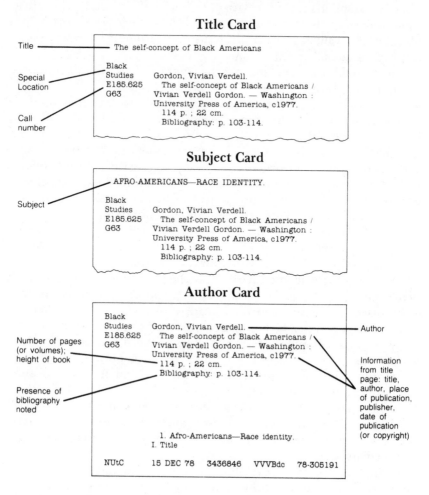

Title Card

Subject Card

Author Card

quick. Or in cases when you can get by with a substitute book on the subject, the reference librarian can help you locate the section where you can browse.

Many students do not realize that libraries usually shelve oversize books in locations separate from smaller books of a similar nature. If you see a + or ++ marking, or an F (for folio) in the catalog, you must locate the oversize section, not the regular section. Art, music, travel, and highly illustrated cultural books are examples of volumes that might be placed in an oversize section.

The serials catalog will guide you to periodical publications (popular magazines, scholarly journals, newspapers). Items will be listed by

**FIGURE 2   BASIC OUTLINES OF THE CLASSIFICATION SYSTEMS   159
WITH EXAMPLES OF SUBDIVISIONS**

Dewey Decimal Classification System

000 General
　　030 General
　　　　encyclopedias

100 Philosophy and Related
　　150 Psychology
　　160 Logic

200 Religion
　　220 Bible

300 The Social Sciences
　　330 Economics

400 Language
　　420 English and
　　　　Anglo Saxon

500 Pure Sciences
　　530 Physics

600 Technology
　　620 Engineering

700 The Arts
　　750 Painting

800 Literature and Rhetoric
　　810 American Literature

900 General Geography and
　　History
　　970 General History of
　　　　North America

Library of Congress Classification System

A General Works
　　AE Encyclopedias

B Philosophy and Religion
　　BS Bible

C History—Auxiliary Sciences
　　CB History of civilization

D History (except America)

E America and U.S.(General)

F U.S. local and other
　　American nations

G Geography and
　　Anthropology

H Social Sciences
　　HB Economics

J Political Science

K Law

L Education

M Music

N Fine Arts
　　ND Painting

P Language and Literature
　　PA Classical languages
　　　and literature

Q Science
　　QD Chemistry

R Medicine
　　RD Surgery

S Agriculture

T Technology

U Military Science

V Naval Science

Z Bibliography

160 FIGURE 3 THE JOURNAL INDEX ENTRY

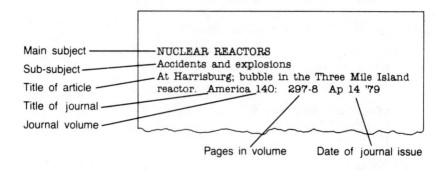

Main subject ⎯⎯⎯⎯ NUCLEAR REACTORS
Sub-subject ⎯⎯⎯⎯ Accidents and explosions
Title of article ⎯⎯⎯ At Harrisburg; bubble in the Three Mile Island
reactor. America 140: 297-8 Ap 14 '79
Title of journal ⎯⎯⎯
Journal volume ⎯⎯⎯

Pages in volume   Date of journal issue

their official titles rather than the titles that appear on the cover of the publication and are sometimes abbreviated or translated (figure 3).

The reference desk, as the hub of reference services, is your most important source of information. Here the reference librarian not only can help you with the card catalog or serials catalog but also will direct you to encyclopedias, bibliographies, handbooks, directories, indexes, dictionaries, yearbooks, atlases, gazetteers, biographies, and guides of many kinds. Also, the reference librarian may be able to help you with the mechanized information retrieval that is becoming increasingly necessary for some writing projects. If your research topic is the economics of Malaysia in the early twentieth century, the reference librarian may be able to help you refine your topic sufficiently and categorize its elements to allow a computer search that will produce a printout of a bibliography of your topic. (This process may or may not involve a charge, so check this out before you progress very far.) The reference librarian will also be able to guide you to language learning materials, microforms, slide, tape, and record collections, and many other audiovisual materials waiting to be used by you. You only need to know what is available, how to find it, and how to use it. Get your local library's guide pamphlet, get a library use handbook, take a course if necessary, and, above all, ask for your librarian's help.

TAKING NOTES

Some people argue that taking notes interferes with listening in class and slows down studying at other times. In fact, experiments have shown that when one group of students only listens or reads intently and the other group takes notes or marks texts, there is little difference in test performance—provided that the examination is given immediately afterward.

Forgetting, though, is our enemy. Three men heard a lecture, and **161** the next day at lunch were discussing what a great lecture it was. One of them marveled at the speaker's acute insight into five problems in our society. Another of them agreed, and they started enumerating the points. They stopped, embarrassed. Between those two men they could come up with only two of the speaker's ideas. The third man, however, pulled out a notebook and supplied the other three points, and the men were able to discuss all of the speaker's main ideas at some length. Without the notebook, they would have lost those points in the great sea of forgetting.

After examining the conclusions of many other researchers into human memory, a distinguished psychologist found a basic theme: Unless detail is organized through reflection under meaningful categories, it is quickly forgotten. Notes, well-taken and reflected upon, are important weapons against forgetting.

What form should your notes take? The proper answer seems to be: the form that is right for you, the one that allows you to reflect upon the material and to expand your knowledge of it. Study guides vary in suggested approaches. You may select from those possibilities the methods that seem best suited to your general style. Rather than providing a shopping list of tips, we will concentrate on a few features of note-taking that seem to us most important.

"Taking notes" is the term we commonly use, but we probably should be saying "making notes." The difference is that making notes is an activity that goes beyond mere recording. It is an active and continuous process until the term is over. First, it involves attentive listening. From the mass of the instructor's words you should always try to select the main ideas and record the essence of them.

Then, after the lecture—as soon as possible—you should edit your notes. While the lecture is still in your memory, through your own system of symbols, underlining, or numbering, identify the major points and expand upon them by writing any necessary additional notes. If you omit this step of editing immediately after class, a step that should require only a few minutes of your time, you are seriously degrading the value of your note-taking.

A third stage in the process is to reflect, integrating in your mind the notes you take in class with all of your other aids to reflection on the course material. During the class itself the instructor may have referred several times to the textbook. You, the wise student, will have noted those places in the text for future reference. And during your study outside class you will have made some marks in your text, and perhaps some notes. Also you may have made notes relating to reading from other sources. During your periodic reviews you should try to draw all of this material together and reflect on what seem to be the main points. If you have listened attentively, then edited your

162 notes, then reflected upon them, you have greatly enhanced your opportunity to perform well in the course.

TAKING TESTS

When you take tests, the quality of your preparation will of course affect your grade. So ask yourself some questions. Have you developed the habit of studying your past tests to determine not just what you missed but why? Have you kept up with your assignments and, using your notes and test markings, spaced your reviews to facilitate remembering? Through careful preparation, have you developed an attitude that this examination is going to be a challenge, yes, but certainly not a defeat? If you have done all of these things, you have taken major steps toward a good grade. Now your technique in actually taking the exam is the other ingredient of a successful outcome.

In most books on effective study, there will be a section on test-taking. We will not go into methods of approaching various categories of test questions, as a book on taking tests will do, but we will emphasize several important principles that apply to all categories.

Many students do poorly on tests because they do not properly size up the nature of the problem at hand. Concerned, nervous, perhaps even panicked, they start shakily with question one and work toward the end, trying to answer the questions sequentially with equal diligence to each and every question. If you take this approach, what happens if you run out of time and discover that the unanswered questions carry greater weight than the ones you have been carefully answering? Despite your good work on part of the test, you have only done a part, and your grade will reflect your lack of skill in taking tests.

Before you start to answer the questions, survey the entire test. The weighting system often is given, and you will want to identify the sections with the most weight. Note the recommended time if this guidance is provided. If not, knowing how long you have for the entire test, you can quickly sketch out a work schedule, allocating time to each of the sections in proportion to its weight. In making this tentative work schedule, allow time for checking and revising your work. About one-fifth to one-quarter of the total seems to work well for most students. It only takes a few minutes to prepare a schedule of progress through the exam, marking each section with the scheduled arrival time as a check on your actual progress when you begin answering the questions. It is time well spent.

The most common cause for poor performance, assuming that a student has prepared adequately, is *failure to read the problem*. First, you must read and understand the directions for each category of questions. This advice seems so obvious that you might wonder why it is necessary to emphasize the point. Yet, time after time, good stu-

dents disappoint themselves on tests by failing to read directions. If,   **163**
for example, you fail to note that the instructions allow more than
one correct answer, you lose points when you choose only the best
answer. And if the directions say answer A *and* B, and you misread
them as answer A *or* B, you lose points.

Reading the problem implies more, though, than just reading the
directions, which are the mechanical means to a correct answer. Reading the problem implies also perceiving the thrust of the question
asked so that you can attempt to answer the question *as it is stated,*
not as you *think* it is stated or *wish* it were stated. Especially on essay
questions, students tend to wander away from the point the instructor wants answered or developed. Don't expect that the questions
you asked yourself during your study of the course material will
come out exactly that way on the exam. By asking those questions
you have prepared yourself in a variety of related areas, and now you
must tailor that preparation to meet the needs at hand: *answering
the question the instructor asked.* Sketching an outline of an answer
will help you keep your writing relevant as it progresses. Don't be
faced with this comment on your corrected exam paper: "That's a
good answer, but unfortunately not to the question I asked." Not
knowing an answer is a forgivable sin. If you simply don't know, write
something and take your chances. Probably your vacuous answer will
be worth more than a blank space would get you. What is nearly un-
forgivable, though, is to know, but through not reading the problem,
to give the wrong answer. *Read the problem.*

The time you program for review and revision is important to your
success, so guard against your encroachments on it. If you find during
examinations that you are having to choose continually between completing additional test items and reviewing and revising, you probably
are not attacking your exams well in terms of assessing the weight of
individual parts and allocating the time you should spend on them.

Taking tests may not be the greatest entertainment in town, but
you can get satisfaction from the results. Good preparation and technique bring better results.

ANNOTATED BIBLIOGRAPHY OF STUDY AIDS

Effective Study

Robinson, Francis P. *Effective Study,* 4th ed. Harper & Row, Pub-
lishers Inc., 10 East 53rd Street, New York, NY 10022. Paperback,
304 pp, $12.50. SQ3R method of studying explained. Chapters on
skills in reading, writing, mathematics.

164 Staton, Thomas F. *How to Study,* 7th ed. Distributor: How to Study, P.O. Box 6133, Montgomery, AL 36106. Paperback, 72 pp, $2.25. PQRST method. Section on note-taking and chapter on taking tests.

Reading

Miller, Lyle L. *Increasing Reading Efficiency,* 4th ed. Holt, Rinehart & Winston, 383 Madison Avenue, New York, NY 10017. Paperback, 333 pp, $14.95. A workbook devoted to reading exercises and comprehension tests.

Writing

McCrimmon, James M. *Writing with a Purpose,* 7th ed. Houghton Mifflin Co., 2 Park Street, Boston, MA 02107. Text ed., 501 pp, $15.50. Also available in short ed., $14.50. Instructor's guides, resource book available at extra cost. A classic text, used for many years in composition classes. Can be used independently. From use of individual words to writing research papers. Includes handbook of grammar and usage.

Speaking and Listening

Shuter, Robert. *Communicating: Concepts and Skills.* Holt, Rinehart & Winston, 383 Madison Avenue, New York, NY 10017. Paperback, 288 pp, $17.95. Clearly written basic text on communication skills covering such topics as nonverbal communication, listening, public speaking, group communication, interviewing, and interpersonal communication.

Mathematics

Carman, Robert A., and Marilyn J. Carman. *Basic Mathematical Skills: A Guided Approach,* 2nd ed. John Wiley & Sons Inc., 605 Third Avenue, New York, NY 10158. Paperback, 576 pp, $21.95. Good for brushup.

Computer Basics

McWilliams, Peter A. *The Personal Computer Book,* 5th ed. Prelude Press, P.O. Box 69773, Los Angeles, CA 90069. Paperback, 335 pp, $9.95.

———. *The Word Processing Book: A Short Course in Computer Lit-* **165**
eracy, 8th ed. Prelude Press (see above). Paperback, 320 pp, $9.95.

Using the Library

Gates, Jean K. *Guide to the Use of Books & Libraries,* 4th ed.
McGraw-Hill Book Co., 1221 Avenue of the Americas, New York,
NY 10020. Paperback, $6.95.

11.

Balancing Your Career, Home, and Study Demands

How can I earn a living, have a home life, and study too?

Contributed by **Nancy Hawks,** *summa cum laude graduate of Adelphi University, Garden City, NY*

TIME: A PRICELESS COMMODITY

The last chapter discussed how you might use your time well while actually engaged in study. But how do you even get the time to study?

Douglas E. Buck graduated from Whatcom Community College and Evergreen State College and is now studying for a master's degree at City College, Seattle, WA. Douglas believes you actually have more time than you think you do. However, he says your anxiety levels are high because of uncertainties and the pressure of trying to balance your career, home, and study demands.

Now that you are enrolled, you will have to do some reorganizing of your life—maintaining previous schedules just won't work. Budgeting your time and energies is a must. You might profit from analyzing your major activities and determining their relative importance. You will need to choose those you can eliminate entirely, pick the ones to be cut back, and decide which are to be retained because they are essential to you and the people around you. For instance, you may decide to relinquish your PTA duties and work less around the house, yet retain your place in the weekly tennis group since you consider it important to your physical and mental health. Despite the way it sometimes seems, we are in charge of ourselves and how we spend our time. Unnecessary intrusions upon our precious time will not occur if we do not allow them to. A pleasant but firm "no" may be difficult **167** to manage at first, but didn't a quick "yes" also begin as a habit?

A student at a trade school in California, who is also the mother of three young boys, found studying difficult until she laid down the law: "I definitely discourage interruptions. The only information I want to receive is about anyone or anything on fire. Or if anyone is bleeding. And bloody noses don't count!"

Adult students need to create space for themselves in their daily existence—mental and emotional space. It will determine to some degree the success they will achieve as students. Set aside a few hours of each day as strictly your own for study. It has to be done, so *do* it!

Anne Seavey, an accounting student at Bentley College, Waltham, MA, says: "Time is the villain that must be dealt with if one is to succeed."

Time: villain or friend? Only *you* can decide which it's going to be.

YOUR EMPLOYER AND YOU

Openness and understanding are important keys to a successful employer/employee relationship. Initially, the attitude of your employer toward you in your new role as a student may be negative. He or she may wonder whether you will be able to meet the demands of studying and still continue to be an effective employee. Your performance over a period of time will, of course, answer the question.

Purely by accident, a student in an Oklahoma business school made a very positive connection with her employer from which they both benefited:

> I didn't tell a soul I had decided to go back to school until I had actually registered. Finally I mustered up my courage and told Hank, my supervisor, that I was now a part-time student. As I was explaining I had worked out a schedule that wouldn't interfere with my hours on the job, I could see he was puzzled and somewhat annoyed. I felt very uncomfortable, even a little guilty, when I left his office. A few days later I was eating lunch at my desk and trying to wade through a tough reading assignment. I must have groaned out loud because Hank stopped short on his way out to lunch and asked what was the matter. I said, "This!" and I began reading to him. When I finished the page he was smiling broadly. It turned out that he was totally familiar with the subject and began to explain it to me. When he had finished I realized that I understood it completely. I felt wonderful. So did Hank. And from that day on he's been my biggest booster. I think he's prouder of me than *me*!

It can be extremely difficult to juggle full-time employment with full-time schooling. If one or the other can be part-time, so much the better.

Fortunately, many students are employed by companies that have tuition-refund programs. And in some companies, employees are even released for part or full days so that school requirements can be met.

If you are unsure of your company's educational support program, or anticipate any type of work/school conflict and are uncertain about your employer's cooperation, we think you should speak to your supervisor or personnel officer as soon as possible. If early resolutions of potential problem areas in employment appear unlikely, you may be wise to begin seeking another job—one more compatible with your role as a student.

YOUR FAMILY AND YOU: RIGHTS AND RESPONSIBILITIES

Most of us experience apprehension when we undergo a major change in our lives. And it is not unusual that others—especially members of our family—will be affected.

If you have not already done so, we suggest that you and your spouse discuss your plans at length. At the very least, higher education means an investment of time and money. There will be questions about household duties and responsibilities. Subsequent discussion might include children in the household since they, too, will be affected by your new arrangements. Older children probably will be expected to assume additional chores. Child-care plans should be explained to younger children. Of course you may hear moans and groans, but they can be changed to expressions of support.

Linda Mitchell, who attends Brescia College in Owensboro, KY, has four children. She says:

> If I had to choose the toughest aspect about going to college it would be the adjustments in home life. Everyone in my family had to form new habits. I had to learn to use my time wisely; housework, cooking, and studying had to be intertwined without too much clashing. The kids took on more of the housework, and my husband had to get used to my absences. At first, there were a lot of head-on collisions, but we soon learned that by pulling together as a team we could keep things running *almost* smoothly. I found that if all members are involved there is less resentment and more willingness to help. As a result of our combined efforts we have formed a new closeness as a family. The gains have far outweighed the problems.

The degree of support and cooperation you will feel from your family will vary greatly, perhaps even from day to day. Disputes involving rights and responsibilities may sometimes seem insoluble. Your confidence in yourself will ebb and flow. Sabina Leonard is a nursing student and mother of five children who confesses that there were times when she broke down, cried, and declared that she would not attend another class: "I felt that it just wasn't worth the aggrava-

tion. But I always went back." Sabina believes that "making a go of   **169**
school without famiły support is much more difficult, but not impossible."

Remember, you will not be able to be all things to everyone at all
times. You can continue your education with greater confidence if
you condition yourself and your family to your new role.

THE SINGLE PARENT

Single parenting is a tough assignment under any circumstances
since the single parent usually feels responsible for supplying all of
his or her children's needs. Because there isn't a spouse to share the
financial burdens as well as the daily chores, including child care, getting through school as a single parent can be a difficult and lonely en-
deavor. Ironically, it is the single parent who most frequently requires
higher education to attain greater financial stability. A woman in New
England explained her situation this way: "I married Phil during my
sophomore year, dropped out of school, and took a secretarial job so
he could finish. Now we are divorced, my skills are rusty, and I have
no recent job experience. Besides, the pay scale around here for office
work is just plain inadequate. One day I woke up and realized that
my anger and bitterness were getting me nowhere. That's when I decided to go back and finish school. I hope that by next year I'll have
my B.A. *and* a decent job."

Two important factors are sending women back to school: Marriages
are being dissolved at a fast pace, and women are still outliving men
during an age in which higher education for women has become widely
accepted. Virginia Mills of Henderson, KY, said: "After my husband
died I was faced with the necessity of becoming self-supporting. I
would have returned to an office job, but I wanted something more
fulfilling. I decided to return to college to prepare for a job as a special education teacher. The youngest two of my three children could
not understand why I simply didn't go out and take a job. I tried to
explain that sometimes immediate gratification must be delayed so
that a better life in the future may be attained."

Under certain circumstances, being a single parent while studying
can be a plus. There is one less role to fill. You do not have a husband
or wife to please, cater to, or consider. Your leisure time is more your
own. Naturally your social life will be somewhat curtailed, but this
too can be turned into an advantage. Certainly you will become more
selective since you won't be accepting invitations out of sheer boredom—as an adult student you won't have *time* to be bored!

Dottie, of Omaha, NE, explained that she really stops and thinks
before accepting a date now that she's back in school. "If I'm really
interested in the person, I'll find the time. If not, my excuse of an

early morning class, or an upcoming test, or the necessity of spending some time with my children is quite satisfactory. I don't hurt anyone's feelings. Besides, my reason for not being available is probably true!"

CHILD CARE

Several types of child care are available to most parents who go to school. Your decision about which kind is most suitable for both you and your child might be based upon such factors as the age of the child, care hours necessary, quality of care, cost, and, finally, your personal preference. The following are major options that you might wish to explore.

Cooperative Child Care

This is a kind of barter system that can be either informal or structured. You may be able to make reciprocal arrangements with the parent of one of your child's playmates to take turns "sitting" for each other. This is an excellent way of introducing the young child to the idea of being away from you since he or she will be in familiar surroundings. A more formal exchange of child care involves a group of parents who rotate child care among themselves. Each parent is required to contribute a certain amount of time or, in some instances, a fee so that qualified staff may be hired.

Private In-Home Care

The advantage of this arrangement is that the child remains at home and maintains a more normal schedule. A lack of playmates may be a disadvantage. Also, this type of care can be quite costly. If you cannot make your own arrangements for a reliable person, check into the possibilities of an agency. Several are usually listed in the telephone directory of a large city. Be sure to investigate their requirements for their employees.

Family Day-Care Homes

This type of group care is a common arrangement for children under three years of age. The care giver is usually a woman who prefers to earn money at home. In some states certain requirements must be met in order to obtain a license to provide day care in a private home.

Community Day-Care Centers

The advantage of a center is that the service is usually more stable since substitute teachers can be called in when necessary. These centers usually provide group care for children three years of age and up. Inspected and licensed, they are usually run by a professional director. They may be located through welfare agencies, the Community Chest, churches, settlement houses, or Head Start programs.

Private Nursery Schools

Usually limited to the three-to-five-year-old age group, nursery schools tend to emphasize the preparation of the preschooler for future formal education. They often provide transportation (at additional cost), and their daily and hourly sessions are flexible.

Child-Care Centers on Campuses

Many colleges and schools have established child-care centers on their campuses to accommodate students with young children. These centers are often sponsored by the school's education department or by the parents in the campus community. In the latter case, the adult student either volunteers his or her services during times of no class commitments or pays a nominal fee.

Once you have selected your preference in child care, it may be a good idea to make some trial runs. If a private sitter sounds right for you and your child, begin interviewing candidates and using them. Observe the interaction between those persons and your child. If out-of-home care appeals to you, why not visit various facilities, bringing your child with you and leaving him or her for short periods? Be cautious, though. There may be unscrupulous people running some child-care facilities. Be sure you are very satisfied with everything you see, and talk at length to other parents if possible.

In any case, no matter what arrangements you finally make, it would be good insurance to have a backup child-care plan in mind. You might need it.

MARRIAGE PARTNERS IN SCHOOL TOGETHER

Reluctance of some adults about going to school may be partly due to apprehensions of competing with fellow students. It is a possibility that you will encounter some rivalry and occasional instances of one-upmanship. It is more likely, however, that feelings of friendship, or at least friendly competition, will prevail.

Many classes evolve into minisocieties with members sharing a "we're all in this together" feeling. Books, papers, and notes can become positively dog-eared from being passed around. Not just pens, but shoulders to cry on, may be freely loaned. Such interdependence often produces great warmth.

If it is good that adult students are willing to help one another, it is especially good when those adult students happen to be married to one another. Mark and Dee Scanlon, parents of two small girls, attend Roger Williams College in Bristol, RI. They note: "To maintain some sort of routine at home, you might each consider attending school on different nights, thus permitting the children to have at least one parent at home. This gives each parent the opportunity to help his or her children with any school problems and projects that they might have. And after the children are in bed, there's time alone for studying or other activities. If it is possible for a husband and wife to attend school together, they can find it to be a very enjoyable experience."

Jayne and Paul Castle of Stockton, CA, the parents of four children (three of whom live at home), also attend college together. Paul goes to California State College, Stanislaus, Extension in Stockton two nights a week, and both Jayne and Paul are part-time students at San Joaquin Delta College in Stockton, where they are both active in the Evening Student Association. Paul is employed full-time and Jayne operates a child-care business in their home. The Castles describe some of the unique problems they've encountered in attending college simultaneously and some of the solutions they've come up with:

> Our 8-year-old daughter is quite proud that every member of our family goes to school, and our 17-year-old son has changed his mind about not going to college since we've both enrolled. But being parents, marriage partners, and college students all at once has not been easy. Our biggest problems are coordinating our schedules and finding time to spend together. Jayne keeps a calendar listing both of our activities so that we don't take two cars to campus at the same time. We have established a rendezvous point at one of the campus snack bars where we can meet before and after classes. Our joint involvement in the Evening Student Association has provided the opportunity to share common interests every other Friday, as well as to travel together (sometimes with the children) to conferences and conventions. It is interesting to note that six of the nine directors of the Evening Student Association are actually three married couples. We feel our joint college involvement has enhanced our marriage and family relationships.

Many couples who are continuing their education have full-time jobs and are parents as well. If you are in this category, you can be almost certain that more than the usual tensions will develop at some point. One partner or the other, when under great stress, is almost sure to question whether it is really important for the other partner to go to school at the same time—whether, perhaps, it would not be

better for the *other* person to wait. There is little additional advice
beyond that already offered, but we can state with assurance that
most dual-career couples come to this juncture and successfully resolve
the problem short of divorce or long-term damage to their relationship.

ESTABLISHING YOUR HOME STUDY AREA

A niche somewhere in your home where you will be able to study
in relative privacy is a necessity for most students. The two essential
elements of a home study area are sufficient space and an atmosphere
conducive to study. Rosemarie Sunderland, a graduate of the College
of New Rochelle in New York State, reflects:

> You need to know yourself well enough to decide whether you concentrate
> best with total quiet or regular, routine noises or music drowning out these
> noises. Once you know this much, you need a place where you can come as
> close as possible to your ideal setting. Though the space may be small and
> compact, it must be set aside just for studying and be yours throughout the
> course of your studies. Even five minutes can be used constructively if you
> don't have to run around first cleaning an edge of a table and scrounging for
> a pencil. Try to plan your study area as carefully as you would plan for a dinner
> party or a poker game. You don't want to be caught short of anything! If you
> can, set up your area as far away from the main traffic of the home as possible
> lest you be caught in a traffic jam—or many of them!

If space is at a premium in your home—as it is with most of us—you
will probably have to draw on your imagination to create it. Are there
children who would survive if they were doubled up for the duration
of your school career, thus freeing up a bedroom? Or how about fin-
ishing off a portion of the attic or cellar? The garage might yield a
corner that could be insulated, with the addition of an electric heater
for very cold days. Perhaps a section of a room can be partitioned off
either permanently or temporarily with a screen. We heard of a man
who appropriated the playhouse that his daughter had outgrown. And
how about the woman in Florida who spend most of her study time
in her son's backyard tree house? (She "bought" it from him with a
new ten-speed bicycle.) Her neighbors thought she was a little strange,
but she got excellent grades on the papers she wrote among the leaves.
To equip your home study area, we suggest the following items:

- Typewriter—in good condition, with a new ribbon
- Wastebasket
- English handbook
- Dictionary—recent edition
- Thesaurus—also recent
- Pens, pencils, felt-tipped highlighting markers—for underlining
  important points in your textbooks

- Scratch paper (children's past school papers and notices are ideal)
- Typewriter paper—of good quality, preferably erasable
- Folders—either plastic or cardboard, for research papers
- Stapler, hole puncher, paper clips

Rosemarie Sunderland thinks that you need a chair "comfortable enough to study in, but uncomfortable enough to keep you awake."

The next step in establishing your study area may be to educate your family not to disturb your study equipment. Few things are more frustrating than reaching for something that isn't there. "My family finally learned not to borrow *anything* of mine," related one Texas student. "But only after I made repeated threats of death, destruction—even divorce!"

In time you will probably learn to study anywhere you happen to be. But your home study area will be your base—a very important one.

Now we come back to the question posed at the beginning of the chapter: "How can I earn a living, have a home life, and study too?" We could answer, "With difficulty." And in many respects that would be true. The back-to-school experience, as reflected in these past chapters, can be a complex one, of course. But many, many adults in the United States and indeed all over the world are involved in that experience. And in being involved, in coping, they are growing as individuals, continually developing more of their capacity to be the persons they can be. In the next chapter we'll explore how you can further enhance your ability to cope.

Editorial note: Nancy contributed this chapter in the original edition also. Now that a few years have passed we wondered if Nancy's college experience had in fact substantially changed her life. Here's her answer.

"You wanted to hear about the effect higher education has had on my career and self-satisfaction. So, I'll tell you. . . I enjoyed the education I received at Adelphi University, and the summa cum laude B.A. certainly looks good on my résumé. Yet my greatest satisfaction deals with more than book learning and a degree. It is how I feel about myself. The process of returning to school at the age of 41 and being a *successful student* totally stoked my ego, and my self-confidence has been quite boundless ever since.

"Since graduating, I moved to Santa Barbara, California, with my two daughters, found a place to live, and took a job with Santa Barbara County. I managed to be promoted three times but, after a few years, I was getting restless and ready for a new challenge.

"Imagine my delight when a close friend and former business associate made me an offer: she and three other independent business

people were in need of secretarial support; would I consider going into   **175**
business for myself and move into their office complex with them? I
just couldn't refuse. Even though it was a risk, in that they would be
using only a portion of my time and I needed to find additional clients,
I decided to quit my county job and do it.

"I formed my own business, Secretarial Office Support (SOS), with
an office in the heart of the downtown business area in an old adobe
which was built about 200 years ago. My new toy is a word processor,
and I am thoroughly enjoying my brand-new career at the age of 48.
Also, I'm doing some interesting community work.

"I have a friend who, at age 47, is a new student. I saw Phyllis the
other day and she sparkles with more life than I've seen in her for
years. I am so excited for her, and talking to her has brought back
lots of wonderful memories.

"I am convinced that if I hadn't gone back to school and gained
my self-confidence all this would never have happened. I would still
be stuck somewhere, hiding out from life and afraid to explore new
horizons. I thank all the forces that directed me to become an adult
student, and I'll always be grateful for the great experience.

"Am I beginning to sound like a recruiter? Well, why not?"

Student Profile

ARLENE Le BLANC of Montreal, Quebec, Canada

*I am most impressed with the helpful resources at
my college—courses in basic study skills, basic math,
and group behavior. The school offers guidance
of every kind.*

Learning was rather difficult for me, so having to leave school at
15 years of age proved to be no problem. My ability as a "jack-of-all-
trades" saw me through a ten-year period. Love, marriage, and two
children occupied me for the next ten years. During this time at
home I realized how little I knew and how much I wanted to learn.

At 36 years of age I started studying French, took some aptitude
tests, and wrote to England for my school marks. The test scores
proved quite low, and my marks came back from England with this
written across the page: "Shows marked weakness." Just after
receiving this nice bit of information I failed a French exam. So I sat

back, patted myself on the back, and said, "Well, Arlene, you tried." I couldn't handle the failure. It just seemed to reinforce how poorly I did in school.

Two years later my discontent at not learning anything was stronger than ever. It was now or never. I enrolled in a course for adults wishing to return to school. After receiving lots of confidence from a superb teacher, I started searching again for an appropriate school program.

With no particular degree in mind and not wanting to enter a university (too costly and too scary), my choices were limited. Evening courses are very tiring for me, so I was really looking for a daytime program. A preuniversity college in the area said it would accept me during the day, but I didn't have the nerve to sit in a classroom with 17- and 18-year-olds.

Trying to find the right program at a convenient college proved frustrating, but finally everything worked out. Dawson College here in Montreal has set up a tuition-free program for mature students. It's a daytime course of two full days a week, leaving time for family and studying. It is not too heavy a course, which is ideal for people like me who need to be eased back into the educational structure. The program incorporates basic study skills, basic math, and group behavior. The course boosts one's confidence while teaching one how to study again. The course can lead to a one-year preparatory science program, which in turn can lead to a diploma. The responsibility lies with the individual to do as much or as little as he or she wishes, but most students take their responsibility seriously.

I am most impressed with the helpful resources available at Dawson. The college offers learning centers where one can go for help in writing book reports and term papers, in reading skills, and in other academic areas. All the professors are very approachable, and there are guidance counselors on staff to help out with any kind of problem. School was never like this when I was young!

My children are amazed that I should want to go back to school, but I try to impress upon them that one is never too old to learn. Even if one does not have a particular degree in mind, I feel that learning for learning's sake is a goal in itself.

My best-laid plans for balancing home life, traveling time, and studies sometimes go awry, but I find this to be a plus as each individual in the family accepts more responsibility. This in turn makes for a more caring atmosphere.

To sum it all up, I would say that it is rewarding to be back at school regardless of where or what it leads to. My plans for the future? The possibilities are endless. I will continue taking academic courses to increase my knowledge.

There is a big, wide world out there and I intend to be part of it.

12.
Utilizing Your Resources for Coping

What are my personal resources for coping, and what school resources may help me?

RESOURCES

In several places we have referred to resources for coping. Now let's pursue this further to help ensure that you are not overlooking some of them. Resources for coping lie within you, around you in your home environment, and at your school. Your success in school will be directly related to how well you utilize those resources. Students enrolled in programs involving independent study will find that many of the following sections will apply to them as well as to students in traditional programs. Near the end of the chapter we focus on the unique problems of those of you in nontraditional programs.

ADULT ASSETS

Adults have many advantages over younger students. Comparing adults with traditional students, educators often list the following as strengths of adult students:

- More experience. As one adult student puts it, "Having lived longer and experienced more is the most important advantage an adult student has." This advantage gives adults a natural basis for discussions that is lacking in classes of younger students. The youngster in a history class may have only the sketchiest notion of where Vietnam is, whereas the adult may have fought there. The adult has lived longer, probably read more, heard more, and talked more about matters that relate to classroom learning than has the younger student.

- Greater eagerness to learn. Adults appreciate more what they have missed and do not want to miss any more of life and learning.
- More intensive commitment. They are probably sacrificing more—time, money, energy—than the younger students, and they want to make that sacrifice worthwhile.
- Less time to waste. Too much time has already gone by, and they want to make wise use of what is left. They will organize, complete assignments, and follow through. They will spend more time on studies and avoid excessive socializing.
- Better sense of goals. Younger people often do not know where they are going. Experience points out directions, clarifies paths, identifies goals.
- More willingness to question. The general life experience of the adult student may be equal to that of the teacher. The adult student, therefore, is more prone to question the assumptions of the teacher, and those questions are likely to lead the class into more profound examination of material than is the case with the younger class of students. Teachers often find this profundity of exploration exciting. "I'd been saying the same thing for years to young students," one teacher said. "Then an adult student questioned me and I realized I was wrong. It was an exhilarating reawakening."
- Greater expectation of good teaching. The adult who has committed more of his own resources than the younger student expects good teaching. Teachers of adults are likely to be better prepared, and the student thereby benefits more.
- Greater appreciation upon completion. Once a successful learning experience has been completed, adults are more prone to express their sincere appreciation to the instructor. Knowing this, and being after all only human, the instructor usually is going to try very hard to make the course worthwhile for adult students. "I will never forget the man who told me at the end of the term that my wonderful course and teaching had changed his life," said a professor from a college in southern Utah. "At that moment, I think I would have taken no salary for the rest of my teaching career if I could only have been assured of such a look on just one of my students' faces at the end of each of my courses."
- In short: Maturity, self-discipline, motivation are assets of adults.

ADULT LIABILITIES

Two liabilities seem to be the chief causes of adult failure in going back to school. The first is:

- Greater susceptibility to fear of failure. The stakes seem higher to adults. With more to lose, with more insight into the consequences of failure, adults can inhibit their chances of success by **179** succumbing to anxiety.

You, and we, recognize anxiety for the formidable enemy it can be, yet we know it can be overcome. Virginia Mills of Brescia College in Kentucky says that she would like to reassure adults who desire to continue their education not to let fear control their lives.

Adults want so much to succeed that they sometimes lose their perspective. In a previous chapter Dennis Gerard Ellis gave you some excellent advice on getting straight A's. Now we want to give you some advice on *not* getting straight A's: Put your performance in perspective. Did you do the best you could under the circumstances? Does a B, C, D, or even an F mean the end of everything for you? Many adults drop out of their programs before giving themselves a chance because they fear they have failed or soon will fail. Remember the race of the turtle and the hare? The turtle was behind in the beginning, but he did not equate that with failure, and he finally won the race. Among the multitude of adult students who have succeeded in school are many, many examples of difficult, slow starts, overcome by perspective and patience.

The second liability is:

- Greater external pressure. Adults bring a more complex world with them to their studies. They are subjected to a greater number of outside pressures to quit than are younger students.

Younger students are pressured by parents and friends to "stick it out." Adult students often find the reverse to be true. Women especially are susceptible to coercion.

"Why don't you stay home and act like a mother?" says the mother of an adult student.

"We can't afford any more of this tuition," says the husband.

"Mom, why don't I ever have any clean socks?" asks the teenage son.

And so on, and so on. One woman, normally a mild-mannered, soft-spoken person, gathered her family around her one evening—parents, husband, children—and said, "Now hear this! I want this degree, and you're going to start helping me get it. I'm doing something for me for once, and so help me God, if I have to, I'll walk out of that door and never come back in order to get it. Now which do you want?" All of the overt and most of the subtle coercion stopped, and she graduated.

SELF-KNOWLEDGE: YOUR STRENGTHS AND WEAKNESSES

Recognizing the assets and liabilities of adults in general should be helpful to you. But of even greater help is taking stock of yourself.

180   Sven, a chemistry major in an Ontario university, found that he had to make a conscious assessment of himself and act on it in order to succeed. After two semesters he was barely passing, yet he knew he could do better. During the early months of the summer he took long walks to think the matter through. He knew he was not highly intelligent, but he had always had good common sense, and he was persistent in his approach to problems. He needed to be able to make his persistence more effective, he came to realize. Sven had been divorced two years before, and his ex-wife habitually dropped in to see him, sometimes bringing a boyfriend. Sven thought that he handled the situation well, that it did not bother him. But his long walks and conscious exploration of his strengths and weaknesses relative to his schoolwork revealed that he was indeed bothered. He needed to be able to concentrate better across long periods of study time, and the frequent visits of his ex-wife not only cut into his available study time, but worse, disrupted his inner tranquility despite his apparently calm exterior. Realizing this after his periods of introspection, Sven called her and terminated their relationship entirely. During the next semester, now liberated in mind, he was able to concentrate effectively on his studies and significantly improve his grades.

Perhaps if you believe you are not able to be objectively analytical of yourself you should see a psychologist. This person could test you and work with you in assessing your strengths and weaknesses. Your school may even have the capability to do this in the personal counseling office (more on this later). Insight into yourself is an excellent tool for coping with school, and one you should not neglect to use.

INTERPERSONAL RELATIONSHIPS

You may know your strengths and weaknesses very well, but if you do not put this knowledge to use in interpersonal relationships it does you little practical good. "You" are not only the totality of individual qualities you possess when alone, but objectively "you" are those qualities and the impact you make on all other people.

It is to your advantage to affect instructors, administrators, and other students positively. But how can you know their reactions to you?

First, by being alert, by being more aware of others than you ever have been, you can assess to a significant degree the nature of your interpersonal relationships. This does not mean that you have to be sugar sweet to everyone. It only means that you have to be effective in dealing with people.

Patricia was a student in a college in South Dakota, enrolled in a psychology class in behavior modification. Part of the course was lec-

ture, part lab. The lab was intended as an extended practical exercise   **181**
in actually modifying the behavior of the students. Each student,
through testing, was first to identify an aspect of personality for behavior modification, then work on the modification through lab exercises and encounters in daily situations. The lab was graded pass or
fail, and the sole criterion for the grade was a practical test at the end
of the course to determine if the chosen aspect of behavior had in fact
been modified.

At the beginning of the course, tests had revealed that Patricia
would become angry and attack others when criticized. She chose
this aspect of her personality to modify. At the end of the term the
professor gave his exam covering the lecture portion of the class, and
later called Patricia into his office.

"I am sorry to say you got a C in the exam. Since you had been
doing A work, I would like to hear your explanation. Did you slack
off at the end of the course?"

Patricia flushed and said, "If I got a C the problem wasn't my answers. It was your questions. If you knew how to write comprehensible
questions, I'd have gotten an A. Your questions were stupid!" She
walked out.

A few days later she inquired about when she would be scheduled
to complete the lab portion of the course.

"You have already done it," the professor said. "You actually got
an A in the exam, but you got an F in the lab. You would do well, I
think, to repeat the lab next semester."

Patricia had not learned to be effective in dealing with others. Even
when her problem had been isolated and she had consciously worked
at modifying this aspect of her behavior, she had not been alert to her
potential effect on others. Her reply to her professor was intended to
diminish, not enhance, his stature. Had this not been a laboratory
situation, he probably would have been offended, and Patricia still
would have lost, not gained, from the encounter.

Another means of judging the effectiveness of interpersonal relationships is to ask others to give you their assessments. How do they
think you affect others?

Your approach could be general: "Professor Smith, how did I do
this past term?" This might eventually lead into an analysis of how
she viewed your interaction with her and the class. But you might get
a more meaningful answer if you apply insights to your personality
and ask specific questions: "Professor Smith, I have been told that I
often antagonize people by monopolizing class discussion. Did you
feel that this was a problem this semester?" Professor Smith's answer,
along with similar assessments, your analysis of them, and your behavior modification, could be an important ingredient in your future
success.

182 FAMILY, FRIENDS, OTHER STUDENTS AS HELPERS

Let's come back to the topic we looked at earlier, and consider it in more detail. When commenting on their school experiences, adult students almost always turn to the topic of helping and being helped. Many adults say essentially what Mary Lou Isernhagen of Kansas State University says: "The encouragement I received from my family was an important factor in my decision to return to school and to stay in school through the completion of my program."

In those cases where your family is not sympathetic to your problems, you may have to start making some withdrawals from that bank of family relationships to which you have been contributing all these years. Just as you have owed others, *they owe you.* It may be crucially important for you to let that fact sink in deeply: *They owe you.* Your investment in higher education is an investment in your family as well as yourself.

As we said earlier, there are risks, of course, and a few adults have found they gained their educational goals but lost other things. In some cases, husbands and wives have turned against one another, and children against mothers or fathers, under the added stress of an adult in the family going to school. "My husband divorced me, and my children hold me responsible for it. But for the first time in my life I feel like something other than an adjunct to everyone else's existence. I am a person. *I am me!*" This woman who graduated from a university in Montreal had never worked outside the house until she went to the university. Now she is the public relations officer for an organization in Quebec. "I create, I relate to others, I am alive!" She hopes that someday her husband and children will come to see that she, as well as they, deserved to be fulfilled as a person.

Friends, like family, can be a powerful resource for coping, or a detriment. A university psychologist suggests, "The friend who will give you a lift to school when your car is in the shop for repairs, who will take your children in an emergency, who will encourage you to persevere is the kind you will need. Just as you have to be selective and conservative with your time in order to study, you may have to focus your friendships more wisely. Don't invite trouble by hanging onto past friendships that you know to be detrimental to your success. Rather, seek friends who will be helpful. There are such people and, if you persist, it is quite likely you will find them."

Other adult students can aid you, perhaps more than you realize is possible. Carpools, shared baby-sitting, assistance with schoolwork—these are obvious types of physical aid. Less obvious, perhaps, is the psychological uplift you can get from other students. Virginia Mills of Brescia College in Kentucky was tempted to quit because of extraordinary pressures that developed soon after her enrollment, but another student played a major role in keeping her in college: "Hav- **183** ing made a good friend at Brescia helped me, and I was calmed by having a friend to share with." Another adult student said, "The encouragement I received from my classmates was one of the main reasons I was able to hold out. I made so many wonderful friends. I'll never forget them. It was like leaving a 'family' each time a class ended."

Some schools have programs of peer counseling that are greatly helpful to new students. Evelyn Greengross of the College of New Rochelle's School of New Resources tells about their Student Resource Center:

> Students very often feel isolated in their world with what they believe are problems unique to them. In reality they discover mutual problems, and very often their shared ideas lead to solutions or new discoveries that would not be possible otherwise. In a setting such as this, people feel free to discuss work-related or home-related problems that may strongly influence their school performance or general attitude toward life. In a student resource center, many students find that an empathetic listener helps them find their own solutions to problems that might otherwise have been destructive.

If your school has such a program, use it. If it doesn't, let the administration know one would be helpful, or perhaps even start one yourself.

SCHOOL RESOURCES: GETTING HELP

Few institutions in our society are as well equipped to assist people in coping with stress as an educational institution, especially one with resident students. Although schools and colleges are not all organized alike, they do tend to have some elements in common, and an understanding of school structure and resources will assist you in getting help.

In a medium-sized or large institution, there are usually one or more vice presidents under the president. Then come deans and directors of administrative offices. Reporting to the academic dean will be academic division or department chairpersons or directors. In smaller schools, duties will be concentrated in fewer staff members. Here is the essential structure that can provide help, assuming that it is operating reasonably well and the people in it want to help.

President

Busy person that he or she is, the president would never intentionally let a student go without needed help. The president may be the only person in the school structure who has the responsibility and authority to get office A and office B working together to solve your problems.

Administrative Assistant to the President

The president may have an assistant who has the implied authority of the president, if not the direct authority himself, to get office A and office B working together to your benefit. Titles vary; the administrative assistant may be called something else, but the function of this person is to coordinate people's efforts and to follow through on problems, including yours.

Vice Presidents and Deans

The second ranking officer in the institution, often called the executive vice president, will have broad supervisory authority and may be able to help you as effectively as the president. Other vice presidents or deans generally want to help too (but unfortunately important things sometimes do not get done because students do not provide direct input to them).

Counseling Services

Any higher education institution, no matter how small, necessarily invests much of its resources in counseling. Whether or not counseling staffs are large, counseling services exist. At a four-year private college with an enrollment of 1,300 full-time and 2,000 part-time students, the president was considering a suggestion to integrate all counseling services on campus. He asked his administrative assistant to explore the matter and provide him with a list of all the people on campus involved in formal counseling of students. This president had been in office for several years, but when he received the list he was astounded. It contained almost *200* names.

"What is this?" he demanded of his assistant.

"You asked for everyone who does formal counseling. After you study it, tell me which names you want struck."

The list had been categorized with a summary of duties for each category. The categories included:

Primary:

- Faculty (92). Contracts require academic advising as integral to teaching duties.
- Academic Advising Office (2). Academic advising.
- Counseling Services (2). Personal counseling.

- Placement Services (1). Career and employment counseling. **185**
- Health Care (2¼). Physical and mental care and counseling; part-time clinical psychologist.
- Dean of Students Office (3). Student affairs.
- Resident Assistants (22). Dormitory assistance and general counseling.
- Educational Opportunity Program (3). Special counseling for educationally and/or economically disadvantaged students.
- Financial Aid Office (2). Financial affairs.
- Registrar's Office (4). Academic records and regulations.
- Office of Continuing Education and Summer Sessions (2). Adult counseling.

Ancillary:

All academic administrators from the academic dean to program directors; all other chief administrators down to assistant directors; Admissions Office; Physical Education and Athletics Office; librarians; secretaries of all the above.

That seasoned president learned something that day. In his many years as a college administrator, he had never been as aware of the extent of counseling services on a college campus as he was when he surveyed that list. Similar resources exist in your school to serve you.

Academic Advising

The academic advising process at its most basic level begins when you contact a teacher and say, "Would you help me?" If this person cannot help, you have other resources. You could try your major adviser (or program adviser, faculty adviser, or program coordinator—there are many names for this person). He is available to ensure that you get the academic counsel you need in order to formulate and complete a viable course of studies in fulfillment of the requirements of your program. Some advisers are content never to see you; others insist on frequent meetings or letter or phone contacts. Thank God if you have the latter. (One word of caution: Whereas schools expect their advisers to act professionally, they usually warn you, "While you may seek the advice of a counselor, final responsibility for any decision reached or action taken *is yours*.") The student who does not seek periodic counsel with an adviser is reckless with his or her destiny.

The academic advising office is another resource, and one too little used by most students. One of your first visits as a student should be to this office. Probably the office will have a handout listing services

186 and procedures. Read it, but don't stop there. Ask questions about the services and see as many of the advisers as you can, if only for a few minutes to introduce yourself. Who those people are and how they relate to you is important. You should assess their ability to help you so you can turn to them if you feel your major adviser does not or cannot give you the help you need.

Although most of your academic problems can be treated effectively by your classroom teacher, major adviser, or the academic advising office counselors, some cannot. These people can put you in contact, though, with department and division chairmen, the registrar, and the dean.

But, you say, you do not want to bother those busy people—better to suffer in silence. Nonsense. The dean, for example, may be the only person in academic administration with sufficient authority to help you. An educational institution, like any other organization, has rules and regulations that govern its existence. But at certain levels, administrators may waive those rules and regulations in the interests of common sense, justice, or compassion. Deans will not lightly waive a requirement or counter a decision made at a lower level. Nor will they make a decision without input from others. Consequently, they will normally expect that you have taken your problem through channels. If you have done so, though, and are dissatisfied, it is their obligation to investigate the matter and act justly.

How often do individual student problems get to the dean's desk? More often than you think. And sometimes such problems are indicative of a weakness in the system that must be corrected. By persisting and utilizing your school's resources for academic advising, you may have helped not only yourself but all the students of the school for years to come.

Financial Aid Counseling

Contributed by **Carol Mackintosh,** *Director of Financial Aid, Utica College of Syracuse University*

Many financial aid offices offer a broad range of services beyond the primary function of providing information concerning aid and aid applications. Most can help you with bureaucratic problems that you may have in processing student-based grants such as the Pell Grant. Generally, a financial aid counselor can help with finding a lender if you wish to process a Guaranteed Student Loan. Many offices provide a job-finder service to help students find part-time jobs in the local community during the school year or during the summer vacation. A counselor may be able to advise students as to how to arrange their academic course load to minimize expenses. The financial aid office can provide you with documentation that you may need for dealing with agencies such as social services or the Food Stamp Administration. Most financial aid offices can help you understand your bill from the business office and payment options available to meet that bill. Many financial aid counselors are aware of new legislation or litigation that may apply to your situation and will keep you informed if the laws or cases will affect your aid. Often offices are familiar with public and private health-insurance plans that students may want to utilize. Some offices can make provisions for a student to receive an emergency short-term loan.

One of the most complicated problems you may encounter in school is coordinating your academic and financial matters. This is particularly true if you are a student who attends some academic terms part-time and some full-time or if you have a term of poor academic performance. You will need to get advice from both your academic advising office and your financial aid office.

Consider the case of Alfred, a student who made full use of his college's counseling services. He had decided to go to college after he left the armed forces, and he made normal academic progress for three years, financing his education through a combination of his wife's employment, his own part-time employment, the G.I. Bill, a small Pell Grant, and a Guaranteed Student Loan. At the end of his third year, he and his wife had a child, and his wife did not return to work. Alfred sought the help of an academic adviser and a financial aid counselor. Together they made new arrangements for Alfred to finish school. Alfred would go to school three-fourths time and increase his hours at work. He and his academic counselor arranged that Alfred's graduation would be only three months later than originally planned. And he and the financial aid counselor made arrangements for him to use the college's division of continuing education which offered a lower tuition rate. They also filed a supplemental Pell Grant application that showed a decrease in income due to the wife's discontinued employment, and this allowed Alfred to receive an increase in his grant. They also notified the Veterans Administration about the new baby so that Alfred could receive additional payments for a third person in his family. Finally, they processed a request for an increase in the Guaranteed Student Loan. Consequently, Alfred did not have to leave college, contrary to his initial fears.

While there are several ways a financial aid officer can help you, there are limitations. The financial aid office is constrained by government regulations and its own budget. You cannot expect the office to change regulations or overspend its budget. You can expect, though, that the office will help you in every way possible.

188   Personal and Psychological Counseling

Contributed by **Robert E. Woods,** *Director of Counseling, Utica College of Syracuse University*

No matter what age a student is, school attendance may be accompanied by symptoms of anxiety and stress. Many of the stresses faced by some adults who return to school have been discussed earlier in the book. You should be aware that most schools provide you with a mental-health service to assist you in coping. This service may range from a staff of psychiatrists and psychologists at a large university to a single counselor at a small trade school who may deal with financial aid, placement, and student social life in addition to personal counseling. The name given to this service may vary from campus to campus; "counseling center" and "psychological services" are common titles.

Once you have located the source of help, you will want to determine whether the available help is appropriate to your particular concern. Psychiatrists, psychologists, and counselors are different kinds of therapists, trained to do different things. Within each category of therapy are scores of techniques and approaches to practice. The following explanations can serve as a general guide that may enable you to choose a therapist or at least be aware of the type of service you are likely to get.

Psychiatrists are licensed physicians with a specialty in treating mental illness. They are the only mental-health professionals who can prescribe drugs.

Psychologists are trained to assess the emotional and behavioral characteristics of people and to help them overcome difficulties. Not all psychologists engage in counseling; some specialize in research and teaching exclusively. In most schools, however, you will find at least one psychologist available for counseling.

Counselors are trained to help with problems associated with stress, such as marriage and family difficulties or anxiety arising out of a particular situation. They can help you to talk about your concerns and to reach satisfactory conclusions. Generally, counselors do not engage in long-term therapy or treat severe personality disorders, but they can identify the need for such treatment and make appropriate referrals.

Since the titles of these professionals are often confusing or vague, it's always a good idea to ask a potential therapist or counselor to discuss his or her training and style of practice. Any ethical therapist will be willing to do this.

An ethical issue that may concern you is confidentiality. Except under extraordinary circumstances, mental-health professionals are bound by a code of ethics that requires them to keep counseling information confidential. Thus, you can be assured that your teachers and others will not be informed of your personal concerns.

A final word of advice: Don't be timid or hesitant about using this **189** service. Higher education institutions take care to hire only trained professionals for these sensitive positions. Counselors and therapists, after all, can have a strong impact on how students view the institution. Happy students are more likely to persist in their studies than unhappy ones. If personal concerns are keeping you from living up to your full potential, visit the counseling center. It may be the key to your success.

CHALLENGING THE @!#—*?! COMPUTER

We think that computers are great, but the advent of computer processing of academic information has added a new dimension to bureaucracy in higher education systems. In theory, the computer promises to solve the problems of inefficiency and ineptitude by collecting, storing, retrieving, and processing data in a fraction of the time it takes people to perform these functions. In practice, however, the computer often leaves much to be desired. The technological capability is there, but the human element has not been eliminated—as the saying goes, "garbage in, garbage out." Too often the computer printout will contain at least as many errors as the old manual systems. But the computer has a unique feature that is relished by some staffs —it can't talk back. The computer may have become the latest "copout" for the system. When something goes wrong, the computer can be blamed.

Remember that computers are tools used by people to do a job. A computer malfunction does not release the person from his or her responsibility to get the job done, and it certainly should not transfer the burden to you. Delays ultimately are caused by people, not computers. If all else fails, and the situation is urgent, there can be no acceptable reason for not handling your problem manually; after all, isn't this how it was done before the computer? You might have to be insistent, and with the right person, but you are entitled to obtain the proper results from the @!#—*?! computer, and you can.

STUDENTS' RIGHTS: FIRST AMENDMENT, DUE PROCESS

In recent years, landmark court rulings have opened the doors for students to exercise their constitutional right of free expression in schools. The First Amendment to the Constitution, according to a United States Supreme Court decision (*Tinker* v. *Des Moines Independent District*), permits students to air their views on any subject provided they do not " 'materially and substantially' disrupt the work and discipline of the school."

190   Due process is another fundamental right of all Americans. Employees of public postsecondary schools are bound by the Fourteenth Amendment to provide any student who is accused of misconduct with a fair and impartial hearing.

Usually private schools also try to assure students of fair treatment through establishment of procedures similar to those in the following excerpt from a student-faculty handbook:

> *Due Process*
> Alleged offenders of . . . Rules, Regulations and Procedures shall be guaranteed due process, which is defined as follows:
>
> 1. The student shall be given adequate notice in writing of the specific ground or grounds and the nature of the evidence on which the disciplinary proceedings are based.
> 2. The student shall be given an opportunity for a hearing in which the disciplinary authority provides a fair opportunity for hearing the student's position, explanations, and evidence.
> 3. No disciplinary action shall be taken on grounds which are not supported by substantial evidence.
>
> Note: Any student may appeal any decision made by a disciplinary authority or hearing board. . . .

Thus you are entitled to certain fundamental rights as a student, including freedom of expression and, at most schools, due process. However, you are required to abide by the rules and regulations of your school. Problems may arise when official policies, procedures, or directives conflict with your basic constitutional rights. You can usually resolve such disputes through the judicial process provided by your school. If you are unable to obtain satisfactory results by appealing to the appropriate hearing board (assuming one exists), you then have the right to take legal action.

WOMEN'S EDUCATIONAL EQUITY

Establishing educational equity for women is generally recognized as the starting point from which the eventual elimination of sex biases, and consequential sex discrimination, in our country might be achieved. With this objective in mind, federal laws and regulations prohibiting sex discrimination in educational institutions have been adopted. The major piece of legislation affecting students is Title IX of the Education Amendments of 1972. The following information was extracted from the "PEER Summary of the Regulation for Title IX Education Amendments of 1972" published by the Project on Equal Education Rights:

> Title IX says: "No person . . . shall, on the basis of sex, be excluded from participation in, be denied the benefits of, or be subjected to discrimination

under any education program or activity receiving federal financing assis-   **191**
tance...." Letters charging that discrimination has occurred may be sent to
the Director, Office for Civil Rights, U.S. Department of Education, 330
Independence Avenue, S.W., Room 3256N, Washington, D.C. 20201, or to the
Director of the Regional Office for Civil Rights responsible for enforcement
in that state....

Although significant gains have been made since the passage of Title
IX, sex discrimination sometimes seems to remain deeply ingrained
in our educational system. Extensive literature on sex discrimination
against students is available from the following sources:

Project on the Status and Education of Women
Association of American Colleges
1818 R Street, N.W.
Washington, DC 20009

PEER (Project on Equal Education Rights)
9th Floor, 1413 K Street, N.W.
Washington, DC 20005

Women's Educational Equity Act Program
Publishing Center, Education Development Center
55 Chapel Street
Newton, MA 02160

AGE DISCRIMINATION ACT

The Age Discrimination Act of 1975 prohibits exclusion of any individual from participating in federally funded programs or activities
on the basis of age. While factors not directly related to age (such as
physical health) might still limit admission of some older people, you
cannot legally be denied admission to most higher education institutions because you are too old.

Should you be denied admission because of your age to a school
that accepts federal funds, you must first seek recourse through the
school's administration. If, after you've pursued all available avenues,
the school still refuses to reverse its decision, you may then file suit
charging violation of the Age Discrimination Act of 1975. Procedures
for filing complaints vary from school to school depending upon which
federal agencies have provided financial assistance to the institution.
Schools are required to provide students with proper information on
how to exercise their rights. Should you not be satisfied with this information, we suggest you contact the nearest office of the U.S. Commission on Civil Rights for advice on how to proceed.

192 PRIVACY ACT: ACCESS TO YOUR OFFICIAL RECORDS

The Family Educational Rights and Privacy Act of 1974 guarantees you access to your school records, and provides the means for you to have inaccurate or inappropriate notations in your files changed or deleted. The law also prohibits disclosure of most information about you to outside organizations or individuals without your written consent. School officials may not deny you the right to see any record of your academic or personal progress, even if the record is designated "confidential" (unless you have signed a waiver of your right to access to a specific piece of information). School officials are entitled to see your records, but only those officials who have a legitimate educational interest and need for access to information about you.

To provide you with an example of the type of information your school might compile about you, we have included this excerpt dealing with the Privacy Act from a university's student-faculty handbook:

> The following educational records are maintained by the University and are considered as subject to this law:
> (a) Student Folders—Dean of Students Office for all undergraduate students, Graduate Dean's Office for all graduate students. Your department or school may also maintain a file . . . for enrolled students.
> (b) Permanent Record Cards—The Dean of Students Office, undergraduates only.
> (c) Academic Transcripts—Office of the Registrar for all students.
> (d) Placement Folders—Office of Counseling and Career Development for all students and alumni.
> (e) Health Records—Infirmary, Psychological Services Clinic, Social Work Services Clinic.

If it is not practical for you to inspect your records personally, you can request copies, and the school must furnish them (although you may have to pay the copying costs). Copies of your academic transcript are always available to you (usually at a nominal fee) from the registrar. If you wish to challenge any entry other than a properly recorded grade on your transcript or other school records, you have the right to a hearing within a reasonable time after you request it. Should you have a complaint that is not resolved to your satisfaction by the school, you can write to the Family Educational Rights and Privacy Act Office, Department of Education, 400 Maryland Avenue, S.W., Washington, DC 20202.

ADULT STUDENT ORGANIZATIONS

Acting individually, adult students have some of the resources necessary to effect changes in a malfunctioning school system. Acting together, their resources are greatly multiplied.

Change can be accomplished through organized student governments, lobbying, and use of the media. However, strong leadership is
needed to overcome the problem of student apathy. Work and family
demands, coupled with the often transient nature of attendance, cause
apathy to be particularly acute among adult students. Yet significant
progress toward forming adult organizations is being made in higher
education institutions throughout the United States.

Adult students, through organizing, have brought about many
changes when things were not going right, such as proper library staff-
ing in the evenings or on weekends, to serve adult students; weekend
and evening hours in the bursar's and registrar's offices, the bookstore,
and the cafeteria; and the creation of a counseling staff for continuing education students where none had existed. If your school does
not have an effective adult student organization, perhaps you should
start one, now.

RESOURCES FOR STUDENTS IN NONTRADITIONAL PROGRAMS

What about students in nontraditional programs? Do they have to
go it alone? Not at all. Although the resources probably will not be
as extensive and certainly will not be as close at hand as they would
be in an on-campus program, essential services for aiding students do
exist.

Earlier we said that if you are in an external degree or other nontraditional program you probably have an assigned adviser with whom
you communicate by correspondence, telephone, computer link, or
cassette. If your problems are beyond the scope of this person's expertise, he or she normally will refer you to the appropriate person
at the institution who can help you. It is important to use your adviser, but it is equally important to realize that if you are not getting
the help you need from this person you have recourse. You may ask
for help from a person higher up the chain of authority: for example,
your adviser's immediate superior, the dean, or the president. Or you
may ask to have another adviser assigned to you. In nontraditional as
well as traditional programs, the ultimate responsibility for decisions
is yours. So use your assigned adviser, of course, but if you are not
getting the help you need, don't be reluctant to go elsewhere in the
institution. Remember, the head of the school wants you to succeed,
not fail; so get help by whatever means are necessary. And you should
expect the same kind of support from family and friends as you would
if you were enrolled in a traditional program. In fact, because your
institutional support structure may not be as convenient for you,
you may need more of their help.

Student Profile

ANTHONY F. FARMA of Needham Heights, Massachusetts

As an evening student, I was told, "If you want to discuss your program you must make an appointment during daytime *appointment hours."*

At the age of 42, with a growing family of five children and plans to embark on self-employment, I decided that a return to college was necessary. Economics dictated that I could take two or three evening courses a semester to avoid straining the family budget and denying my children an opportunity to further their own educational goals. I was fortunate to pick Suffolk University near my home in Boston, Massachusetts.

Anyone who had seen my high school record would have been reluctant to predict I could ever have received A's in anything except recess. However, with maturity came a philosophy that everything you do is worth 100 percent effort. I received A's in both of my first two courses at Suffolk University.

Naturally the high marks encouraged me to continue. The academic atmosphere was intoxicating, and I was actually enjoying Saturday afternoons in the library doing research papers and reading. The doors of knowledge began opening, with each one more exciting than the last. Soon the routine of work, classes, and weekend study became ingrained in my life as it does with all evening students. However, there was something missing in my college experience.

I noticed that some of my classmates were complaining of problems regarding services that were not being provided, and the attitude of certain administrators toward evening students. I was fortunate not to have run into any of these problems and considered the complaints natural in an urban university—certainly having nothing to do with me.

Then it happened!

In an effort to save precious time, I called my adviser to clarify my forthcoming semester courses. His secretary said she was sorry but her boss would not talk to me on the phone. As an evening student, I was told, "If you want to discuss your program you must make an appointment during *daytime* appointment hours."

Needless to say my Italian temper was put to its severest test. Then and there the plight of the much maligned evening student became my personal battle. I began to explore avenues to change the

attitudes of the administrators and faculty at this small urban **195**
university and to seek ways to help my fellow students.

My chance arose because the evening student government at that
time was in desperate trouble due to a lack of good public relations
and the normal apathy evidenced by most evening and part-time
students. Before long I was elected president of the Evening Division
Student Association (EDSA).

After taking office I realized that without sufficient funding no
organization can ever reach its full potential. With the support of the
Evening Division Student Association board, EDSA developed a new
constitution that allowed for a collection of $5.00 per year per
part-time student. This money, which was under the direct control of
the EDSA board, allowed us to properly advertise and develop new
programs and provide scholarship services for officers.

In prior years the Evening Division Student Association had had
trouble filling its twelve-member board. Now, with a healthy budget
and an enthusiastic board, we had more than enough people to run
for the positions.

The combined efforts of dedicated adult students resulted in
significant accomplishments. These included an Oktoberfest, reduced
parking rates for evening students in the surrounding garages, and a
well-attended and enjoyable Recognition Night dinner dance.

Once the commitment to be totally involved was made, it was just
a short step for me to look beyond Suffolk University to the
problems and concerns of evening and part-time adult students in
other universities. I attended a meeting at Northeastern University of
the United States Association of Evening Students (USAES). At the
next meeting of the EDSA board I enthusiastically recommended
our joining USAES. A vote was taken and we became members.

Within the space of two years, through a series of circumstances,
I was elected president of the New England Region of USAES.
Liaison was established with my congressman (a former evening
student), and he was sympathetic to our cause. Through this
contact I was able to keep a close watch on the happenings in
Washington and how they would affect our population. At several
national meetings, legislation workshops were held in which letter-
writing techniques and campaign strategies were discussed. For the
first time the organization was having its collective voice heard in
Congress.

At the same time I was concentrating on expanding the New
England Region, and results were starting to show. By the end of my
second elected term, the membership of the region had increased by
100 percent.

Several members of USAES encouraged me to run for president of
the National, so I did and was elected. Following my term as

196   president of the United States Association of Evening Students, I can
       look back at appearances before congressional committees, an
       increase in membership, and plans for additional expansion which
       will, I'm sure, bear fruit.

13.

Reassessing Your Goals and Performance

After having been in school for some time, I wonder—am I going in the right direction, achieving all I can, and getting the most satisfaction out of school and life?

REVIEWING GOALS, PRIORITIES, DECISIONS, ACTIVITIES

Your chances for success both in your studies and in your future career are enhanced if, after having been in school for some time, you deliberately review your goals, priorities, decisions, and activities. Your choices of school and curriculum were based on what you believed some time ago, and not necessarily on what you know and feel now. Ask yourself if those decisions are still valid, considering your current outlook on life, your newly acquired training and knowledge, and your personal and professional aspirations. Assuming that you have given your new lifestyle a sufficient chance so that you can draw legitimate conclusions, you should conduct this review as soon as possible. If your reassessment indicates that you should change course, it is better to find out sooner rather than later. The longer you wait, the more difficult and costly any changes will become for you.

ASSESSING THE PRESENT

Your answer to the question, "What should I be doing now in order to get where I want to go?" necessarily involves the three major concerns in your present existence. They are career, school, and personal and family relationships.

198   Career Relationships

Planning for your future career is important, but you must also pay attention to your present employment. You cannot afford to become so engrossed in your educational and career plans that you lose sight of this basic fact. Martin, a Colorado sales executive, had recently been promoted to territorial vice president with responsibility for directing a team of 20 district sales managers. Soon after his promotion he decided to enroll in a bachelor of business administration degree program at a local university. This would please his employer, he thought. Carrying a 12-credit load throughout the academic year, he was determined to earn straight A's, and he did. Unfortunately, Martin was so preoccupied with his course work that he neglected his duties, and within a year he was demoted to his former position.

School must be kept in proper perspective as it relates to your daily activities. Watch for danger signals: Have you discovered yourself talking often about school during lunch hour or cocktails with the boss? Is your superior making comments (even innocent-sounding ones) about your being enamored of school? Have you found yourself thinking of course work when you should have been concentrating on company work? If so, you might be wiser to cut back on course work and give adequate attention to your present career. Even if your ultimate objective is to change careers, finding a new job is considerably easier for an individual who is already employed and who can get a good recommendation from a current employer.

School Relationships

Your assessment of present relationships at school should involve not just program and credit review to ensure that you are on the right track to graduation and later a career, as discussed earlier. It should also take into account your total school environment.

After having been in school for some time, you should ask yourself if you are being as effective as possible in your dealings with others. If not, can you find any pattern to your problems? If you can, you are well equipped to discuss the matter with various people—individual instructors in whom you place confidence, or academic and personal counselors, or a dean. Out of these discussions might come solutions.

But what if, after having made such an assessment, you believe sincerely that the fault lies not in you but in the school? Have you considered transferring to another institution? It is a routine procedure, and certainly is nothing of which to be ashamed. Even if you have to lose some ground you had fought hard earlier to gain, transferring might be the right action to take.

When assessing your present school relationships, if you find your- **199** self in an unsatisfactory situation, you have certain choices. You can accept the situation and live with it. Or you can change yourself in order to adapt to it. Or you can effect changes in the other elements of the situation so they are compatible with you. Or you can walk away from it. Consider your alternatives carefully, and then decide.

Personal and Family Relationships

Contributed by **Stephanie Phillips,** *Associate in Science degree with honors from Dutchess Community College, Poughkeepsie, NY*

Now that you have experienced a term or so of higher education, and probably cleared those initial hurdles of personal and family con- sternation, nevertheless you should reassess your personal and family relationships. Penny Meek, of Twin Lakes, CO, says: "My husband and I have had to reevaluate our expectations and goals as individuals and as a couple. We found at times each of us had to give a little more than we normally might have. As a result, I feel we have developed a nontraditional marriage and family."

In some personal relationships, and in some families, perhaps the smoothness with which everything is proceeding is only a surface condition. Or if the surface is churning, it may not be too late to pour oil on the troubled waters. Sabina Leonard of Trocaire College recognized that serious consequences can result from neglecting to reassess present relationships. Recently, more and more women have been going back to college, and, as Sabina put it, it sometimes seems that "once they have their degree they divorce their husbands. I know that this must bother my husband because he teases me about my divorcing him as soon as I graduate. I usually tell him I have a list of things to do after graduation. First is to buy new shoes; second, divorce Bud. We both chuckle and it's okay for the moment, but he wouldn't tease if it didn't bother him. I make the time to reassure him often that he is more important than my schooling."

Adults in school work and achieve. Credit for the achievement right- fully may go as much to others who are close to the student as to the student personally. If this is so in your case, be sure you let your sup- porters know of your appreciation.

ACHIEVEMENT AND SATISFACTION

How important is achievement? And what is the relationship be- tween achievement and satisfaction? These questions, to be sure, are important to all of us.

200   Achievement is a means by which we can demonstrate our worth to society and elicit recognition from our fellow human beings. Does recognition of our achievements, however, provide the satisfaction we seek? Maybe, and maybe not. We can be recognized without being appreciated and respected. What then is the point of achievement if we can't be assured of the appreciation and respect of others?

Here is what some adult students have told us about their feelings of educational achievement and satisfaction.

Stephanie Phillips dropped out of high school at the age of 16 to get married. Eleven years later, she enrolled in Dutchess Community College with the support of her husband and two children. The going was rough, but achievement made her efforts worthwhile: "Throughout my college education, I experienced many changes and a lot of growth. My actual accomplishments are a matter of record. My grade-point average was a 3.95, I earned a scholarship to continue my education, and I received a letter of acceptance to Vassar College in Poughkeepsie, New York. In comparison, my growth as an individual can't be measured by a grade-point average."

Virginia B. Mills was widowed at age 45 after 25 years of marriage. A mother of three children, she was faced with the necessity of becoming self-supporting. Despite considerable difficulty in obtaining financial aid and in coping with family responsibilities and her father's illness, she persevered. As she approached her final semester at Brescia College, Owensboro, KY, looking forward to graduation with honors, she described her feelings: "In just six weeks I will be a degreed and certified special education teacher. Two years ago when I looked at the schedule, I could not believe I could do it all, and now, I just have one semester of student teaching to go. Now I feel comfortable in school, and, more important, in life. Even if I should never go into teaching, I have a confidence and competence that have made me a fuller, stronger, and more outgoing person. I have discovered my potential and I realize that I am an intelligent person."

Wilma J. Dickey of Mission, Kansas, discovered that her "nesting urge was threadbare" at age 41, and she entered college. She said: "There is no way that I can adequately express what attending Johnson County Community College did for my life. It gave me confidence; it gave me purpose. It gave me friendships; it gave me joy. I relate any good thing in both my professional and personal life today to that year, as the new beginning. Whether I will ever continue and earn a four-year degree, I still do not know. For now, I feel fulfilled."

Now that we've reviewed these descriptions of achievement and satisfaction experienced by this representative sampling of adult students, perhaps we can draw some conclusions. How important is achievement? We think it is important to everyone. Does achievement lead to satisfaction? Probably, but not necessarily. Achievement

without a worthy purpose can be empty. Will lack of recognition **201**
minimize the satisfaction you realize through your achievements?
Probably not. If the accomplishment is truly significant, lack of recognition should not detract from your sense of self-satisfaction.

But some people might yet ask, "Why bother?" The following
excerpts from John W. Gardner's book *Excellence: Can We Be Equal
and Excellent Too?* might help you to clarify your reasons for being
an adult student.

> We fall into the error of thinking that happiness necessarily involves ease,
> diversion, tranquility—a state in which all of one's wishes are satisfied. For
> most people happiness is not to be found in this vegetative state but in *striving
> toward meaningful goals*. The dedicated person has not achieved all of his
> goals. His life is the endless pursuit of goals, some of them unattainable. He
> may never have time to surround himself with luxuries. He may often be tense,
> worried, fatigued. He has little of the leisure one associates with the storybook
> conception of happiness.
>
> But he has found a more meaningful happiness. The truth is that happiness
> in the sense of total gratification is not a state to which man can aspire. It is
> for the cows, possibly for the birds, but not for us.
>
> We want meaning in our lives. When we raise our sights, strive for excellence,
> dedicate ourselves to the highest goals in our society, we are enrolling in an
> ancient and meaningful cause—the age-long struggle of man to realize the best
> that is in him. Man reaching toward the most exalted goals he can conceive,
> man striving impatiently and restlessly for excellence, has achieved great reli-
> gious insights, created great works of art, penetrated secrets of the universe
> and set standards of conduct which give meaning to the phrase "the dignity
> of man."

14.
Viewing Your New Horizons

What lies ahead—continuing my education, perhaps graduate school, a new career, continued personal growth?

GAZING INTO THE CRYSTAL BALL

You are nearing graduation. That license as a practical nurse, or your associate degree in electronics technology, or your bachelor's degree in accounting which qualifies you to sit for the CPA exam, is just around the corner. What is on the horizon? If you have trained for a career at a trade or technical institute, should you go on to get an associate or bachelor's degree? If you have the associate degree almost in hand, should you continue for your bachelor's? If that is within grasp, what about graduate school? Should you enter a new phase in your current career or shift careers entirely?

Questions like these undoubtedly are ones you have been pondering as graduation nears. At your school, your academic advising staff and career and placement counselors should be able to assist you in planning your course of action. With this kind of help, and other types we will suggest, what lies in the crystal ball should become more distinct for you to see. This chapter takes you down the two paths that most students tread in the latter stages of their program. One leads to further higher education, perhaps including graduate school, and the other directly to a career.

HIGHER EDUCATION ALTERNATIVES FOR GRADUATES OF TECHNICAL, BUSINESS, AND OCCUPATIONAL PROGRAMS

With your certificate, diploma, or associate degree you will be well qualified to build on that base if that is your wish. Have you considered adding another related field to your newly gained expertise so that **203** you will be even better qualified in your career? For example, as you took your courses to become an electronics technician, perhaps you felt a need to learn more about computer technology specifically. Remember that there are many courses and programs in which you can enroll to gain this added expertise. Review the early chapters for information about directories and approaches that may help you. Well-trained technicians in any field are hard to find, and your career potential is great.

ALTERNATIVES FOR GRADUATES OF DEGREE PROGRAMS

If you want to continue learning, a higher-level undergraduate degree or graduate school may not be right for you, at least not yet. Undergraduate courses that you were not able to take as part of your degree curriculum might provide your best source of satisfaction. You might even be able to advance your career objectives more effectively by taking selected undergraduate courses. Sharpening your skills in areas that are directly applicable to your work could provide your quickest route to success.

Some colleges, universities, and vocational schools offer certificate programs designed to enhance the potential of college graduates for employment in certain professional fields. These programs usually involve modules of four to eight courses (12-24 credits) in a specific field. Such programs are especially well suited for individuals with undergraduate degrees in disciplines with limited career opportunities. Since certificate programs take less time to complete than most graduate degree programs, they are particularly appealing to many adults.

Some colleges and universities will allow a student to apply credits earned through a postbaccalaureate certificate program toward the requirements for a graduate degree. Thus a professional program might provide quick access to a new career as well as a stepping-stone to a master's or doctoral degree. If graduate credit is important to you, though, be sure to check on credit transferability since many postbaccalaureate certificate programs are composed of undergraduate courses only. Also, the better course of action in many cases might be to get a second bachelor's degee that will allow entry to a particular career field. Often the second degree can be obtained with only somewhat more credit hours than would be accumulated in a certificate program. But an even better approach than to get a second degree at the same level or a certificate might be to get a graduate degree, especially if it requires only a few more credit hours than the second degree or certificate, which is frequently the case.

When you took that major step forward and decided to continue your education, graduate school became a realistic possibility for you. Mary Ellen Schwender of Oceanside, NY, says: "When I started I was only going to try for the associate degree. Now I have that degree and soon will have my B.A. degree. And here I am, thinking about graduate school."

Many adult students have decided that higher education need not stop with a bachelor's degree, regardless of one's age. Evelyn M. Greengross, aged 60, of Mamaroneck, NY, says: "From the experiences of earning my B.A. degree I have developed a direction for myself. I have been accepted in a master's degree program in counseling the aging at the University of Bridgeport. This degree will enable me to pursue a professional career based upon the experiences that were developed and nurtured during my four exciting years at the School of New Resources, College of New Rochelle."

Coauthor Charles McCabe, a high school dropout, entered college on a "provisional basis" at age 31. Because of his limited formal education, he was quite concerned about his ability to do college-level work as an adult. Yet within less than two and a half years he had earned his high school equivalency diploma, his Associate in Arts degree, and his Bachelor of Science degree with a double major (graduating summa cum laude, number one in his class of 141 nontraditional students), and he was admitted to a highly selective executive M.B.A. degree program at Pace University in New York City. Chuck completed his M.B.A. degree within two years, then immediately began pursuing a doctorate in professional studies in management at Pace University.

Success stories such as these are abundant—the list could go on and on. Can such a story be about you? Absolutely! We're convinced that virtually any adult who has demonstrated the motivation and perseverance required to earn a baccalaureate degree can succeed in graduate studies.

Two types of graduate degrees may be attained—academic and professional. Your college library will contain guides to graduate studies. Some guides will be specialized for such fields as political science, management, psychology, law, and medicine. Others will be comprehensive such as the several annual guides to graduate study in various fields, published by Peterson's Guides. Such references will greatly assist you in choosing a graduate program.

As you look for an appropriate graduate program, don't forget to consider external degrees. A growing number of accredited colleges and universities offer such programs, awarding the Master of Business Administration, Master of Fine Arts, Master of Science, Doctor of Education, Doctor of Philosophy, and other degrees in various fields. (You can send a self-addressed, stamped envelope to ETC Associates,

External Graduate Degrees, 507 Rider Road, Clayville, NY 13322,   **205**
for information on how to locate graduate external degree programs.)

PREPARING FOR THAT NEW CAREER

As we noted previously, career planning and placement services are
often provided by the institution in which you enroll, usually at no
cost to students and alumni. To find out what career services your
school has to offer, first check the school's bulletin. Typically you
will find a policy statement such as the following, which was included
in the Northrop University (Inglewood, CA) bulletin:

> The Placement Office offers career counseling and guidance to help the
> graduating student make career decisions and provides information on the
> employment opportunities and practices of numerous companies and federal
> agencies. The office maintains a library of career descriptions, complete with
> company and community information. Materials are furnished for employer
> contacts; on-campus interviews are arranged and the student is assisted in ré-
> sumé preparation and the arrangement of off-campus interviews.
>
> There are no fees and all graduates of the University are entitled to free life-
> time service which includes job referrals, preparation of a professional résumé,
> and assistance with correspondence.

Specific information and literature describing the various services
that are provided can be obtained from the career center, or its equivalent, at your school. Some career centers, such as the one at Pepperdine
University in Malibu, CA, provide psychological testing (vocational
and personal) to aid students in self-assessment. Pepperdine also offers
a one-credit course on exploring career options. And most schools
vigorously promote on-campus recruiting. Kent State University in
Ohio explains in its bulletin that "the on-campus recruiting program
attracts representatives who visit the campus to interview candidates
for full-time employment in business, industry, government, human
services, and education." We recommend that you first determine the
degree of assistance your school's career center can provide you. To
supplement this service, or ensure that all options have been explored,
you may then wish to investigate other career services, such as those
outlined earlier.

CAREER OPPORTUNITIES FOR WOMEN

Contributed by Judith Weber Wertheim, *M.S. in Counseling, C. W. Post College;
currently a career counseling consultant for the South Huntington and Harbor-
fields libraries and the Suffolk Cooperative Library System, NY*

This decade presents women with opportunities and challenges in
the world of work that are greater and more exciting than ever before.
But if women expect a greater share of the financial pie, they must

rethink and redirect their career choices and goals. The women's movement, various pieces of antidiscrimination legislation, and economic need have spurred women to consider entering the more lucrative, and frequently more stimulating, nontraditional fields. By this we mean fields that have been almost exclusively dominated by men.

Let us consider some of the fields offering the best prospects for employment—the growth fields. Department of Labor projections predict good long-range opportunities in the professional and technical areas. Concern for all types of energy production and conservation, and interest in environmental protection, have created strong demands for scientists and engineers. Prospects for mining and petroleum engineers and for geologists are particularly bright. Science technicians of all types, with specializations partly dictated by local needs, are in short supply. Computer specialists will continue to be marketable, as will economists. All the above are in the nontraditional designation for women. In other areas relatively new to women, financial management, banking, and accounting are exceedingly promising. Women hold about 90 percent of the jobs as tellers in banks, but less than 2 percent of the senior officer positions. There is a great deal of catching up to do!

The "graying" of our population will create expanded opportunities in health care, health-care support, and related fields. Specifically, some of the greatest demands will be for physicians and osteopaths, therapists, hygienists, nurses, laboratory technologists, and health administrators.

A large population of healthy, retired people will stimulate the travel, tourism, and recreation industries.

The importance to women of setting career goals unfettered by centuries of prejudice should be obvious. You must realize that for a woman to be considered a success in positions previously held almost exclusively by men, she most often must use her intelligence to greater effect, and work harder than her male peers. In considering your future employment be sure to understand and evaluate carefully the degree of commitment expected and necessary for your particular choices. Confront honestly your readiness, willingness, and ability to accomplish your goals, or you cannot expect to achieve them.

HUNTING FOR THAT NEW JOB

Ugh! What a task!

Job hunting, without doubt, can be one of the most stressful experiences in life. It is a season of seemingly endless trauma for most people. Yet, the task may be made less wearing if you prepare intelligently for it.

This would be a good time for you to review chapters 1 and 2. **207**
When we discussed career matters involving long-range considerations,
we referred to a variety of aids that will also be helpful as you search
for that new job on the horizon. At this point we will concentrate on
two additional aids—books or other publications that will help you,
and computer information and guidance systems.

One of the most widely used books in the job-hunting category is
*What Color Is Your Parachute? A Practical Manual for Job-Hunters
and Career-Changers,* by Richard N. Bolles. It should be in your library
or bookstore, or you can order it from Ten Speed Press, Box 7123,
Berkeley, CA 94707, $8.45 (including shipping and handling). Al-
though the book has its detractors, and some of their criticisms seem
justified, it nevertheless presents the world of the job hunt in a graphic,
maplike manner that is easy to follow, and there can be no doubt
that many people have benefited greatly from taking Bolles's advice.
The book has such chapters as "Rejection Shock," "You Must Keep
at It," and "The Quick Job-hunting Map." Another popular book is
John Munschauer's *Jobs for English Majors and Other Smart People*
($8.20, including shipping, from Peterson's Guides). This book con-
centrates on showing the job-hunter how to understand employers'
needs and tells the reader how to be the right applicant—in other
words, how to seize opportunities.

Now let's come back to computer information and guidance systems. In the early chapters of this book we treated them mostly in
terms of long-range career applications and of identifying higher education programs and institutions. But some of them also can help
you get a job, and are "state-based"; that is, their information is not
presented just in general and national terms, but is adapted for your
state and locality. A widely used system is one we earlier mentioned,
Career Information System. It provides not only educational information but also employment information. In addition to descriptions of
job duties, CIS contains: local employment and outlook information;
average entry and average maximum wage rates; employers' hiring
practices regarding skills and experience required; alternative methods
of preparation for employment; related occupations; researching
firms, and résumé preparation and other job-search techniques. For
more information about CIS, see the address in chapter 1; for other
services, contact the types of counselors we recommended in the earlier
chapters, or write to the Guidance Services Office of your state's department of education or labor. Also visit your local state employment office. Did you think they were in the business of finding jobs
only in unskilled fields? Not so. In their files or computer data banks
they will list many types of available jobs, including some that might
call for your newly gained higher education credentials.

208   GRADUATION AT LAST!

During those last several months of school, no doubt you have been busily (frantically?) preparing for further education (maybe graduate school) or for that new career. At the same time you have been juggling all of the other important aspects of your life, including trying to make it successfully to graduation. If you have attended a school that holds a commencement, you have had to order your cap and gown. You have had to make sure that Aunt Mabel gets an invitation and that she has a room reserved on the first floor of the nearby motel because she can't walk up the stairs. And so on, and so on, and so on. And suddenly the day is upon you. **Graduation!**

What is it like? Has it all been worthwhile?

So many adult students have commented on the significance of graduation, there can be no doubt that it stands as one of the few truly important highlights of a lifetime.

"At last the struggle was over," recalls Dorothy June Harris, a 54-year-old mother of six children, of Flat River, MO. "The Dean of Instruction introduced me as 'the grandmother who came back to school and proved to all of us that age is no barrier to learning if a deep motivation is present.'"

Lawrence Gaskins, a former prison inmate, and now a respected member of his community, testifies: "The proudest day of my life was when I received my associate degree."

When you join the ranks of graduates, along with Dorothy June Harris and Lawrence Gaskins and all those many other successful adult students, undoubtedly you too will beam with pride. You've made it after all!

SUNSET, SUNRISE? LIFELONG LEARNING AND YOU

Will your graduation be a bright new day dawning, or a glorious sunset? Can it be both?

Our world seems to be changing at a rate that is too fast for the average person to keep up with. This phenomenon was recognized years ago by Alvin Toffler, author of the now-classic book *Future Shock:*

> The rapid obsolescence of knowledge and the extension of life span make it clear that the skills learned by youth are unlikely to remain relevant by the time old age arrives. Super-industrialized education must therefore make provisions for life-long education. [p. 407]

Our federal and state governments and our colleges and universities have undertaken to solve this problem. For example, the American

Association of Community and Junior Colleges has set forth a *Bill of* **209**
Rights for the lifelong learner:

Bill of Rights
Every adult American has the right to continue to learn throughout life;

Every adult American has the right to equal opportunity for access to relevant learning opportunities at each stage of life;

Diversity and access to educational opportunity are important to democracy in the United States;

Any index of the quality of life in the United States includes opportunities for growth and self-actualization as a right of the learning society;

Neither age, nor sex, nor color, nor creed, nor ethnic background, nor marital status, nor economic status, nor disability should create barriers to the opportunity to continue to grow through participation in organized learning activities;

Coping, living, and working are dimensions which exemplify the range of learning needs of the learning society;

Public investment in the learning society is an investment in human capital and in human condition.

Thus our society has realized that education is not a privilege to be reserved for the young. Adults possess invaluable experiences that, coupled with continuing education, represent intellectual wealth that should be cherished at least as highly as the potential of youth. We must not waste this valuable human resource. And we should not deprive any segment of our society of the right to a satisfying and rewarding life by curtailing education that is an important source of continuing growth and development.

Ronald Gross, author of *The Lifelong Learner,* summarized the significant attitude changes taking place in our society:

We Americans as individuals seem to be developing a fresh hunger for experience, for growth, for personal cultivation. Men and women of all ages today feel the urge to seek more in life—to shape a larger self, that quest I call lifelong learning. [pp. 168-69]

Indeed, a multitude of adults are realizing their aspirations through lifelong education. When Douglas E. Buck of Bellingham, WA, received his bachelor's degree from Evergreen State College, he recalls feeling that "it was a very rewarding learning experience. My degree was an end to a personal goal. However, education is a never-ending process. We all learn something new every day, and wouldn't life be boring if we didn't?"

Lifelong learning clearly represents our society's educational direction. This trend will continue for several reasons: First, technological and cultural change is accelerating at such a rapid pace that continuing education is necessary if we are to maintain our way of life and standards of living. Second, average life spans are being continuously extended due to advances in science and medicine; thus the gap from the traditional end of formal education to death is widening while the rate of obsolescence of knowledge is increasing. Third, the "graying of America" will bring with it greater dependence upon older people to provide impetus for scientific and social advancement. Fourth, if America is to maintain its position of leadership among industrialized nations of the world, we must fully utilize *all* of our valuable human resources. In fact, we must develop a new social ethic in which productivity and commitment to excellence are once again cherished.

Socrates said, "The unexamined life is not worth living." That statement, twenty-four hundred years old, seems invigoratingly fresh as we—adult students, all of us—set about the remainder of our lives of lifelong learning, looking always for new horizons.

Student Profile

ROBERT H. NORTON of Holliston, Massachusetts

It was a challenge getting an external master's degree at the same time I was trying to develop my own business. But I did it, and in the process found a new "inner me."

I guess my life as a young man was like most others. I went to MIT, joined a fraternity, and lived the "good life." It was too good: I never finished MIT.

I was not unintelligent, however, and was able to garner my share of good jobs. But I did not last more than three years at any of them. It seems that I was never able to complete what I started. Then I came into the insurance field, where I've been ever since, and found that I'd need to get more education. I completed a Chartered Life Underwriter (CLU) certificate program, Advanced CLU program, and other related studies. My income increased, my position advanced, and my family grew to eight kids. Then came a major turning point in my life: I decided to finish my college education. By now I had completed another certificate program (Chartered Financial Consultant), and I enrolled in an advanced degree program, Master of Science in Financial Services, at the American College in Bryn Mawr, Pennsylvania.

At first I feared the decision because I did not even have a   **211**
bachelor's degree. Fortunately, though, the college had procedures
by which a person could demonstrate readiness for admission by
taking a series of examinations, and I passed.

All of the American College courses, except for one brief
residency at the end of the program, are designed for self-study if the
student wants them this way. I chose to complete about one-half of
my studies entirely independently, and the other half in small classes
of six to eight students in locations convenient to my home and
business. Then I took the residency and was awarded my degree. So
great was the experience that, before completing the residency, I
decided to go on to get a Master of Science in Management, realizing
that this additional education would be of immeasurable value in
running my financial planning firm.

And so, at age 54, I have found a new quality of life. I had known
it existed, but it had been elusive during my earlier years. I'm
convinced that without obtaining my external master's degree, it
would still be missing. Forget about my increase in income, or
owning my own company, or finding a prestigious spot in my
industry, town, and environs. Through education I have found a new
"inner me."

Glossary of Terms in Higher Education

academic year The traditional school year, usually September through May, typically divided into two (semester or trimester) terms of equal length. However, many different schedules are now offered to accommodate accelerated and weekend courses. In addition, many institutions offer one or more summer sessions during June, July, and August.

accreditation The official recognition granted by one of the regional, state, or specialized accrediting associations for having satisfied the standards established by the association. Criteria usually include extent and suitability of educational programs and curriculums; caliber of faculty and administration; and quality of library, classroom, and other facilities.

administrative rank The designated status of an institutional official. The titles most typically used (in order of hierarchical rank and formal authority) are:

1. President, Chancellor
2. Vice President, Vice Chancellor*
3. Dean, Provost*
4. Director, Chairperson*
5. Coordinator

Sometimes the added designation of associate or assistant (or occasionally deputy) is applied to the levels marked with an asterisk.

admission Acceptance of a candidate for enrollment, especially into a formal course of study leading to a certificate, diploma, or degree. (Also see *enrollment, matriculation.*)

admissions tests, standardized The nationally recognized tests used as part of the selective admission procedure or, by some institutions, as a device for validating nontraditional work. The two major college

213

214 entrance tests are the American College Testing Program examination (ACT) and the College Board's Scholastic Aptitude Test (SAT).

adult student A student generally of age 25 or older who has had a break of several years' duration in formal schooling.

Application for Federal Student Aid The form designed by the federal government for use in applying for the Pell Grant. May be used for the same purpose as the FAF or FFS as well as to process institutionally administered aid.

associate degree A degree granted for completing a two-year, full-time course of study or the equivalent (generally at least 60 semester credits).

audit To attend a credit course on a noncredit basis (usually at a reduced tuition) without being graded.

baccalaureate or bachelor's degree A degree granted for completing a four-year, full-time course of study or the equivalent (usually 120–130 semester credits).

bible college A college offering primarily bible study and leading to certification or degrees in the Protestant ministry, and usually subject to accreditation by the American Association of Bible Colleges.

branch campus A unit of an institution located at a place other than its main campus and offering courses for credit and programs leading to certificates, diplomas, or degrees.

bulletin The periodic publication containing compact descriptions of the educational programs offered during a forthcoming semester or other period. (Also see *catalog.*)

bursar The administrator responsible for billings and collections of tuitions and fees payable by students.

business or specialized institute (or school) Usually a privately owned, profit-making institution of higher education with occupational programs in business fields, generally at the certificate or associate degree level, although sometimes also at higher levels, and subject to accreditation by the Association of Independent Colleges and Schools.

calendar The arrangement of the academic year. The three common types are the semester system, the quarter system, and the trimester system (see separate definitions). Bulletins often include calendars listing the beginning and ending dates of classes, recognized holidays, registration, preregistration, add/drop dates, and dates of final examinations.

career An occupation or profession pursued over a significant number of years.

career guidance Counseling in career concerns, administered either by a trained career counselor or self-administered using a computer career guidance system or other means such as a battery of diagnostic instruments.

catalog (sometimes called *bulletin*) The annual publication containing compact descriptions of the educational programs, resources, and services provided by an institution, as well as details of the school's official regulations and policies. The catalog is an important source of information that the student should carefully review and retain for future reference.

certificate A credential issued by an institution in recognition of completion of a curriculum other than one leading to a degree or diploma.

class types The types of classes found at most schools are: classroom, lecture hall, seminar, laboratory, and studio. Nontraditional classes, such as televised lectures followed by telephone communication between individual students and the instructor, are being employed by an increasing number of schools.

closed (closed section) A section or course that has been filled to capacity; no further registrations will be accepted.

college Usually, a degree-granting institution of higher education offering instruction above the level of the secondary school. Sometimes also applied to institutions offering certificates or diplomas.

community college An institution of higher education offering certificate, diploma, and two-year associate degree programs. Generally publicly owned and serving the needs of the community in which it is located. Credits earned are often transferable toward a bachelor's degree at a four-year college or university. However, credits earned for a terminal certificate, diploma, or degree program often are not transferable.

concentration An area of specialization chosen by the student. (See *major* and *minor.*)

consortium A group of educational institutions associated to serve their common interests. Attending an institution that belongs to a consortium affords certain benefits such as interschool library privileges, an opportunity to take courses not offered by the school in which the student is enrolled, and the possibility of additional social, cultural, and educational opportunities.

continuing education Extension of education for persons who have completed or withdrawn from full-time secondary or postsecondary school programs.

continuing education unit (CEU) A nationally recognized measure used to document the type, quality, and duration of noncredit course work that one has satisfactorily completed. One CEU is equal to ten class hours completed in a continuing education course. CEUs may be accepted by some schools to satisfy certain requirements for degree or certificate programs.

cooperative education The integration of classroom work and practical experience through alternate class attendance and employment in

216   business, industry, government, or other agencies through contractual agreement between the student's institution and the outside agency.

core curriculum Established by the school, a group of fundamental courses that are required for all candidates for a given certificate, diploma, or degree.

correspondence education Education undertaken by an individual at a distance from the source; involves transmitting written and sometimes audio study material and examinations. Sometimes called distance learning.

counseling The giving of advice, opinion, or instruction with the intent of affecting the beliefs, behavior, or course of action of another person. Career, academic, financial aid, and personal counseling are the most common types involving adult students.

course An organized series of instructional and learning activities dealing with a subject.

course outline See *syllabus.*

credit A unit of academic award applicable toward a degree, certificate, or diploma offered by an institution of higher education.

credit hour See *semester hour.*

curriculum (program) The formal educational requirements necessary to qualify for a degree, diploma, or certificate. May include general education or specialized study in depth, or both.

dean An official presiding over the faculty of an institution, an area of study, or a particular group of students.

dean's list Common designation for the published list of undergraduate students who have achieved an honors grade average for the term.

degree Title bestowed as official recognition for the completion of a specified curriculum of two or more years in duration or, in the case of an honorary degree, for a certain attainment. (See also associate, baccalaureate, master's, and doctoral degrees.) Some common degrees include:

undergraduate degrees

A.A.	Associate in Arts
A.A.S.	Associate in Applied Science
A.S.	Associate in Science
B.A.	Bachelor of Arts
B.S.	Bachelor of Science
B.B.A.	Bachelor of Business Administration
B.E.	Bachelor of Engineering
B.Ed.	Bachelor of Education
B.F.A.	Bachelor of Fine Arts
B.P.S.	Bachelor of Professional Studies
B.Tech.	Bachelor of Technology

graduate academic degrees

M.A.   Master of Arts
M.S.   Master of Science
M.Phil.   Master of Philosophy
Ph.D.   Doctor of Philosophy

graduate professional degrees

M.Arch.   Master of Architecture
M.A.T.   Master of Arts in Teaching
M.B.A.   Master of Business Administration
M.Ed.   Master of Education
M.F.A.   Master of Fine Arts
M.L.S.   Master of Library Science
M.P.A.   Master of Public Administration
M.S.   Master of Science
M.S.W.   Master of Social Work
D.D.S.   Doctor of Dental Surgery
Ed.D.   Doctor of Education
J.D.   Doctor of Law
M.D.   Doctor of Medicine
D.V.M.   Doctor of Veterinary Medicine

For a complete listing of academic degrees and abbreviations, see *American Universities and Colleges* (Appendix III, pp. 1760-70), published by the American Council on Education, Washington, DC, available in the reference section of most libraries.

department A unit of the school's faculty organized to provide courses of study in a specific discipline such as English, automotive technology, or banking.

diagnostic instrument A device, usually written, which helps reveal individual strengths and weaknesses in particular areas of concern, and thus enables individuals to take informed courses of action.

diploma An academic award granted for completion of a curriculum other than one leading to a degree or certificate. In Canada, a diploma often represents the equivalent of an associate degree in the United States.

division A group of related academic disciplines (such as the social sciences, the arts, the humanities, and the natural sciences). Sometimes also an administrative unit of an institution.

doctoral degree or doctorate Any academic degree carrying the title of "doctor." The doctorate is the highest academic degree in a given discipline or profession, generally requiring three or more years of graduate work and completion of a course of study culminating in the preparation of a dissertation approved by a faculty committee.

218   **double major or dual major** Official recognition that a student is pursuing or has satisfied the minimum requirements for majors in two disciplines of study.

drop To decrease one's course load for a particular term by one or more courses.

drop date The deadline by which a student may choose, without incurring academic penalty, to decrease his or her course load for a particular term.

education The procedure or result of acquiring broad general knowledge, as well as specific knowledge, and developing the powers of reasoning and judgment.

elective A course chosen at the discretion of the student to fulfill part of the requirements for a degree.

enrollment The act of registering for a course or program of study. (Also see *admission, matriculation.*)

entrance examination A standardized examination taken to gain entrance to an institution of higher education, usually prepared and administered by a testing service.

experiential learning Conceptual knowledge acquired through life experience for which academic credit may be granted.

extension center A site other than the principal center of an institution or any of its branch campuses at which curriculums leading to degrees, diplomas, or certificates are not offered, but at which courses for credit are offered on a limited and temporary basis for the convenience of students.

external degree An academic award earned through any of the following: extrainstitutional learning, credit by examination, special experiential-learning programs, self-directed study, and satisfactory completion of campus or off-campus courses. In some programs the learning is attained in circumstances outside of the sponsorship or supervision of the awarding institution. Generally credit is granted for documented learning from such sources as work and life experience and noncollegiate courses previously completed.

faculty rank title The institutionally designated title or grade of a faculty member. The categories most typically used (in descending order of professional achievement) are:

1. Professor ("full professor")
2. Associate Professor
3. Assistant Professor
4. Instructor
5. Other (such as lecturer)

The modifiers *adjunct* and *clinical* are sometimes used in conjunction with faculty titles to mean visiting or part-time classroom or laboratory instructors respectively. The term "instructor," or "teacher," is often also used generally to mean any of the ranks above.

Family Financial Statement (FFS) A form designed by the American College Testing Program to provide information for determining a student's eligibility for financial aid. Completing the FFS (or FAF or Application for Federal Student Aid) is usually the first step in applying for financial aid.

fees Charges assessed in addition to tuition to cover costs of administration, required course materials and equipment, or student services and programs (such as application fees, lab fees, and student activity fees).

fellowship A gift of money to a student, ordinarily for support of graduate study. The recipient is rarely required to demonstrate financial need. The award is designed to support free inquiry on the part of the student in a field of interest, and to provide for educational and living expenses of a full-time student.

final examination A test given at the end of a course that may count for a large percentage of a student's grade. The final exam may be cumulative (covering the entire course content) or noncumulative (including only material studied since the midterm or last major exam).

financial aid Any source of monetary assistance sponsored by federal, state, or local governments, or provided by educational institutions, business institutions, or private agencies or individuals. Provides students with ways to meet the costs of attending school, and includes loans, grants, and work-study programs.

Financial Aid Form (FAF) This form is designed by the College Board and is used for the same purpose as the Family Financial Statement (FFS).

financial need The difference between your cost of going to a particular school and the money you (and your spouse, if you have one) can provide for your college costs.

full-time Status of an undergraduate student who takes at least 12 credits during a conventional academic term. For financial aid purposes, 6 credits might be considered as full-time status during the summer if at least 12 credits are taken during the preceding spring and following fall terms.

General Educational Development (GED) tests See *high school equivalency examinations.*

grade-point average (GPA) or quality-point index (QPI) A system of measuring students' average grades for academic rating purposes. Points are given for each credit hour of course work undertaken based on the grade earned.

graduate degree Any academic degree conferred by a graduate division or graduate school of an institution of higher education (such as

220 M.A., M.S., Ph.D., Ed.D.). Also includes first professional degrees (such as the M.D., D.D.S., or J.D.), which are conferred by professional rather than graduate schools.

graduate school A college or unit of a higher education institution which offers study beyond the baccalaureate level. If the study is in a technical or professional area, such as medicine, the term "professional school" may be used.

graduate study A program of study beyond the bachelor's degree usually in pursuit of a master's or doctoral degree.

graduation A formal procedure, often including a ceremony, for awarding an academic credential.

graduation requirements A specified group of minimum achievements or other qualifications needed for a student to qualify for a certificate, diploma, or degree. For a bachelor's degree, for example, a college might require the following: (1) successful completion of 120 credits, at least 30 of which must be earned in residence; (2) a cumulative grade-point average of 2.0 or better; (3) completion of all specified courses in the core curriculum and major area of concentration selected for the degree; (4) payment of all tuition and fees incurred.

grant A gift of money to a student with no requirement of repayment or of services to be rendered. Also called a scholarship.

Guaranteed Student Loan (GSL) A program of the federal government that provides for low-interest deferred-payment loans for students attending eligible institutions of higher education in the United States and abroad, as well as thousands of vocational, technical, business, and trade schools.

gut course (slang) A course with a light work load requiring relatively little effort to complete successfully.

higher education Education undertaken beyond high school (secondary school). Also called postsecondary education.

high school equivalency examinations Examinations approved by a state department of education or other authorized agency that are intended to provide an appraisal of a student's achievement or performance in the broad subject matter areas usually required for high school graduation. The General Educational Development tests (GED) are the most widely recognized high school equivalency examinations, and are administered by the department of education in states, commonwealths, and territories of the United States and in Canadian provinces. The tests are prepared by the General Educational Development Testing Service, One Dupont Circle, Washington, DC 20036.

honors Recognition of academic excellence achieved by a student. At the undergraduate level, one of the following Latin terms traditionally designates graduation with honors: *cum laude* (with honors), *magna cum laude* (with high honors), and *summa cum laude* (with highest honors). At the graduate level, one term only, graduation with distinction, is generally used.

honors program A particularly challenging program offered to students who have demonstrated superior academic ability in their fields of specialization. Students who succeed in satisfying the stringent requirements of an honors program are generally graduated with honors.

incomplete A temporary designation assigned to a student's record of a course in which the student was unable for a valid reason to take the final exam or complete a required course assignment. The student must make arrangements with the course instructor to make up the exam or submit the missing assignment within a certain time period (determined by school policy) to have the incomplete changed to a regular grade.

independent study Study undertaken by an individual without the immediate assistance of an instructor. The study may, however, be formally guided at a distance through correspondence, telephone, and other contacts.

information and guidance system A computer-assisted method for imparting career and/or academic information and guidance.

institutional aid form The school's own form of application for financial aid. Students usually must complete both the institutional aid form and the FFS, FAF, or Application for Federal Student Aid to receive financial aid.

interdisciplinary A curriculum or course of study that includes two or more academic disciplines.

intersession The period between academic terms during which short, intensive courses might be scheduled to satisfy the special interests of groups of students, or to provide an additional opportunity for acceleration of progress. Many schools use the "4-1-4" plan, that is, a four-month term in the fall (September to December), one month of school during what normally is the intersession break (January), and a four-month term in the spring (February to May).

junior college (two-year college) A higher education institution that is authorized to offer undergraduate curriculums below the baccalaureate level that normally lead to the associate degree.

liberal arts The broad scope of academic disciplines encompassed by the humanities, the social sciences, and the natural sciences (generally exclusive of professional fields of study).

load (credit, course) The credit hours or courses required for graduation divided by the number of semesters or terms normally required for graduation determines the normal full-time load. A heavier than normal load is usually permitted when a student demonstrates exceptional academic ability. A lighter than normal course load for a full-time student may require special permission.

loan, student See *Guaranteed Student Loan* and *National Direct Student Loan.*

lower-division courses Introductory-level courses usually taken during the first two years of college study.

222   **major** A student's primary area of concentration. Can be in a specific discipline or some combination of disciplines (a combined major). Usually one-quarter to one-half of the student's degree program must be taken in the established major.

master's degree A degree granted for completing a one- to two-year, full-time course of study usually encompassing 30 to 60 semester credits beyond the baccalaureate degree.

matriculation Registration following acceptance of an individual in a certificate, diploma, or degree program. Not generally used in referring to enrollment in individual courses. (Also see *admission, enrollment.*)

minor A secondary concentration in a specific discipline or field of study, usually requiring about half the number of credits required for a major.

National Direct Student Loan (NDSL) A low-interest loan available through joint sponsorship of the federal government and the individual postsecondary institution.

noncollegiate instruction Instruction offered by an institution, agency, or organization other than one engaged primarily in higher education.

nonmatriculated Status of a student who has been admitted to a school and allowed to take courses on either a credit or noncredit basis but not as an official certificate, diploma, or degree candidate. Nonmatriculated students are often referred to as special students. Students may be able to take courses and accumulate credits toward a credential while matriculation is pending due to some unfulfilled admissions requirement.

nontraditional higher education Off-campus education, pursued at a distance from an institution, and involving significant independent study.

occupational education Education designed to impart sufficient knowledge and skills to enable a person to acquire at least an entry-level job in a trade, technical, or other skills-oriented field. Also called vocational education.

open admissions A liberal admissions policy under which all applicants are accepted (space permitting) so long as they meet minimum requirements mandated by the state education department, such as holding a high school diploma.

part-time Status of a student who takes fewer than 12 credits during a conventional academic term.

pass-fail option A provision enabling a student to take a course with annotation of having passed or failed, rather than receiving a letter grade. Pass-fail is sometimes excluded in computing a student's grade-point average (GPA).

Pell Grant A federal grant for the support of undergraduate study.

Eligibility requires attendance at an approved institution on at least a half-time basis and demonstrated financial need.

Pell Grant Application See *Application for Federal Student Aid.*

percentile A measure of the relative standing of a student among all students in the same category. Scoring at the 70th percentile on the verbal portion of a standard graduate school admission exam, for example, means that only 30 percent of all students who took the same exam in the current testing group scored higher in verbal skills than the individual scoring 70.

postgraduate study Usually taken to mean study beyond the master's degree but below the doctorate. For the completion of a postgraduate program, a certificate of advanced graduate study, an advanced professional certificate, or a diploma of advanced graduate study may be awarded.

postsecondary education See *higher education.*

preregistration The plan by which students select and are assigned courses for a succeeding term well in advance of the official opening date of registration for the term.

prerequisite A course that must be taken, or a requirement that must be satisfied, before a student will be permitted to take a more advanced course in the same field of study.

probation, academic A warning (as opposed to a penalty) resulting from unsatisfactory scholarship, and an opportunity to improve. Academic probation usually involves the compulsory reduction of the academic load, interviews for diagnosis of difficulties, and academic counseling.

professional degree The first degree satisfying completion of the minimum academic requirements for practice of a profession. Includes certain bachelor's, master's, and doctoral degrees.

proficiency examination A test taken by a student to demonstrate competence in the subject matter of a course in order to receive equivalent credit for that course.

program (curriculum) The formal educational requirements necessary to qualify for a degree, diploma, or certificate. May include general education or specialized study in a particular field, or both.

provisional registration Permission to attend classes pending the adjustment of standing.

quarter A period of about 10 weeks representing one-fourth of a school year (as compared to a semester or trimester, which is usually about 16 weeks in length).

rank, class The position of a student in relation to others being graduated in that class as determined by a comparison of academic records.

registrar The college administrator responsible for supervising course and program admissions and enrollments, academic recording, and certification.

224   **registration** Official enrollment in a course or program, or approval of a student's curriculum.

residence Pursuit of full- or part-time study in classes on campus. At some institutions it means living in the school's dormitories.

residence requirement A minimum period of required attendance at a school to qualify for a certificate, diploma, or degree awarded by that school, often stated in terms of credits. For example, 30 credits of course work might be required to be completed "in residence" at a particular college in order to qualify for a degree.

rolling admissions A system by which admission applications are evaluated upon receipt throughout the year and applicants are notified as soon as a decision can be made, as compared to notification of all applicants soon after a specified deadline for admission applications.

satellite center Same as *branch campus.*

schedule, class The list of courses and sections offered, together with the names of the instructors, the days, hours, and places of meeting.

scholarship A gift of money to a student, ordinarily for the support of undergraduate study. It is granted in recognition of academic or other distinction and may require that the recipient be in need of financial assistance. The donor may specify particular conditions or restrictions in addition to demonstrated financial need.

school Loosely, any educational institution, Also, a division of a university organized to provide training in a professional field (such as school of business, school of nursing).

section A division of a course into two or more classes, each having the same subject matter, but not necessarily taught by the same instructor, or at the same hour.

semester Traditionally half an academic year, usually about 16 weeks, beginning in August/September or January/February.

semester hour A unit representing one hour of classroom instruction per week for a semester of not less than 15 weeks. One credit, point, or other academic unit is traditionally granted for the successful completion of each semester hour. This basic measure must be adjusted proportionately to translate the value of academic calendars and formats of study other than that of the traditional two-semester academic year (this includes summer sessions and independent study).

summer session A session not a part of the academic year (September through May).

Supplemental Educational Opportunity Grant (SEOG) A federally funded grant administered by the school for undergraduate students who have exceptional financial need not entirely satisfied by the Pell Grant.

survey course A course designed to provide a general overview of an area of study. Completed by a student either prior to undertaking specialized work in a given field, or to provide broad, general concepts about an area in which one does not plan to specialize.

syllabus A sequential outline of topics to be covered by the instructor, **225** and assignments to be completed by the students during a course.

tenure The institutional designation that serves to identify the status of the employee with respect to permanence of position. A faculty member on tenure normally cannot be discharged except for extreme reasons such as moral turpitude or the financial exigency of the institution.

term The period of time that a course runs with specific beginning and ending dates. Usually a semester, trimester, or quarter.

trade or technical institute (or school) An institution of higher education offering occupational programs in trade and technical fields, usually granting certificates but not degrees, and subject to accreditation by the National Association of Trade and Technical Schools.

traditional higher education On-campus education involving classroom work and direct contact with instructors.

transcript A student's official record of courses taken, credits earned, and grades received, which is maintained by the registrar. Students are entitled to unofficial copies of their transcripts upon request (usually upon payment of a nominal fee). Official transcripts imprinted with the school's seal will be sent at the student's request to admissions offices of other schools and to prospective employers.

transfer Admission to a new school with acceptance of previously earned credits toward the degree, diploma, certificate, or program requirements of the new school.

trimester A period of about 16 weeks representing one-third of a school year. A school using the trimester system is on a normal academic schedule during the summer months when schools operating on a traditional semester system would be closed except for summer session courses. Two trimesters constitute an academic year.

tuition The amount of money charged to students for instructional services. Tuition may be charged on a per-term, per-course, or per-credit basis. Fees (see definition) may also be charged to students.

undergraduate study Study at the associate or baccalaureate level.

university A higher education institution that confers graduate as well as undergraduate degrees in various fields of study. A university has at least two colleges or professional schools granting doctorates and doing research at an advanced level.

upper-division courses Advanced courses usually taken as part of a student's major during the last years of college study.

Veterans Administration (VA) Educational Benefits Benefits paid for student financial assistance at approved postsecondary educational institutions for three types of beneficiaries: (1) surviving spouse and children, (2) discharged veterans, and (3) active armed-service employees in special programs.

vocational education See *occupational education.*

withdrawal A release from enrollment. A student may usually with-

226 draw from a course officially within a specified period without being graded. Withdrawal without permission will probably result in a failing grade.

work-study A plan of part-time work for which a student receives pay. May be on or off campus, usually has no relationship to the student's degree program, and is generally given as part of financial aid.

Bibliography of Career References

An enormous body of career and job-hunting references exists. The following are only some of the most commonly used sources, all of which are revised annually or periodically. See *Books in Print* in the reference section of your library for the most recent information, including date of publication and ordering information. This abbreviated reference list has been extracted from bibliographical material prepared for this book by Janet Wagner, Reference Department, Library, Hofstra University, Hempstead, NY.

College Placement Annual. College Placement Council. Information on positions customarily offered to college graduates by principal employers. Includes more than 1,200 corporate and governmental employers.

Dictionary of Occupational Titles. United States Department of Labor. Standardized job descriptions with coding arrangement for occupational classification. Breakdown of occupations by category.

Encyclopedia of Associations. Two volumes. Denise S. Akey, ed. Gale Research Company. Comprehensive coverage of more than 17,000 nonprofit American membership organizations of national scope.
    I. Parts I and II. National Organizations of the United States
    II. Geographic and Executive Indexes

Encyclopedia of Business Information Sources. Paul Wasserman, ed. Gale Research Company. A detailed listing of sourcebooks, periodicals, organizations, directories, handbooks, bibliographies, on-line databases, etc.

228 *Encyclopedia of Career and Vocational Guidance.* Three volumes. William E. Hopke, ed. Doubleday and Company. Detailed information on planning your career, and careers and occupations.

Jobs for English Majors and Other Smart People. John L. Munschauer, Peterson's Guides. Shows the job seeker how to understand the needs of the employer and how to demonstrate the ability to meet those needs. A practical book for the current job market.

Occupational Outlook Handbook. United States Department of Labor. Basic reference source on job descriptions, training and education required, advancement possibilities, employment outlook, earnings and working conditions, sources of additional information. Also see *Occupational Outlook Quarterly.*

Peterson's Annual Guides to Graduate Study. Five volumes. Amy J. Goldstein, ed. Peterson's Guides. Information on over 25,000 graduate programs in nearly 300 fields of study at all accredited degree-granting institutions in the U.S.
  I. Graduate and Professional Programs: An Overview
  II. Graduate Programs in the Humanities and Social Sciences
  III. Graduate Programs in the Biological, Agricultural, and Health Sciences
  IV. Graduate Programs in the Physical Sciences and Mathematics
  V. Graduate Programs in Engineering and Applied Sciences

Standard and Poor's Register of Corporations, Directors and Executives. Three volumes.
  I. 40,000 corporate listings, with names, titles, and functions of officers, annual sales, number of employees, etc.
  II. Individual listings, directors and executives, biographical information on 70,000 individuals.
  III. Indexes: Standard Industrial Classification Code additions.

What Color Is Your Parachute?: A Practical Manual for Job-Hunters and Career-Changers. Richard Bolles, Ten Speed Press. Step-by-step approach to methods of career exploration and change, and job-hunting strategy. Emphasizes self-assessment and finding the "right" job.

Where to Start: An Annotated Career-planning Bibliography. Madeline T. Rockcastle, ed. Career Center, Cornell University, published by Peterson's Guides. Lists and describes the career-planning resources used by Cornell's Career Center, which has one of the best career and job-hunting libraries in the country. Comprehensive coverage of sources by career field as well as general resources.

Have You Seen These Other Publications from Peterson's Guides?

Peterson's Annual Guides/Undergraduate Study
Guide to Four-Year Colleges 1986
SIXTEENTH EDITION
Editor: Andrea E. Lehman
Data Editor: Eric A. Suber

The largest, most up-to-date guide to the over 1,900 accredited four-year colleges in the United States and Canada. Contains concise college profiles, a reader guidance section, and two-page "Messages from the Colleges" that are found in no other guide.

8½" x 11", 2,239 pages   Stock no. 3398
ISBN 0-87866-339-8   **$12.95** paperback

Peterson's Annual Guides/Graduate Study
Graduate and Professional Programs: An Overview 1985
NINETEENTH EDITION
Series Editor: Diane Conley

Covers the whole spectrum of U.S. and Canadian graduate programs in a single reliable volume. A special table correlates over 1,350 schools with the graduate and professional degrees they offer.

8½" x 11", 885 pages   Stock no. 2340
ISBN 0-87866-234-0   **$15.95** paperback

The Independent Study Catalog: NUCEA's Guide to Independent Study Through Correspondence Instruction 1983–1985
Editor: Joan H. Hunter

A new edition of the ultimate education "wishbook" for people who want to study on their own without the restrictions of regular class attendance. Students can choose from more than 12,000 correspondence courses offered by 72 colleges and universities. Credit and noncredit courses are available at the elementary, high school, undergraduate, and graduate levels.

8½" x 11", 120 pages   Stock no. 1808
ISBN 0-87866-180-8   **$5.95** paperback

Who Offers Part-Time Degree Programs?
SECOND EDITION
Editor: Karen C. Hegener

The only handy reference book that covers part-time undergraduate and graduate degree programs offered by colleges and universities throughout the United States. It provides a complete, up-to-date overview of daytime, evening, weekend, summer, and external degree programs at more than 2,000 institutions.

8½" x 11", 424 pages   Stock no. 2855
ISBN 0-87866-285-5   **$7.95** paperback

Finding a Job in Your Field: A Handbook for Ph.D.'s and M.A.'s
Rebecca Anthony and Gerald Roe

This practical and thorough guide is the only book written especially for holders of advanced degrees to explain how they should prepare for academic and professional employment. It includes an assessment of the job choices available, advice on organizing a job search, tips on how to write effective vitas and résumés, advice on how to interview with search committees, and other specific and very helpful information.

6" x 9", 144 pages   Stock no. 2782
ISBN 0-87866-278-2   **$8.95** paperback

Liberal Arts Power! How to Sell It on Your Résumé
Burton Jay Nadler

This is the first résumé book written exclusively for generalists, liberal arts students, recent graduates, and career changers. Using about 30 sample résumés, the author shows how job hunters can demonstrate their skills and match them to specific jobs.

8½" x 11", 127 pages   Stock no. 2545
ISBN 0-87866-254-5   **$6.95** paperback

Where to Start: An Annotated Career-planning Bibliography
FIFTH EDITION, 1985–87
Madeline T. Rockcastle

This book is published by Cornell University's Career Center, which houses one of the best career libraries in the nation, and describes the career-planning publications used there. It covers books, periodicals, audiovisual resources, and other materials and is an invaluable tool for human resource managers, counselors, and librarians in both corporate and academic organizations.

8½" x 11", 278 pages   Stock no. 3843
ISBN 0-87866-384-3   **$12.95** paperback

Jobs for English Majors and Other Smart People
John L. Munschauer

This book recognizes the realities of the job market for the generalist, the inexperienced, the career changer. The author offers down-to-earth advice about such common concerns as when to send and when not to send a résumé, how to identify alternative careers, and how to create a job when there is no advertised opening.

5½" x 8½", 180 pages   Stock no. 1441
ISBN 0-87866-144-1   **$6.95** paperback

How to Order

These publications are available from all good booksellers, or you may order direct from **Peterson's Guides, Dept. 5615, P.O. Box 2123, Princeton, New Jersey 08540.** Please note that prices are necessarily subject to change without notice.

- Enclose full payment for each book, plus postage and handling charges as follows:

Amount of Order	4th-Class Postage and Handling Charges
$1–$10	$1.25
$10.01–$20	$2.00
$20.01–$40	$3.00
$40.01 +	Add $1.00 shipping and handling for every additional $20 worth of books ordered.

Place your order TOLL-FREE by calling 800-225-0261 between 8:30 A.M. and 4:30 P.M. Eastern time, Monday through Friday. From New Jersey, Alaska, Hawaii, and outside the United States, call 609-924-5338. Telephone orders over $15 may be charged to your charge card; institutional and trade orders over $20 may be billed.

- For faster shipment via United Parcel Service (UPS), add $2.00 over and above the appropriate fourth-class book-rate charges listed.

- Bookstores and tax-exempt organizations should contact us for appropriate discounts.

- You may charge your order to VISA, MasterCard, or American Express. Minimum charge order: $15. Please include the name, account number, and validation and expiration dates for charge orders.

- New Jersey residents should add 6% sales tax to the cost of the books, excluding the postage and handling charge.

- Write for a free catalog describing all of our latest publications.